Undergraduate Topics in Computer Science

Undergraduate Topics in Computer Science (UTiCS) delivers high-quality instructional content for undergraduates studying in all areas of computing and information science. From core foundational and theoretical material to final-year topics and applications, UTiCS books take a fresh, concise, and modern approach and are ideal for self-study or for a one- or two-semester course. The texts are all authored by established experts in their fields, reviewed by an international advisory board, and contain numerous examples and problems. Many include fully worked solutions.

For further volumes:
www.springer.com/series/7592

Daniel Page · Nigel Smart

What Is Computer Science?

An Information Security Perspective

 Springer

Daniel Page
Department of Computer Science
University of Bristol
Bristol, UK

Nigel Smart
Department of Computer Science
University of Bristol
Bristol, UK

ISSN 1863-7310   ISSN 2197-1781 (electronic)
Undergraduate Topics in Computer Science
ISBN 978-3-319-04041-7   ISBN 978-3-319-04042-4 (eBook)
DOI 10.1007/978-3-319-04042-4
Springer Cham Heidelberg New York Dordrecht London

Library of Congress Control Number: 2013958156

Introduction

Computer Science is a diverse subject: it covers topics that range from the design of computer hardware through to programming that hardware so it can do useful things, and encompasses applications in fields such as Science, Engineering and the Arts. As a result, a modern Computer Science degree will often see students study topics that could be described as applied Mathematics (e.g., cryptography), applied Physics (e.g., quantum computing), Psychology (e.g., human-computer interaction), Philosophy (e.g., artificial intelligence), Biology (e.g., bio-informatics) and Linguistics (e.g., speech synthesis); such a list could go on and on.

On one hand, this diversity means trying to capture what Computer Science *is* can be quite hard and the subject can be misunderstood as a result. A prime example is that ICT, a subject often taught in schools, can give a false impression of what Computer Science would be about at University: if ICT gives the impression that a Computer Science degree would be about *using* a word processor for example, the reality is it relates more closely to *creating* the word processor itself. The knock-on effect of this potential misunderstanding is that recruiting students to do Computer Science degrees is much harder work than you might think.

But on the other hand, the same diversity is *tremendously* exciting. Bjarne Strous-trup, inventor of the C++ programming language, is quoted as stating that "our civilisation runs on software" and therefore, by implication, the Computer Scientists who create it do likewise. From the perspective of other fields this might seem like a wild claim; for example, an Engineer might argue various wonders of the ancient world were realised without assistance from computers! However, the increasing ubiquity of computing in our lives somewhat justifies the statement. Beyond software running on desktop and laptop computers, we are increasingly dependent on huge numbers of devices that have permeated society in less obvious ways. Examples include software running on embedded computers within consumer products such as automobiles and televisions, and software running on chip-and-pin credit cards. All of these examples form systems on which we routinely depend. From domestic tasks to communication, from banking to travel: Computer Science underpins almost *everything* we do, even if you cannot see it on the surface.

Beyond the challenge this presents, it has tangible advantages in terms of employment: Computer Science graduates are regularly snapped up by industries as diverse as finance, media and aerospace for example. The reason is obvious: of course they are highly skilled in the use and creation of technology, but more importantly they have been trained to understand and solve problems, and to challenge what is possible. These skills in particular turn out to be the "gold dust" that distinguishes graduates in Computer Science from other subjects; they also represent the main reason why such a high proportion of those graduates become entrepreneurs by developing their own ideas into their own businesses.

So our goal here is to answer questions about, and encourage you to be interested in, the subject of Computer Science. More specifically, we want to answer questions such as "what is Computer Science" and "why should I study it at University". Of course, to some extent the answers will differ for everyone; different topics within the subject excite different people for example. But rather than give a very brief overview of many *topics*, our approach is to showcase specific topics all roughly relating to one *theme*: information security. This is a slightly subjective choice, but it turns out to allow a very natural connection between lots of things you are already familiar with (e.g., how compact discs work, or the problem of computer viruses) and theory in Computer Science that can help explain them. In each case, we try to demonstrate how the topic relates to other subjects (e.g., Mathematics) and how it allows us to solve *real* problems. You can think of each one as a "mini" lecture course: if you find one or more of them interesting, the chances are you would find a Computer Science degree interesting as well.

Intended Audience

This book attempts a careful balancing act between two intended types of reader, who have related but somewhat different needs. Clearly the book can still be useful if you fall outside this remit, but by focusing on these types we can make some assumptions about what you already know and hence the level of detail presented.

Students   Our primary audience are students looking for an introduction to Computer Science. Two examples stand out:
1. A student studying Mathematics (perhaps ICT or even Computer Science) in later years of secondary or further education.

     In this case our goal is to give a taste of what Computer Science is about, and to provide a connection to your existing studies. Either way, we view you as a target to recruit into a Computer Science degree at University!
2. A student in early years of a Computer Science degree at University, or taking flavours of such a degree from within another subject (e.g., as an optional or elective course).

     In this case our goal is to (re)introduce topics and challenges you may already be faced with; offering a new, and hopefully accessible perspective can help understand basic concepts and motivate further study by illustrating concrete applications.

Teachers   Our secondary audience are teachers. Anecdotally at least, we have found two use-cases that seem important:

1. Where there is a lack of specialist staff, non-specialists or early career staff members are often tasked with teaching Computer Science. In some cases, for example with content in Mathematics, there is clear synergy or even overlap. Either way however, this task can be very challenging.

   In this case the book can be used more or less as a student would. Although you might absorb the material quicker or more easily, it still offers an good introduction to the subject as a whole.

2. Even *with* specialist staff, it can be hard to find and/or develop suitable material; there are an increasing number of good resources online, but still few that focus on fundamentals of the subject and hence form a link to University-level study.

   In this case, the book can act as a useful way to enrich existing lesson plans, or as further reading where appropriate. The tasks embedded in the material, in particular, offer potential points for discussion or work outside the classroom.

Overview of Content

Some books are intended to be read from front-to-back in one go; others are like reference books, where you can dive into a specific part if or when you need to. This book sits somewhere between these types. It is comprised of various parts as explained below, each with specific goals and hence a suggested approach to reading the associated material.

Core Material

The first part is concerned with the fundamentals of Computer Science, and outlines concepts used variously elsewhere in the book. As a result, each chapter in this part should ideally be read in order, and before starting any other part:

Chapter 1   introduces the idea that numbers can be represented in different ways, and uses this to discuss the concepts of data compression, and error detection and correction. The example context is CDs and DVDs. Both store vast amounts of data and are fairly robust to damage; the question is, how do they do this?

Chapter 2   is a brief introduction to the study of algorithms, i.e., formal sets of directions which describe how to perform a task. The idea is to demonstrate that algorithms are fundamental tools in Computer Science, but no more complicated than a set of driving directions or cookery instructions. By studying how algorithms behave, the chapter shows that we can compare them against each other and select the best one for a particular task.

Chapter 3   uses the example of computer viruses to show how computers actually work, i.e., how they are able to execute the programs (or software) we use every day. The idea is to show that there is no magic involved: even modern computers are based on fairly simple principles which everyone can understand.

Chapter 4   highlights the role of data structures, the natural companion to algo-
           rithms. By using the example of strings (which are sequences of characters) the
           chapter shows why data structures are needed, and how their design can have a
           profound influence on algorithms that operate on them.

Chapter 5   deals with one of the most ubiquitous and influential information sys-
           tems available on the Internet: Google web-search. Using only fairly introductory
           Mathematics, it explains how the system seems able to "understand" the web and
           hence produce such good results for a given search query.

The second part focuses specifically on examples drawn from cryptography and
information security. After completing the first part, the idea is that each chapter in
the second part can be read more or less independently from the rest:

Chapter 6   gives a brief introduction to what we now regard as historical schemes
           for encrypting messages. The goal is to demonstrate the two sides of cryptog-
           raphy: the constructive side where new schemes are designed and used, and the
           destructive side where said schemes are attacked and broken. By using simple
           programs available on every UNIX-based computer, the chapter shows how his-
           torical cryptanalysts were able to decrypt messages their sender thought were
           secure.

Chapter 7   discusses the idea of randomness: what does random even mean, and
           when can we describe a number as random? The idea is that random numbers
           often play a crucial role in cryptography, and using just some simple experiments
           one can demonstrate the difference between "good" and "bad" randomness.

Chapter 8   shifts the focus from history to the present day. By giving a more com-
           plete overview of a specific area in Mathematics (i.e., the idea of modular arith-
           metic) it describes two modern cryptographic schemes that more or less all of us
           rely on every day.

Chapter 9   introduces the concept of steganography which relates to hiding secret
           data within non-secret data. This allows a discussion of how computers represent
           and process images (e.g., those taken with a digital camera) and how simple
           steganographic techniques can embed secret messages in them.

Chapter 10   approaches the idea of security from a different perspective than the
           description in Chap. 8. As well as reasoning in theory about how secure a system
           is, we *also* need to worry about whether the physical system leaks information or
           not. The example scenario is guessing passwords: can you break into a computer
           without having to try every possible password, i.e., use any leaked information
           to help you out?

Supplementary Material

In addition to electronic copies of each core chapter, various supplementary material
is available online at

http://www.cs.bris.ac.uk/home/page/teaching/wics.html

This includes additional chapter(s) extending the range of topics covered, plus Appendices providing extra introduction and explanation for topics we think might need it.

Perhaps the single most important instance is an Appendix supporting the use of BASH within examples and tasks. If you have no experience with BASH, which is common, the examples can be confusing. As such, we have written a short tutorial that includes a high-level overview of BASH itself, plus lower-level explanations of every command used in the book. The best approach is arguably to use it for reference as you read through each chapter: whenever you encounter something unfamiliar or confusing, take some time to look through the Appendix which *should* provide an explanation.

Embedded Tasks

To ensure the content is as practically oriented as possible, various tasks are embedded into the material alongside the fixed examples. These fall into various categories:

 These tasks represent implementation challenges, usually with a clear or fixed answer or outcome. In some cases the task might act as a prompt to reproduce or extend an example; in other cases the task might ask you to design something, e.g., an algorithm based on an information description of something in the material.

 These tasks outline topics that represent a good next step on from the material presented: you are interested in the material but want to learn more, or about a specific aspect in more depth, these give some suggestions of what to look at.

They often present open-ended challenges or questions, and as a result often make good discussion points. Either way, the idea is that you stop reading through the material, and attempt to solve the task yourself (rather than rely on the resources provided).

Some tasks of this type will be harder than others, but none are designed to represent a significant amount of work: if you get stuck on one, there is no problem with just skipping it and moving on.

Notation

Throughout the book we have tried to make the notation used as simple and familiar as possible. On the other, hand some notation is inevitable: we need a way to express sets and sequences for instance.

Ranges

When we write $a \ldots b$ for a starting point a and a finishing point b, we are describing a **range** that includes all numbers between (and including) a and b. So writing $0 \ldots 7$ is basically the same as writing $0, 1, 2, 3, 4, 5, 6, 7$. If we say c is *in* the range $0 \ldots 7$ we mean that

$$0 \leq c \leq 7$$

i.e., c is one of $0, 1, 2, 3, 4, 5, 6$ and 7.

Sequences

We write a **sequence** of **elements** called A, which you can think of as like a list, as follows

$$A = \langle 0, 3, 1, 2 \rangle.$$

This sequence contains elements which are numbers, but it is important to keep in mind that elements can be *any* objects we want. For example we could write a sequence of characters such as

$$B = \langle \text{`a'}, \text{`b'}, \text{`c'}, \text{`d'}, \text{`e'} \rangle.$$

Either way, we know the size of A and B, i.e., the number of elements they contain; in the case of A we write this as $|A|$ so that $|A| = 4$ for instance.

In a sequence, the order of the elements is important, and we can refer to each one using an **index**. When we want to refer to the i-th element in A for example (where i is the index) we write A_i. Reading the elements left-to-right, within A we have that $A_0 = 0$, $A_1 = 3$, $A_2 = 1$ and $A_3 = 2$. Note that we count from zero, so the first element is A_0, and that referring to the element A_4 is invalid (because there is no element in A with index 4). Using $\perp$ to mean invalid, we write $A_4 = \perp$ to make this more obvious.

Sometimes it makes sense to save space by not writing all the elements in a given sequence. For example we might rewrite B as

$$B = \langle \text{`a'}, \text{`b'}, \ldots, \text{`e'} \rangle$$

where the continuation dots written as $\ldots$ represent elements `c' and `d' which have been left out: we assume whoever reads the sequence can fill in the $\ldots$ part appropriately. This means it should always be clear and unambiguous what $\ldots$ means. This way of writing B still means we know what $|B|$ is, and also that $B_5 = \perp$ for example. Another example is the sequence C written as

$$C = \langle 0, 3, 1, 2, \ldots \rangle.$$

When we used continuation dots in B, there was a well defined start and end to the sequence so they were just a short-hand to describe elements we did not want to write down. However, with C the continuation dots now represent elements either we do not know, or do not matter: since there is no end to the sequence we cannot necessarily fill in the ... part appropriately as before. This also means we might not know what $|C|$ is, or whether $C_4 = \bot$ or not.

It is possible to join together, or **concatenate**, two sequences. For example, imagine we start with two 4-element sequences

$$D = \langle 0, 1, 2, 3 \rangle$$
$$E = \langle 4, 5, 6, 7 \rangle$$

and want to join them together; we would write

$$F = D \parallel E = \langle 0, 1, 2, 3 \rangle \parallel \langle 4, 5, 6, 7 \rangle = \langle 0, 1, 2, 3, 4, 5, 6, 7 \rangle.$$

Notice that the result F is an 8-element sequence, where $F_{0...3}$ are those from D and $F_{4...7}$ are those from E.

Sets

The concept of a **set** and the theory behind such structures is fundamental to Mathematics. A set is an unordered collection of **elements**; as with a sequence, the elements can be anything you want. We can write a set called A by listing the elements between a pair of braces as follows

$$A = \{2, 3, 4, 5, 6, 7, 8\}.$$

This set contains the whole numbers between two and eight inclusive. The size of a set is the number of elements it contains. For the set A this is written $|A|$, so we have that $|A| = 7$. If the element a is in the set A, we say a is a **member** of A or write

$$a \in A.$$

We know for example that $2 \in A$ but $9 \notin A$, i.e., 2 is a member of the set A, but 9 is not. Unlike a sequence, the ordering of the elements in a set does *not* matter, only their membership or non-membership. This means we *cannot* refer to elements in A as A_i. However, if we define another set

$$B = \{8, 7, 6, 5, 4, 3, 2\},$$

we can be safe in the knowledge that $A = B$. Note that elements cannot occur in a set more than once.

As with sequences, it sometimes makes sense to save space by not writing all the elements in a set. For example we might rewrite the set A as

$$A = \{2, 3, \ldots, 7, 8\}.$$

Sometimes we might want to write a set with unknown size such as

$$C = \{2, 4, 6, 8, \ldots\}.$$

This set is infinite in size in the sense there is no end: it represents all even whole numbers starting at two and continuing to infinity. In this case, the continuation dots are a necessity; if we did not use them, we could not write down the set at all.

Frequently Asked Questions (FAQs)

I have a question/comment/complaint for you.   Any (positive *or* negative) feedback, experience or comment is very welcome; this helps us to improve and extend the material in the most useful way. To get in contact, email

page@cs.bris.ac.uk

or

nigel@cs.bris.ac.uk

We are not perfect, so mistakes are of course possible (although hopefully rare). Some cases are hard for us to check, and make your feedback even more valuable: for instance
1. minor variation in software versions can produce subtle differences in how some commands and hence examples work, and
2. some examples download and use online resources, but web-sites change over time (or even might differ depending on where you access them from) so might cause the example to fail.
Either way, if you spot a problem then let us know: we will try to explain and/or fix things as fast as we can!

Why are all your references to Wikipedia?   Our goal is to give an easily accessible overview, so it made no sense to reference lots of research papers. There are basically two reasons why: research papers are often written in a way that makes them hard to read (even when their intellectual content is not difficult to understand), and although many research papers are available on the Internet, many are not (or have to be paid for). So although some valid criticisms of Wikipedia exist, for introductory material on Computer Science it certainly represents a good place to start.

I like programming; why do the examples include so little programming?   We want to focus on interesting topics rather than the mechanics of programming. So even when we include example programs, the idea is to do so in a way where their meaning is fairly clear. For example it makes more sense to use pseudo-code algorithms or reuse existing software tools than complicate a description of something by including pages and pages of program listings.

If programming really is your sole interest, you might prefer

S.S. Skiena and M.A. Revilla.
Programming Challenges: The Programming Contest Training Manual.
Springer, 2003. ISBN: 978-0387001630.

which offers a range of programming challenges; the excellent online resource

http://projecteuler.net/

is similar, although with greater emphasis on problems grounded in Mathematics.
But you need to be able to program to do Computer Science, right?   Yes! But only
in the same way as you need to be able to read and write to study English. Put
another way, reading and writing, or grammar and vocabulary, are just tools: they
simply allow us to study topics such as English literature. Computer Science is
the same. Although it *is* possible to study programming as a topic in itself, we are
more interested in what can be achieved *using* programs: we treat programming
itself as another tool.
Are there any other things like this I can read?   There are many books about specific topics in Computer Science, but somewhat fewer which overview the subject
itself. Amongst these, some excellent examples are the following:

A.K. Dewdney.
The New Turing Omnibus.
Palgrave-Macmillan, 2003. ISBN: 978-0805071665.

B. Vöcking, H. Alt, M. Dietzfelbinger, R. Reischuk, C. Scheideler, H. Vollmer
and D. Wagner.
Algorithms Unplugged.
Springer, 2011. ISBN: 978-3642153273.

J. MacCormick.
*Nine Algorithms That Changed the Future: The Ingenious Ideas that Drive To-
day's Computers.*
Princeton University Press, 2011. ISBN: 978-0691147147.

There are of course innumerable web-site, blog and wiki style resources online.
Some structured examples include the CS4FN (or "Computer Science for fun")
series from Queen Mary, University of London, UK

http://www.dcs.qmul.ac.uk/cs4fn/

and Computer Science Unplugged series from the University of Canterbury, New
Zealand

http://csunplugged.org/

the latter of which now also offers downloadable and printable books ideal for
use in earlier stages of school.

Acknowledgements

This book was typeset with LATEX, originally developed by Leslie Lamport and based on TEX by Donald Knuth; among the numerous packages used, some important examples include adjustbox by Martin Scharrer, algorithm2e by Christophe Fiorio, listings by Carsten Heinz, PGF and TiKZ by Till Tantau, and pxfonts by Young Ryu. The embedded examples make heavy use of the BASH shell by Brian Fox, and numerous individual commands developed by members of the GNU project housed at

http://www.gnu.org

Throughout the book, images from sources other than the authors have been carefully reproduced under permissive licenses only; each image of this type notes both the source and license in question.

We owe a general debt of gratitude to everyone who has offered feedback, ideas or help with production and publication of this book. We have, in particular, benefited massively from tireless proof reading by Valentina Banciu, David Bernhard, Jake Longo Galea, Simon Hoerder, Daniel Martin, Luke Mather, Jim Page, and Carolyn Whitnall; any remaining mistakes are, of course, our own doing. We would like to acknowledge the support of the EPSRC (specifically via grant EP/H001689/1), whose model for outreach and public engagement was instrumental in allowing development of the material. All royalties resulting from printed versions of the book are donated to the Computing At School (CAS) group, whose ongoing work can be followed at

http://www.computingatschool.org.uk/

We thank Simon Rees and Wayne Wheeler (Springer) for making publication such a smooth process, and additionally Simon Humphreys (CAS) and Jeremy Barlow (BCS) for dealing ably with non-standard administrative overhead of the royalties arrangement.

Bristol, UK   Daniel Page
                                                                                   Nigel Smart

Contents

Part I
Foundations of Computer Science

Compressing and Correcting Digital Media

1

If you talk to most teenage mobile telephone users, they will be experts in data compression [3]. Sadly, money rather than Computer Science is their motivation. **Short Message Service (SMS)** text messages [17] cost the sender some money and, in addition, are limited to 160 characters per-message. Newer messaging services like Twitter derive their limits from SMS (140 characters is actually 160 characters minus 20 for any meta-data), but is less clear where the 160 character limit came from in the first place; it seems the designers just guessed this would be about right in 1985, and now we are stuck with it forever!

Although Twitter messaging is (currently) free, SMS turns out to be a relatively expensive means of communication. For example, Nigel Bannister, a lecturer at the University of Leicester, made a comparison used on the Channel 4 documentary called *The Mobile Phone Rip-Off*: at £0.05 per-message in 2008, transmitting 1 MB of data using SMS costs about £374.49 whereas transmitting the same amount from the Hubble Space Telescope [9] to earth only costs about £8.85!

But I digress. The point is that no matter what means of communication we choose, it makes sense to pack as much information into each message as we can. For example the message

"R U @ hm cuz I wnt 2 cm ovr"

is only 27 characters long and looks like gibberish [18]. To the trained eye, however, it easily translates into the message

"are you at home because I want to come over"

which is a massive 43 characters.

We have **compressed** the message: the first message is shorter than the second, and perhaps costs less as a result. Of course, there is a trade-off or balance between how much we save in terms of communication and how much work we do to compress and decompress the text: typically the more cryptic a text message, the harder it becomes for someone to understand it.

The idea of compressing data is not a new one, but is often hidden by new trends in technology. Only a generation ago for example, before the advent of high-speed

D. Page, N. Smart, *What Is Computer Science?*,
Undergraduate Topics in Computer Science, DOI 10.1007/978-3-319-04042-4_1,
© Springer International Publishing Switzerland 2014

broadband and wireless Internet connections, communication between computers was achieved using a MODEM [13]. The purpose of such a device was to convert digital data into analogue sounds that could be sent along a normal telephone line; this allowed computers to "talk" to each other. However, the speed at which they could talk was slow in comparison to the speed at which they did everything else. Early MODEMs could transmit data at less than 1 kB/s: I can remember transmitting the contents of 880 kB floppy disks to my friend using a MODEM, it *literally* took all day! People quickly realised that compressing the data first could help: if there was less data to send, it would take less time to send it and also reduce their telephone bill. Exactly the same story is true of storage. Again looking back only a generation ago, it would have been seen as quite extravagant to own a 50 MB hard disk. Constrained by cost, people using even smaller hard disks than this realised that they could extend the limits of the space they did have by compressing files which were not in use. It was common practice, whenever they finished writing a document, to first save it onto the hard disk and then compress it so that it took up less space.

These days one can buy a 50 GB hard disk, so it might appear that the need for compression has disappeared: with large bandwidth and storage capacities, who really needs it? The problem is that people have a tendency to fill up *whatever* bandwidth or storage capacity is provided with new forms of data produced by new forms of application! As an example, consider the rise in use of digital photography: armed with digital cameras, people are now used to taking many photographs every time they do something or go somewhere. It is highly likely that the average person takes over 1000 pictures per-year; over a lifetime that is a lot of data to store!

So we can compress data and save money when we communicate or store it. The next problem is, when we receive or read the data how do we know that is what was meant? How do we know there were no errors that may have corrupted the data so that instead of

> "R U @ hm cuz I wnt 2 cm ovr"

the recipient actually gets the even less intelligible

> "Q T ? gl btx H vms 1 bl nuq"

i.e., each character is "off by one". The answer lies in the two related techniques of **error detection** and **error correction** [5]. The idea is that we add some extra information to the data we communicate or store so that if there is an error it is at least apparent to us and, ideally, we can also correct it. Returning to reminiscing about MODEMs, the advantage of an error correction scheme should be apparent: computers used MODEMs to talk over *noisy* telephone lines. We have all used a telephone where there is a bad connection for example. Humans deal with this reasonably well because they can ask the person with whom they are talking to "say that again" if they do not understand something. Computers can do the same thing, but first they need to know that they do not understand what is being said; when the data they are communicating is simply numbers, how can a computer know that one number is right while another is wrong? Error detection and correction solve

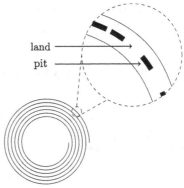

(a) The front and rear surfaces of a real CD.

(b) A conceptual view of the rear CD surface.

Fig. 1.1   An illustration of pits and lands on a CD surface

this problem and are the reasons why after a day spent sending the content of floppy disks via our MODEMs, my friend did not end up with 880 kB of nonsense data he could not use.

The goal of this chapter is to investigate some schemes for data compression and error correction in a context which should be fairly familiar: we will consider data stored on a **Compact Disk (CD)** [2]. This is quite a neat example because when introduced in the early 1980s, the amount of data one could store on a CD and their resilience against damage were two of the major selling points. Both factors (plus some effective marketing) enabled the CD to replace previous technologies such as the cassette tape. The "official" CD specifications are naturally quite technical; our goal here is to give just a flavour of the underlying techniques using the CD as a motivating example.

1.1   A Compact Disk = a Sequence of Numbers

Roughly speaking, you can think of the content of a CD as being a long spiral track onto which tiny marks are etched (as shown in Fig. 1.1): a **pit** is where a mark is made, a **land** is where no mark is made. The physical process by which a writer device performs the marking depends slightly on the CD type. But however it is written, the idea is that a reader device can inspect the surface of a CD and detect the occurrence of pits and lands. It is easy to imagine that instead of talking about pits and lands we could write down the content as a sequence such as

$$A = \langle 0, 1, 0, 1 \rangle$$

where for the sake of argument, imagine a pit is represented by a 1 and a land is represented by a 0. Quite often it is convenient to interpret the CD content represented by A in different ways that suit whatever we are doing with it. To this end, we need to understand how numbers are represented by a computer.

1.1.1 Decimal and Binary Representation

As humans, we are used to working with base-10 or **decimal** numbers because (mostly) we have ten fingers and toes; this means the set of valid decimal digits is $\{0, 1, \ldots, 9\}$. Imagine we write down a decimal number such as 123. Hopefully you can believe this is sort of the same as writing the sequence

$$B = \langle 3, 2, 1 \rangle$$

given that 3 is the first digit of 123, 2 is the second digit and so on; we are just reading the digits from left-to-right rather than from right-to-left. How do we know what 123 or B *means*? What is their value? In simple terms, we just weight each of the digits 1, 2 and 3 by a different amount and then add everything up. We can see for example that

$$123 = 1 \cdot 100 + 2 \cdot 10 + 3 \cdot 1$$

which we might say out loud as "one lot of hundred, two lots of ten and three units" or "one hundred and twenty three". We could also write the same thing as

$$123 = 1 \cdot 10^2 + 2 \cdot 10^1 + 3 \cdot 10^0$$

since any number raised to the power of zero is equal to one.

In our example, the sequence B consists of three elements; we can write this more formally by saying $|B| = 3$ meaning "the size of B is three". The first element of the sequence is B_0 and clearly $B_0 = 3$; likewise for the second and third elements we have $B_1 = 2$ and $B_2 = 1$. It might seem odd naming the first element B_0 rather than B_1, but we almost *always* count from 0 rather than 1 in Computer Science. We can now rewrite

$$123 = 1 \cdot 10^2 + 2 \cdot 10^1 + 3 \cdot 10^0$$

as the **summation**

$$123 = \sum_{i=0}^{|B|-1} B_i \cdot 10^i.$$

In words, the right-hand side means that for each index i between 0 and $|B| - 1$ (since $|B| = 3$ this means $i = 0$, $i = 1$ and $i = 2$) we add up terms that look like $B_i \cdot 10^i$ (i.e., the terms $B_0 \cdot 10^0$, $B_1 \cdot 10^1$ and $B_2 \cdot 10^2$). This means we add up

$$\begin{aligned}
B_0 \cdot 10^0 &= 3 \cdot 10^0 = 3 \cdot 1 &= 3 \\
B_1 \cdot 10^1 &= 2 \cdot 10^1 = 2 \cdot 10 &= 20 \\
B_2 \cdot 10^2 &= 1 \cdot 10^2 = 1 \cdot 100 &= 100
\end{aligned}$$

to make a total of 123 as expected. As a final step, we could abstract away the number 10 (which is called the **base** of our number system) and simply call it b.

An aside: a magic trick based on binary numbers (part #1)

A popular magic trick is based on binary representations of numbers: you might have seen the trick itself before, which is a common (presumably since it is inexpensive) prize inside Christmas crackers. The whole thing is based on 6 cards with numbers written on them:

1	3	5	7	9	11	13	15
17	19	21	23	25	27	29	31
33	35	37	39	41	43	45	47
49	51	53	55	57	59	61	63

2	3	6	7	10	11	14	15
18	19	22	23	26	27	30	31
34	35	38	39	42	43	46	47
50	51	54	55	58	59	62	63

4	5	6	7	12	13	14	15
20	21	22	23	28	29	30	31
36	37	38	39	44	45	46	47
52	53	54	55	60	61	62	63

8	9	10	11	12	13	14	15
24	25	26	27	28	29	30	31
40	41	42	43	44	45	46	47
56	57	58	59	60	61	62	63

16	17	18	19	20	21	22	23
24	25	26	27	28	29	30	31
48	49	50	51	52	53	54	55
56	57	58	59	60	61	62	63

32	33	34	35	36	37	38	39
40	41	42	43	44	45	46	47
48	49	50	51	52	53	54	55
56	57	58	59	60	61	62	63

To pull off the trick, we follow these steps:
1. Give the cards to your target and ask them to pick a number x that appears on at least one card, but to keep it secret.
2. Now show them the cards one-by-one: each time, ask them whether x appears the card or not. If they tell you x does appear on a card then place it in a pile, otherwise discard it.
3. To "magically" guess the number chosen, just add up each top, left-hand number on the cards in your pile.

This means that our number

$$123 = \sum_{i=0}^{|B|-1} B_i \cdot 10^i$$

can be rewritten as

$$123 = \sum_{i=0}^{|B|-1} B_i \cdot b^i$$

for $b = 10$. So to cut a long story short, it is reasonable to interpret the sequence B as the decimal number 123 if we want to do so: all we need know is that since B represents a decimal sequence, we need to set $b = 10$.

An aside: a magic trick based on binary numbers (part #2)

Why does this work? Basically, if we write a number in binary then we are expressing it as the sum of some terms that are each a power-of-two. You can see this by looking at some examples:

$$
\begin{aligned}
1 &= 1 & &= 2^0 \\
2 &= \quad 2 & &= \qquad 2^1 \\
3 &= 1+2 & &= 2^0 + 2^1 \\
4 &= \qquad 4 = & & \qquad 2^2 \\
5 &= 1 \quad +4 = 2^0 & &+ 2^2 \\
6 &= \quad 2+4 = & & \quad 2^1 + 2^2 \\
7 &= 1+2+4 = 2^0 & &+ 2^1 + 2^2
\end{aligned}
$$

$$\vdots \qquad\qquad \vdots$$

Notice that the top, left-hand number t on each card is a power-of-two; all the other numbers on a given card are those where t appears as a term when we express it in binary. Look at the first card for example: each of the numbers $1, 3, 5, 7$ and so on include the term $t = 2^0 = 1$ when we express it in binary. Or, on the second card each of the numbers $2, 3, 6, 7$ and so on include the term $t = 2^1 = 2$.

So given a pile of cards on which x appears, we recover it more or less in reverse. Imagine the target selects $x = 35$ for example. Look at the cards: if we ask the target to identify cards on which 35 appears, we get a pile with those whose top, left-hand numbers are $1, 2$ and $32 \ldots$ when we add them up we clearly recover

$$2^0 + 2^1 + 2^5 = 1 + 2 + 32 = 35.$$

To a target with no understanding of binary, this of course looks far more like magic than Mathematics!

The neat outcome is that there are *many* other ways of representing 123. For example, suppose we use a different value for b, say $b = 2$. Using $b = 2$ equates to working with base-2 or **binary** numbers; all this means is our weights and digit set from above change. We could now express the number 123 as the binary sequence

$$C = \langle 1, 1, 0, 1, 1, 1, 1, 0 \rangle.$$

For $b = 2$, the set of valid binary digits is $\{0, 1\}$. The value of C is therefore given by

$$\sum_{i=0}^{|C|-1} C_i \cdot 2^i$$

as before, which since $|C| = 8$ means we add up the terms

$$
\begin{aligned}
C_0 \cdot 2^0 &= 1 \cdot 2^0 = 1 \cdot 1 &&= 1 \\
C_1 \cdot 2^1 &= 1 \cdot 2^1 = 1 \cdot 2 &&= 2 \\
C_2 \cdot 2^2 &= 0 \cdot 2^2 = 0 \cdot 4 &&= 0 \\
C_3 \cdot 2^3 &= 1 \cdot 2^3 = 1 \cdot 8 &&= 8 \\
C_4 \cdot 2^4 &= 1 \cdot 2^4 = 1 \cdot 16 &&= 16 \\
C_5 \cdot 2^5 &= 1 \cdot 2^5 = 1 \cdot 32 &&= 32 \\
C_6 \cdot 2^6 &= 1 \cdot 2^6 = 1 \cdot 64 &&= 64 \\
C_7 \cdot 2^7 &= 0 \cdot 2^7 = 0 \cdot 128 &&= 0
\end{aligned}
$$

to obtain the number 123 as before.

Now we can move away from the specific example of 123, and try to think about a general number x. For a given base b, we have the digit set $\{0, 1, \ldots, b - 1\}$. Remember that for $b = 10$ and $b = 2$ this meant the sets $\{0, 1, \ldots, 9\}$ and $\{0, 1\}$. A given number x is written as a sequence of digits taken from the appropriate digit set, i.e., each i-th digit $x_i \in \{0, 1, \ldots, b - 1\}$. We can express the value of x using n base-b digits and the summation

$$
x = \sum_{i=0}^{n-1} x_i \cdot b^i.
$$

The key thing to realise is that it does not matter so much *how* we write down a number, as long as we take some care the *value* is not changed when we interpret what it means.

1.1.2   Decimal and Binary Notation

Amazingly there are not many jokes about Computer Science, but here are two:
1. There are only 10 types of people in the world: those who understand binary, and those who do not.
2. Why did the Computer Scientist always confuse Halloween and Christmas? Because 31 Oct equals 25 Dec.

Whether or not you laughed at them, both jokes relate to what we have been discussing: in the first case there is an ambiguity between the number ten written in decimal and binary, and in the second between the number twenty five written in octal and decimal.

Still confused? Look at the first joke: it is saying that the literal 10 can be interpreted as binary as well as decimal, i.e., as $1 \cdot 2 + 0 \cdot 1 = 2$ in binary and $1 \cdot 10 + 0 \cdot 1 = 10$. So the two types of people are those who understand that 2 can be represented by 10, and those that do not. Now look at the second joke: this is a play on words in that "Oct" can mean "October" but also "octal" or base-8. Likewise "Dec" can mean "December" but also "decimal". With this in mind, we see that

$$
3 \cdot 8 + 1 \cdot 1 = 25 = 2 \cdot 10 + 5 \cdot 1.
$$

I.e., 31 Oct equals 25 Dec in the sense that 31 in base-8 equals 25 in base-10.

Put in context, we have already shown that the decimal sequence B and the decimal number 123 are basically the same if we interpret B in the right way. But there is a problem of ambiguity: if we follow the same reasoning, we would also say that the binary sequence C and the number 01111011 are the same. But how do we know what base 01111011 is written down in? It could mean the decimal number 123 (i.e., one hundred and twenty three) if we interpret it using $b = 2$, or the decimal number 01111011 (i.e., one million, one hundred and eleven thousand and eleven) if we interpret it using $b = 10$!

To clear up this ambiguity where necessary, we write literal numbers with the base appended to them. For example $123_{(10)}$ is the number 123 written in base-10 whereas $01111011_{(2)}$ is the number 01111011 in base-2. We can now be clear, for example, that $123_{(10)} = 01111011_{(2)}$. If we write a sequence, we can do the same thing: $\langle 3, 2, 1 \rangle_{(10)}$ makes it clear we are still basically talking about the number 123. So our two "jokes" in this notation become $10_{(2)} = 2_{(10)}$ and $31_{(8)} = 25_{(10)}$.

Actually working through examples is really the only way to get to grips with this topic. Convince yourself you understand things so far by

- converting the decimal literal $31_{(10)}$ into binary, then
- converting the binary literal $01101111_{(2)}$ into decimal.

1.1.3 Grouping Bits into Bytes

Traditionally, we call a binary digit (whose value is 0 or 1) a **bit**. Returning to the CD content described as the sequence of bits called A, what we really had was a sequence which we could interpret as a single (potentially very large) number written in binary. Imagine we write a similar sequence

$$D = \langle 1, 1, 0, 0, 0, 0, 0, 0, 1, 0, 0, 0, 1, 0, 1, 0 \rangle.$$

One could take D and write it to the CD surface directly, or instead we could write it in groups of bits. The second approach would be sort of like constructing and writing a new sequence, for example splitting the bits of D into groups of four,

$$E = \big\langle \langle 1, 1, 0, 0 \rangle, \langle 0, 0, 0, 0 \rangle, \langle 1, 0, 0, 0 \rangle, \langle 1, 0, 1, 0 \rangle \big\rangle$$

or eight,

$$F = \big\langle \langle 1, 1, 0, 0, 0, 0, 0, 0 \rangle, \langle 1, 0, 0, 0, 1, 0, 1, 0 \rangle \big\rangle.$$

So E has four elements (each of which is a sub-sequence of four elements from the original sequence), while F has two elements (each of which is a sub-sequence of eight elements from the original sequence). We call a group of four bits a **nybble** and a group of eight bits a **byte**: E is a sequence of nybbles and F is a sequence of bytes. The thing is, if we write the content of E or F to the CD surface we get the same bits (and hence the same pits and lands) as if we write D: it just depends on how we group them together.

Armed with the knowledge we now have about representing numbers, we can also use a short-hand to write each group as a decimal number. For example

$$G = \langle 3_{(10)}, 81_{(10)} \rangle$$

can be reasonably interpreted as the same sequence as F, and hence D, because

$$\langle 1, 1, 0, 0, 0, 0, 0, 0 \rangle_{(2)} \equiv 1 \cdot 2 + 1 \cdot 1 \qquad = 3_{(10)}$$
$$\langle 1, 0, 0, 0, 1, 0, 1, 0 \rangle_{(2)} \equiv 1 \cdot 64 + 1 \cdot 16 + 1 \cdot 1 = 81_{(10)}$$

As an exercise, look at the four groups of four bits in E: see if you can work out the equivalent of G for this sequence, i.e., what would the same decimal short-hand look like?

The upshot of this is that we can describe the CD content in a variety of different ways on paper, even though when we talk about actually writing them onto the CD surface everything *must* be a sequence of bits. All we need to be careful about is that we have a consistent procedure to convert between different ways of describing the CD content.

Research (task #4)

Another representation of integers used by Computer Scientists, often as a short-hand for binary, is base-16 or **hexadecimal**. Do some research on this representation, and try to explain it within the general framework used for decimal and binary above. Also, explain

1. how we can cope with the fact that we only have ten digits (i.e., 0 to 9) but hexadecimal needs 16, and
2. how and why it acts as the short-hand described.

1.2   Data Compression

Even though it is intended as an amusing example, there *are* serious points we can draw from our previous discussion of text messaging:

- The topic of data compression has a golden rule which, roughly speaking, says to replace long things with shorter things. We can clearly see this going on, for example we have used the short symbol "@" to represent the longer sequence of characters "at".
- *How* were we able to compress and decompress the text at all? Partly the answer is that we know what English words and sentences mean; we can **adapt** our compression scheme because of this knowledge. However, in many situations we are just given a long binary sequence with no knowledge of what it means: it could represent an image, or some text for instance. In such a case, we have no

extra insight with which to adapt our compression method; we only have the raw bits to look at.

- The fact that we *can* find a good scheme to compress the text is, in part, because the English language is quite **redundant**; this is a fancy way to say some things occur more often than others. So for example, if you look at this chapter then you would see that the sequence of characters "compression" appears quite often indeed: if we apply the golden rule of data compression and replace "compression" with some short symbol, e.g., '@', then we will make the document quite a bit shorter.

- The final thing to note is the difference between **lossless** and **lossy** compression. If we compress something with a lossless compression scheme and then decompress it, we always get back what we started with. However, with lossy compression this is not true: such a scheme throws away data thought not to matter in relation to the meaning. For example, if we had a sequence of ten spaces, throwing away nine of them still means the text is readable even though it is not the same.

You may have come across lossy and lossless compression when dealing with digital photographs. When storing or editing the resulting image files, one usually stores them in the **jpeg** or **jpg** format; this is a standard produced by the **Joint Photographic Experts Group (JPEG)** [11]. Such a file usually compresses the image, but it does so in a lossy manner: some information is thrown away. The advantage of this approach is that the file can be smaller: much of the information in the image is so detailed our eyes cannot see it, so any disadvantage is typically marginal.

Armed with this knowledge we can be a bit more specific about how to treat the CD content: we want a non-adaptive, lossless compression scheme. Put more simply, we want to take some binary sequence X and, without knowing anything about what it means, compress it into a shorter sequence $\bar{X}$ so that later we can recover the exact original X if we want to. This will basically mean we can write more data onto the surface of our CD (i.e., longer films, larger files, more music or whatever), though we need to work harder to access it (i.e., decompress it first).

Research (task #5)

There are plenty of good software tools for manipulating images, and many of them are free; a good example is **The GNU Image Manipulation Program (GIMP)**

www.gimp.org

Using such a tool, load a photograph and then save various versions of it: if you use JPEG as the format, you should be able to alter the compression ratio used, and hence the quality. What is the smallest sized version (on disk) you can make? At what point does the image quality start to degrade past what you find acceptable? Does the answer to these questions change if you use a different photograph?

1.2.1 A Run-Length Based Approach

Imagine we wanted to write a decimal sequence

$$X = \langle 255, 255, 255, 255, 255, 255, 255, 255 \rangle$$

onto a CD. The number 255 is repeated eight times in a row: we call this a **run** [16], each run has a **subject** (i.e., the thing that is repeated, in this case 255) and a **length** (i.e., how many times the subject is repeated, in this case 8). Of course, you might argue that this is a contrived example: how likely is it that 255 will be repeated again and again in real CD content? Actually, this happens more often that you would think. Going back to the example, imagine we wrote a digital photograph onto the CD where numbers in the sequence X basically represent the colours in the image; if the image has a large block of a single colour then the colour value will repeat many times. Another example is English text; although it is uncommon to have a run of more than two identical characters in a word (for example "moon" is possible with a run of two 'o' characters), sometimes there *is* a long run of spaces to separate words or paragraphs.

For the sake of argument, imagine there is at least a fair chance of a run occurring from time to time: how can we compress a run when we find one? Think about a simple question: which is shorter, X or a *description* of X written as

"repeat 255 eight times" .

Probably it is hard to say since we know how to write numbers onto the CD, but not the description of X. So we need to invent a scheme that converts the description into numbers we *can* write to the CD; imagine we choose to represent a run description as three numbers where:

1. the first number (the **escape code**) tells us we have found a run description rather than a normal number and therefore need to take some special action (here we use the number 0 as the escape code),
2. the second number tells us the length of the run, and
3. the third number tells us the subject of the run.

Using this scheme, we can compress our sequence X into the new sequence

$$\bar{X} = \langle 0, 8, 255 \rangle$$

where 0 tells us this is a run, 8 tells us the run length is eight and 255 tells us the number to repeat eight times is 255. Compressing X into $\bar{X}$ is a matter of scanning the original sequence, identifying runs and converting them into the corresponding description. To decompress $\bar{X}$ and recover X we simply process elements of the compressed sequence one at a time: when we hit a 0 we know that we need to do something special (i.e., expand a run description specified by the next two numbers), otherwise we just have a normal number.

However, there are two problems. First, since our scheme for describing runs has a length of three, it does not really make sense to use it for runs of length less than three. Of course, runs of length one or zero do not really make sense anyway, but we should not compress runs of length two because we would potentially be making the compressed sequence longer! To see this, consider the sequence

$$Y = \langle 255, 255 \rangle.$$

Our compression scheme would turn this into

$$\bar{Y} = \langle 0, 2, 255 \rangle,$$

which is longer than the original sequence! In short, we are relying on the original sequence containing long runs, the longer the better: if it does not, then using our scheme does not make sense.

Second, and more importantly, what happens if the original sequence contains a 0? For example, imagine we want to compress the sequence

$$Z = \langle 255, 255, 255, 255, 255, 255, 255, 255, 0, 1, 2 \rangle$$

with our scheme; we would end up with

$$\bar{Z} = \langle 0, 8, 255, 0, 1, 2 \rangle.$$

When we read $\bar{Z}$ from the CD and try to decompress it, we would start off fine: we would read the 0, notice that we had found a run description with length 8 and subject 255, and expand it into eight copies of 255. Then there is a problem because we would read the next 0 and assume we would found another run with length 1 and subject 2 which is not what we meant at all. We would end up recovering the sequence

$$Z' = \langle 255, 255, 255, 255, 255, 255, 255, 255, 2 \rangle,$$

which is not what was originally compressed.

To fix things, we need to be a bit more clever about the escape code. One approach is to compress a "real 0" into a run of length one and subject 0. With this alteration we would compress Z to obtain

$$\bar{Z} = \langle 0, 8, 255, 0, 1, 0, 1, 2 \rangle$$

which will then decompress correctly. However, this is a bit wasteful due to two facts: first we know it does not make sense to have a run of length zero, and second if the run length *was* zero there would be no point having a subject since repeating anything zero times gives the same result. So we could reserve a run length of zero to mean we want a real 0. Using this approach, we would compress Z to get

$$\bar{Z} = \langle 0, 8, 255, 0, 0, 1, 2 \rangle.$$

We can still decompress this correctly because when we read the second 0 and (falsely) notice we have found a run description, we *know* we were mistaken because the next number we read (i.e., the supposed run length) is also 0: there is no need to read a run subject because we already know we meant to have a real 0. In other words, the sequence $\langle 0, 0 \rangle$ is an encoding of the actual element 0.

1.2.2   A Dictionary-Based Approach

A run-length approach is fine if the original sequence has long runs in it, but what else can we do? One idea would be to take inspiration from our original example of text messaging. Abusing our notation for CD content for a moment, roughly what we want to do is compress the sequence

$$X = \langle \text{"are"}, \text{"you"}, \text{"at"}, \text{"home"}, \text{"because"}, \text{"I"}, \text{"want"}, \text{"to"}, \text{"come"}, \text{"over"} \rangle.$$

The way we did this originally (although we did not really explain how at the time) was to construct and use a **dictionary** that coverts long words into short symbols [4]. For example, if we had the dictionary

$$D = \langle \text{"are"}, \text{"at"}, \text{"to"} \rangle$$

then we could compress X into

$$\bar{X} = \langle D_0, \text{"you"}, D_1, \text{"home"}, \text{"because"}, \text{"I"}, \text{"want"}, D_2, \text{"come"}, \text{"over"} \rangle.$$

Essentially we have replaced words in X with references to entries in the dictionary. For example D_0 is a reference to the 0-th entry in the dictionary D so each time we see D_0 in $\bar{X}$, we can expand it out into "are".

If $\bar{X}$ is shorter than X, we could claim we have compressed the original sequence; if we choose longer words to include in the dictionary or words that occur often, we improve how much we compress by. The sanity of this approach is easy to see if we continue to ignore sequences of numbers and consider some real text from Project Gutenberg:

http://www.gutenberg.org/

Among a huge number of potential examples, consider the text of *The Merchant of Venice* by Shakespeare. To analyse the frequency of words, we will combine some standard commands in a BASH terminal. First we fetch the text and save it as the file A.txt:

```
bash$ wget -q -U chrome -O A.txt 'http://www.gutenberg.org/dirs/etext97/1ws1810.txt'
bash$
```

The wget command downloads the file containing *The Merchant of Venice* text from the URL

http://www.gutenberg.org/dirs/etext97/1ws1810.txt

using three options, namely
1. -q tells wget not print out any progress information,
2. -U chrome tells wget to masquerade as the Chrome web-browser so the download is not blocked, and
3. -O A.txt tells wget to save the output into a file called A.txt,

plus the URL

http://www.gutenberg.org/dirs/etext97/1ws1810.txt

Once we have the text, we translate all characters to lower-case so our task is a little easier (i.e., we do not need to consider the upper-case characters as distinct), and save the result in B.txt. This is achieved using the following command pipeline

```
bash$ cat A.txt | tr [:upper:] [:lower:] > B.txt
bash$
```

where the output of cat (the contents of A.txt) is fed as input to tr which performs the translation for us; the output is then redirected into B.txt. In this case, the rule [:upper:] [:lower:] used by tr can be read as "take upper-case letters, translate them into lower-case equivalents".

Now we need a way to count the number of occurrences of words. To do this we first use tr to convert all space characters into EOL characters and delete all punctuation characters; this basically takes the original file and converts it into a version where there is one word per-line. Finally we remove all punctuation and blank lines using tr and grep, and save the result as C.txt. In summary we execute the command pipeline:

```
bash$ cat B.txt | tr [:space:] '\n' | tr -d [:punct:] | grep -v ^$ > C.txt
bash$
```

To get the actual count, we first sort C.txt then use uniq to count the unique occurrences of each word; we sort the result and use head to give us the top 31 most used words:

```
bash$ cat C.txt | sort | uniq -c | sort -n -r | head -n 31 | paste -s
888 the       662 and       656 i         549 of        502 to
476 you       462 a         363 my        306 in        296 is
271 that      263 for       262 me        243 it        231 not
208 be        207 with      188 your      185 but       177 this
174 he        166 have      159 his       151 as        145 portia
144 by        135 will      128 so        128 if        121 are
120 bassanio
bash$
```

This might all seem a bit like magic if you are not used to BASH or the commands themselves. However, the result we get at the end should be more obviously close to what you would expect. For example the words used most are things like "the" and "and". Working down the list we start to find some good candidates for the dictionary. For example "bassanio" is quite long and also used fairly often, so replacing this with a reference to the dictionary would be quite effective.

Of course, a largely similar approach is possible when we return to consider sequences of numbers we want to write onto the CD. Imagine we wanted to write a decimal sequence

$$Y = \langle 1, 2, 3, 4, 5, 5, 5, 5, 1, 2, 3, 4 \rangle$$

onto a CD. First we construct a dictionary, say

$$D = \langle \langle 1, 2, 3, 4 \rangle, \langle 5, 5, 5, 5 \rangle \rangle,$$

and then compress Y to get

$$\bar{Y} = \langle D_0, D_1, D_0 \rangle.$$

Already we can identify two problems. First, the text messages example was a special case since the dictionary was actually in the head of the person reading the SMS message: we did not need to include it *with* the message! Now things are different. To decompress $\bar{Y}$ and hence recover Y, we need to write D to the CD as well because this is the only way to be clear what D_0 means. There is a trade-off as a result: the more elements we add to the dictionary, the more chance we have to compress parts of the sequence *but* also the larger the dictionary becomes. Since we need to write the dictionary onto the CD as well as the compressed sequence, identifying a small set of good candidates for dictionary entries is therefore important, otherwise including the dictionary will cancel out any advantage (in terms of storage space) we get from the compression process.

Second, D_0 is not a number so we cannot currently write it to the CD at all. To solve this, we can use a similar approach as when we looked at run-length encoding; imagine we choose to represent a reference to a dictionary entry as two numbers:

1. the first number (the **escape code**) tells us we have found a dictionary reference rather than a normal number and therefore need to take some special action (here we use the number 1 as the escape code),
2. the second number tells us the dictionary entry we are referring to.

Returning to the sequence Y, given the dictionary D we could compress Y to give

$$\bar{Y} = \langle 1, 0, 1, 1, 1, 0 \rangle$$

where, looking at the first two elements in $\bar{Y}$, 1 tells us this is a dictionary reference, and 0 tells us the reference is to entry 0 (i.e., $\langle 1, 2, 3, 4 \rangle$) for example.

Compressing Y into $\bar{Y}$ is a matter of scanning the original sequence, identifying good candidates for the dictionary and converting them into references. Of course this is a bit harder than when we looked at text: given we are not working with words which we can identify based on spaces around them, how could we decide $\langle 1, 2, 3, 4 \rangle$ is a good candidate? This is beyond the scope of our description; essentially this is the clever part in any dictionary based approach. We would need to perform a scan of the original sequence to capture statistics about the content, and construct the dictionary before a second scan performed the actual compression.

To decompress $\bar{Y}$ and recover Y, we simply process elements of the compressed sequence one at a time: when we hit a 1 we know that we need to do something special (i.e., replace a reference with an element from the dictionary), otherwise we just have a normal number. Again, we would need to do the same thing as in the run-length encoding case to cope with the fact that the escape code 1 might occur in the original sequence; we need to be able to specify that we meant a "real 1" somehow.

1.3   Error Correction

In the previous section we looked at two simple schemes for data compression. But recall this was only *one* reason that CDs became popular; the other reason was that CDs are less prone to damage than previous media such as vinyl or cassette tape. Now we need to turn our attention to the detection and correction of errors. To illustrate the problem, imagine we start off with the short binary sequence

$$X = \langle 0, 1, 1, 1 \rangle$$

which represents (potentially compressed) binary data we want to write onto a CD. Two types of error might occur:
1. There might be **permanent** errors which occur *every time* we try to read X. For example, if we scratch the CD surface then every time we try to read X we get some other sequence because the pits and lands have been destroyed.
2. There might be **transient** errors that only occur *occasionally* when we try to read X. For example, if the CD surface has dust on it then we might read X incorrectly sometimes and correctly other times when the dust is displaced.

To cope with this, we would like to construct a scheme with two properties: first we would like to know when an error has occurred, and second we would like to be able to correct an error once we know it has occurred. To do this we will add some redundant elements to X in order to produce a new sequence $\hat{X}$ which is what we actually write onto the CD.

1.3.1   An Error Detection Approach

To present an error detection scheme we need to introduce two functions:
1. The HAMMING-WEIGHT function [8] counts the number of elements in a binary sequence that are equal to one. So given that

$$X = \langle 0, 1, 1, 1 \rangle,$$

for example, this means HAMMING-WEIGHT$(X) = 3$. We can compute this result by just adding all the elements together, i.e.,

$$\text{HAMMING-WEIGHT}(X) = \sum_{i=0}^{|X|-1} X_i$$

so that

$$\text{HAMMING-WEIGHT}(\langle 0, 1, 1, 1 \rangle) = X_0 + X_1 + X_2 + X_3 = 0 + 1 + 1 + 1 = 3.$$

2. The PARITY function tells us whether the HAMMING-WEIGHT function gives an odd or even result. The idea relies on the XOR (short for "exclusive-or") function [6] that is written using the symbol $\oplus$ and gives us a single output from

two inputs:

$$x \oplus y = \begin{cases} 0 & \text{if } x = 0, y = 0 \\ 1 & \text{if } x = 1, y = 0 \\ 1 & \text{if } x = 0, y = 1 \\ 0 & \text{if } x = 1, y = 1 \end{cases}$$

We compute the PARITY function by simply XOR'ing all the elements together, i.e.,

$$\text{PARITY}(X) = \bigoplus_{i=0}^{|X|-1} X_i$$

so that

$$\text{PARITY}\big(\langle 0, 1, 1, 1 \rangle\big) = X_0 \oplus X_1 \oplus X_2 \oplus X_3 = 0 \oplus 1 \oplus 1 \oplus 1 = 1.$$

In other words, we take the HAMMING-WEIGHT function and replace each $+$ with $\oplus$. As a consequence, you could also think of the result as being given by

$$\text{PARITY}(X) = \text{HAMMING-WEIGHT}(X) \bmod 2.$$

Given a sequence X, an **even parity code** [15] adds an extra element in order to allow detection of errors. Starting with X, we compute the extra element

$$P_0 = \text{PARITY}(X) = X_0 \oplus X_1 \oplus X_2 \oplus X_3$$

and then concatenate it to the end of X to give

$$\hat{X} = X \parallel \langle P_0 \rangle.$$

A more concrete example probably makes this easier to understand. If we start with

$$X = \langle 0, 1, 1, 1 \rangle$$

then since $P_0 = \text{PARITY}(X) = 1$, the result is a new sequence

$$\begin{aligned} \hat{X} &= X \parallel \langle 1 \rangle \\ &= \langle 0, 1, 1, 1 \rangle \parallel \langle 1 \rangle \\ &= \langle 0, 1, 1, 1, 1 \rangle \end{aligned}$$

which we can write onto the CD. Notice that because of our choices, we will *always* have $\text{PARITY}(\hat{X}) = 0$.

Now imagine that sometime after writing $\hat{X}$ to the CD, we try to read the sequence back again. Unfortunately there is an error: instead of getting what we expected, i.e., $\hat{X}$, we get some other sequence $\hat{X}'$ where the error has flipped one element from either 0 to 1 or from 1 to 0. For example, we might get

$$\hat{X}' = \langle 0, 1, 0, 1, 1 \rangle$$
$$= \langle 0, 1, 0, 1 \rangle \parallel \langle 1 \rangle$$
$$= X' \parallel \langle 1 \rangle$$

How can we detect that the error occurred? Because of the way we added the extra element to X, $\text{PARITY}(\hat{X}')$ *should* be zero but because of the error it is one: this mismatch shows that an error occurred. Put more simply, if we recompute

$$P_0' = X_0' \oplus X_1' \oplus X_2' \oplus X_3'$$
$$= 0 \ \oplus 1 \ \oplus 0 \ \oplus 1$$
$$= 0$$

then the fact we get 0 as a result signals that an error occurred: this does not match the original P_0 we added. Notice that

- if we read $\hat{X}$, i.e., there was no error, we can simply strip off the extra element and get back the X we wanted to read, but
- if we read $\hat{X}'$, i.e., there was an error, we cannot tell where the error occurred or how to correct it, so we have to try to reread the CD and hope the error is transient and does not occur again.

This sounds great, but there is a problem: if more than one error occurs then we can be fooled into thinking that there was no error at all. For example, imagine that two elements are flipped and we read

$$\hat{X}' = \langle 0, 0, 0, 1, 1 \rangle$$
$$= \langle 0, 0, 0, 1 \rangle \parallel \langle 1 \rangle$$
$$= X' \parallel \langle 1 \rangle$$

instead of $\hat{X}$. To check if an error occurred, we compute

$$P_0' = X_0' \oplus X_1' \oplus X_2' \oplus X_3'$$
$$= 0 \ \oplus 0 \ \oplus 0 \ \oplus 1$$
$$= 1$$

and are fooled because we get 1 as a result which matches what we were expecting; as a result we use $\hat{X}'$ thinking it is correct. Clearly detection of more than one error is important in reality, and more complex schemes that can achieve this goal *are* possible. But instead we turn our attention to error correction: once we have detected an error, how can we fix it rather than reread the CD and hope for the best?

Implement (task #6)

Throughout the above, we used an even parity code. Provided all the working out is consistent, however, there is no reason to prefer this approach over the alternative: an **odd parity code**. Reproduce the example above using an odd parity code.

Fig. 1.2 A Venn diagram
describing the computation of
error correction bits in a
$(7, 4)$-code

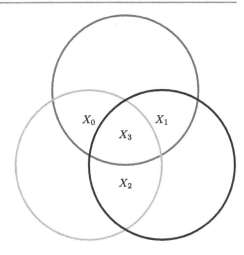

1.3.2   An Error Correction Approach

The **Hamming code** [7], named after inventor Richard Hamming, improves on simple error detection mechanisms by allowing the correction of errors once they are
detected. This requires more than one element to be added to the sequence we start
with. Hamming used the term (n, m)-code to mean a scheme where there were n
elements in the end result, of which m are the original elements and $n - m$ are
added afterwards. Phrased like this, you could view the original even parity code
from above as an $(n, n - 1)$-code because there were n elements to start with, and
we added $n - (n - 1) = 1$ element.

We will concentrate on the specific example of a $(7, 4)$-code introduced in 1950:
this starts with a sequence of four elements and adds three more to realise the error
correction scheme. Starting with X, we compute the three extra elements

$$P_0 = X_0 \oplus X_1 \oplus X_3$$
$$P_1 = X_0 \oplus X_2 \oplus X_3$$
$$P_2 = X_1 \oplus X_2 \oplus X_3$$

and then concatenate them onto the end of X to give

$$\hat{X} = X \parallel \langle P_0, P_1, P_2 \rangle.$$

A reasonable question to ask is why we would choose to compute P_0, P_1 and P_2
like *this* rather than in some other way? The choice is explained neatly by placing
them into the Venn diagram [19] shown in Fig. 1.2. The idea is that the three sets
in the Venn diagram represent the three extra elements we have computed. Each set
"covers" a different combination of the elements from X: the upper set represents
P_0 and covers X_0, X_1 and X_3; the lower-left set represents P_1 and covers X_0, X_2
and X_3; the lower-right set represents P_2 and covers X_1, X_2 and X_3. Notice, for
example, that the element X_0 is only included in the equations for P_0 and P_1, so it

is placed in the intersection of the P_0 and P_1 sets and hence covered only by those sets. As a result, if there is an error and X_0 is flipped then we know that P_0 and P_1 will be affected but P_2 will not.

Again, a more concrete example probably makes this easier to understand. If we start with

$$X = \langle 0, 1, 1, 1 \rangle$$

then since

$$
\begin{aligned}
P_0 &= X_0 \oplus X_1 \oplus X_3 \\
&= 0 \oplus 1 \oplus 1 \\
&= 0 \\
P_1 &= X_0 \oplus X_2 \oplus X_3 \\
&= 0 \oplus 1 \oplus 1 \\
&= 0 \\
P_2 &= X_1 \oplus X_2 \oplus X_3 \\
&= 1 \oplus 1 \oplus 1 \\
&= 1
\end{aligned}
$$

the result is a new sequence

$$
\begin{aligned}
\hat{X} &= X \parallel \langle 0, 0, 1 \rangle \\
&= \langle 0, 1, 1, 1 \rangle \parallel \langle 0, 0, 1 \rangle \\
&= \langle 0, 1, 1, 1, 0, 0, 1 \rangle
\end{aligned}
$$

which we can write onto the CD.

Now imagine that when we try to read $\hat{X}$ from the CD, there is again some error: instead of getting what we expected, i.e., $\hat{X}$, we get some other sequence $\hat{X}'$ where one element has been flipped. For example, we might get

$$
\begin{aligned}
\hat{X}' &= \langle 1, 1, 1, 1, 0, 0, 1 \rangle \\
&= \langle 1, 1, 1, 1 \rangle \parallel \langle 0, 0, 1 \rangle \\
&= X' \parallel \langle 0, 0, 1 \rangle
\end{aligned}
$$

If we recompute

$$
\begin{aligned}
P_0' &= X_0' \oplus X_1' \oplus X_3' \\
&= 1 \oplus 1 \oplus 1 \\
&= 1 \\
P_1' &= X_0' \oplus X_2' \oplus X_3' \\
&= 1 \oplus 1 \oplus 1 \\
&= 1 \\
P_2' &= X_1' \oplus X_2' \oplus X_3' \\
&= 1 \oplus 1 \oplus 1 \\
&= 1
\end{aligned}
$$

Table 1.1 A table detailing error correction for the $(7, 4)$-code

Difference	Error
$\langle 0, 0, 0 \rangle$	None
$\langle 0, 0, 1 \rangle$	$\hat{X}'_6$
$\langle 0, 1, 0 \rangle$	$\hat{X}'_5$
$\langle 0, 1, 1 \rangle$	$\hat{X}'_2$
$\langle 1, 0, 0 \rangle$	$\hat{X}'_4$
$\langle 1, 0, 1 \rangle$	$\hat{X}'_1$
$\langle 1, 1, 0 \rangle$	$\hat{X}'_0$
$\langle 1, 1, 1 \rangle$	$\hat{X}'_3$

and match these against the original P_0, P_1 and P_2 we added to X, this shows there is an error: P'_0 and P'_1 do not match up with P_0 and P_1, but P'_2 does match P_2. Put another way, since we assume only one error has occurred and we know that the values of P'_0 and P'_1 are wrong, this means that the error must occur in the upper *and* lower-left sets of our Venn diagram; in the same way, because P'_2 is correct, this also means that the error did not occur in the lower-right set. There is only one region of the Venn diagram which is covered by the upper and lower-left sets yet not by the lower-right set: this corresponds to X_0, so it must be $\hat{X}'_0$ which is wrong.

Does this work for all possible errors? Given we originally added three extra elements, i.e., P_0, P_1 and P_2, we can deal with at most eight possibilities; these are described by the left-hand column in Table 1.1. Note that one possibility corresponds to no errors occurring, leaving seven others: intuitively this should seem the correct number since we have seven bits in which an error could occur. The issue now is to determine how we can translate the "differences" between P'_0, P'_1 and P'_2 and P_0, P_1 and P_2 into the position of an error as we did for the example above; the right-hand column in Table 1.1 describes the correct translation. In our example, the difference was $\langle 1, 1, 0 \rangle$, i.e., P'_0 and P'_1 were wrong but P_2 was right: the corresponding entry in the table shows that the error was in $\hat{X}'_0$.

1.4 Recasting Error Correction as Matrix Arithmetic

Another way of thinking about the $(7, 4)$-code for error correction is that it simply reuses the even parity code that we used for error detection. In this context, we could say that

$$\langle X_0, X_1, X_3, P_0 \rangle$$

is a **codeword** for the even parity code on the data $\langle X_0, X_1, X_3 \rangle$, and likewise both

$$\langle X_0, X_2, X_3, P_1 \rangle$$

and

$$\langle X_1, X_2, X_3, P_2 \rangle$$

are code words on the data $\langle X_0, X_2, X_3 \rangle$ and $\langle X_1, X_2, X_3 \rangle$. The idea is to recast this in terms of **matrices**. If you have covered matrices before then the following should link the theory you already know to a real-world application; if not, we try to introduce the theory as we go, but you can skip to the next chapter if you prefer.

Basically we would like to generalise and extend the $(7, 4)$-code so far explained in a fairly informal way; perhaps to send more data per-codeword, or to correct more than one error. Doing this with a Venn diagram seems unattractive for two reasons

1. for a human, more complicated Venn diagrams (e.g., in more than two dimensions) are hard to draw and understand, and
2. on a computer, the concept of using Venn diagrams does not easily map onto the types of operation that are available.

To combat both problems, we recast and formalise the basic idea, then let Mathematics take care of achieving the generalisation [1].

1.4.1 An Overview of Vectors

A **row vector** is simply a sequence of elements, e.g.,

$$\mathbf{R} = (r_0, r_1, \ldots, r_{m-1}),$$

where the number of elements is m; we call m the **dimension** of $\mathbf{R}$. A **column vector** is similar, except the elements are written down in a column rather than a row, e.g.,

$$\mathbf{C} = \begin{pmatrix} c_0 \\ c_1 \\ \vdots \\ c_{n-1} \end{pmatrix}.$$

In this case the number of elements in $\mathbf{C}$ is n, so the dimension of $\mathbf{C}$ is n. Note that we use lower-case letters for the vector elements, so, for example, r_i is the i-th element of $\mathbf{R}$; the reason for this is that we want to use $\mathbf{R_j}$ to denote the j-th separate vector in some set.

If we take two row vectors (or two column vectors) which have the same dimension, i.e., $n = m$, we can combine them together. For example, we can compute a **vector addition**, where the idea is to add together corresponding elements of the vectors:

$$(1, 2, 3) + (4, 5, 6) = (1 + 4, 2 + 5, 3 + 6) = (5, 7, 9).$$

Note we cannot add a row vector to a column vector: the operation is only valid when the two vectors have the same type and dimension. However, if we take a row vector and a column vector which have the same dimension, we *can* compute a **vector multiplication** (or **dot product**): the idea is to multiply together corresponding elements of the vectors, and add up all the results. For example

$$(1,2,3) \cdot \begin{pmatrix} 4 \\ 5 \\ 6 \end{pmatrix} = 1 \cdot 4 + 2 \cdot 5 + 3 \cdot 6 = 4 + 10 + 18 = 32.$$

We can write a more general method

$$\mathbf{R} \cdot \mathbf{C} = (r_0, r_1, \ldots, r_{n-1}) \cdot \begin{pmatrix} c_0 \\ c_1 \\ \vdots \\ c_{n-1} \end{pmatrix} = r_0 \cdot c_0 + r_1 \cdot c_1 + \cdots + r_{n-1} \cdot c_{n-1} = \sum_{i=0}^{n-1} r_i \cdot c_i,$$

which captures the same idea more formally. In words, the right-hand side means that for each index i between 0 and $n-1$ (i.e., $i = 0$, $i = 1$ and so on up to $i = n-1$) we add up terms that look like $R_i \cdot C_i$ (i.e., the product of the i-th elements of $\mathbf{R}$ and $\mathbf{C}$). Note we cannot multiply a row vector and a row vector, or a column vector and a column vector: the operation is only valid when the two vectors have different types but the same dimension. Further, we *always* write the column vector on the right, i.e.,

$$\mathbf{R} \cdot \mathbf{C}$$

is valid, but

$$\mathbf{C} \cdot \mathbf{R}$$

is not. These restrictions can be annoying because sometimes we might want to put the column vector on the left, or multiply a row vector by another row vector. The solution is to use a **vector transpose** operation to translate a row vector into a column vector or vice versa. For example

$$(1,2,3)^T = \begin{pmatrix} 1 \\ 2 \\ 3 \end{pmatrix} \quad \text{and} \quad \begin{pmatrix} 1 \\ 2 \\ 3 \end{pmatrix}^T = (1,2,3)$$

where the "T" superscript means "apply transpose to this vector".

1.4.2   An Overview of Matrices

Suppose we have n *separate* row vectors, each of dimension m; that is, suppose we have $\mathbf{R_1}, \mathbf{R_2}, \ldots, \mathbf{R_n}$, where each $\mathbf{R_i}$ has dimension m. If we write the row vectors above each other, we get a "table" or **matrix** with n rows and m columns, i.e., of dimension $n \times m$. For example, if we take the $n = 3$ row vectors

$$\mathbf{R_1} = (1,2,3,4) \qquad \mathbf{R_2} = (5,6,7,8) \qquad \mathbf{R_3} = (9,0,1,2),$$

each of which has dimension $m = 4$, and write them above each other, we get a matrix

$$M = \begin{pmatrix} 1 & 2 & 3 & 4 \\ 5 & 6 & 7 & 8 \\ 9 & 0 & 1 & 2 \end{pmatrix}$$

of dimension 3×4. Alternatively, we could construct the same matrix by taking m column vectors, each of dimension n, and writing them next to each other. For example, if we take $m = 4$ column vectors

$$\mathbf{C_1} = \begin{pmatrix} 1 \\ 5 \\ 9 \end{pmatrix} \qquad \mathbf{C_2} = \begin{pmatrix} 2 \\ 6 \\ 0 \end{pmatrix} \qquad \mathbf{C_3} = \begin{pmatrix} 3 \\ 7 \\ 1 \end{pmatrix} \qquad \mathbf{C_4} = \begin{pmatrix} 4 \\ 8 \\ 2 \end{pmatrix},$$

each of which has dimension $n = 3$ and write them next to each other, we again get

$$M = \begin{pmatrix} 1 & 2 & 3 & 4 \\ 5 & 6 & 7 & 8 \\ 9 & 0 & 1 & 2 \end{pmatrix}.$$

This means a given matrix can be considered either as a collection of row vectors *or* column vectors.

The vector transpose operation we described previously can also be used to perform a **matrix transpose**, i.e., to translate a matrix of dimension $n \times m$ into one of dimension $m \times n$. Basically we just apply the vector transpose to *everything*: given the matrix above, we see that

$$M^T = \begin{pmatrix} 1 & 2 & 3 & 4 \\ 5 & 6 & 7 & 8 \\ 9 & 0 & 1 & 2 \end{pmatrix}^T = \begin{pmatrix} 1 & 5 & 9 \\ 2 & 6 & 0 \\ 3 & 7 & 1 \\ 4 & 8 & 2 \end{pmatrix}$$

because

$$M = \begin{pmatrix} \mathbf{R_1} \\ \mathbf{R_2} \\ \mathbf{R_3} \end{pmatrix}$$

so

$$M^T = \begin{pmatrix} \mathbf{R_1}^T \\ \mathbf{R_2}^T \\ \mathbf{R_3}^T \end{pmatrix}^T = \begin{pmatrix} (1,2,3,4)^T \\ (5,6,7,8)^T \\ (9,0,1,2)^T \end{pmatrix}^T = \left(\begin{pmatrix} 1 \\ 2 \\ 3 \\ 4 \end{pmatrix}, \begin{pmatrix} 5 \\ 6 \\ 7 \\ 8 \end{pmatrix}, \begin{pmatrix} 9 \\ 0 \\ 1 \\ 2 \end{pmatrix} \right).$$

Finally, the vector multiplication operation is also useful in the context of matrices since it allows us to define **matrix-vector multiplication**. Suppose we have a matrix M of dimension $n \times m$. We compute matrix-vector multiplication in one of two ways depending on the type of the vector:

1. A row vector $\mathbf{R}$ with dimension n can be multiplied on the left of the matrix to obtain another row vector of dimension m. To achieve this, we consider M as a set of m column vectors and compute

$$\mathbf{R} \cdot M = \mathbf{R} \cdot (\mathbf{C_0}, \mathbf{C_1}, \ldots, \mathbf{C_{m-1}}) = (\mathbf{R} \cdot \mathbf{C_0}, \mathbf{R} \cdot \mathbf{C_1}, \ldots, \mathbf{R} \cdot \mathbf{C_{m-1}}).$$

Notice that there are m elements in the result, each one computed via the dot product of $\mathbf{R}$ and one of the $\mathbf{C_i}$ vectors.

2. A column vector $\mathbf{C}$ with dimension m can be multiplied on the right of the matrix, to obtain another column vector of dimension n. To achieve this, we consider M as a set of n column vectors and compute

$$M \cdot \mathbf{C} = (\mathbf{R_1}, \mathbf{R_2}, \ldots, \mathbf{R_n}) \cdot \mathbf{C} = (\mathbf{R_1} \cdot \mathbf{C}, \mathbf{R_2} \cdot \mathbf{C}, \ldots, \mathbf{R_n} \cdot \mathbf{C}).$$

Notice that there are n elements in the result, each one computed via the dot product of one of the $\mathbf{R_i}$ vectors and $\mathbf{C}$.

1.4.3 Addition and Multiplication Modulo 2

Recall the XOR function from our discussion of error correction; it gives a single output from two inputs:

$$x \oplus y = \begin{cases} 0 & \text{if } x = 0, y = 0 \\ 1 & \text{if } x = 1, y = 0 \\ 1 & \text{if } x = 0, y = 1 \\ 0 & \text{if } x = 1, y = 1 \end{cases}$$

Although it was useful, you might be forgiven for thinking that XOR is a little ad hoc: where does this *particular* form come from? Another way of thinking about XOR is that it computes a special type of addition. What we are doing is called **modular arithmetic** [14], and we will encounter more formal definitions later in Chaps. 6 and 8. For now, it is enough to think of XOR as addition where we treat all even numbers as 0 and all odd numbers as 1. In more detail, the four cases above can be described as

$$\begin{aligned} 0 + 0 &= 0 \equiv 0 \pmod{2} \\ 1 + 0 &= 1 \equiv 1 \pmod{2} \\ 0 + 1 &= 1 \equiv 1 \pmod{2} \\ 1 + 1 &= 2 \equiv 0 \pmod{2} \end{aligned}$$

Likewise, the AND function

$$x \wedge y = \begin{cases} 0 & \text{if } x = 0, y = 0 \\ 0 & \text{if } x = 1, y = 0 \\ 0 & \text{if } x = 0, y = 1 \\ 1 & \text{if } x = 1, y = 1 \end{cases}$$

can be described as modular multiplication because

$$0 \cdot 0 = 0 \equiv 0 \pmod 2$$
$$1 \cdot 0 = 0 \equiv 0 \pmod 2$$
$$0 \cdot 1 = 0 \equiv 0 \pmod 2$$
$$1 \cdot 1 = 1 \equiv 1 \pmod 2$$

In both cases, when we write $x \equiv y \pmod 2$ this shows the number x on the left is *equivalent* to the number y on the right if considered modulo 2. The idea is that we have translated what looked like ad hoc functions into a more Mathematical setting: the goal is that whereas we previously did all our arithmetic "normally" on vectors and matrices of numbers, now we can do it all "modulo 2" and work with vectors and matrices of bits instead.

1.4.4   Using Matrices for Error Correction

Our original goal was to generalise and extend the $(7, 4)$-code using the concept of matrices as a formal underpinning. We now know enough to do just that. First we need to translate the encoding step: consider

$$G = \begin{pmatrix} 1 & 0 & 0 & 0 & 1 & 1 & 0 \\ 0 & 1 & 0 & 0 & 1 & 1 & 1 \\ 0 & 0 & 1 & 0 & 1 & 0 & 1 \\ 0 & 0 & 0 & 1 & 0 & 1 & 1 \end{pmatrix}$$

which we call the **generating matrix** since it will be used to generate codewords from data; notice it has dimension 4×7. Now suppose we have the data

$$X = \langle 0, 1, 1, 1 \rangle$$

which matches our original $(7, 4)$-code example. To compute the codeword $\hat{X}$, we first write the elements of X as a row vector and then multiply it on the right by the generating matrix G: all operations on elements are performed modulo 2. For example

$$\hat{X} = \mathbf{X} \cdot G = (0, 1, 1, 1) \cdot \begin{pmatrix} 1 & 0 & 0 & 0 & 1 & 1 & 0 \\ 0 & 1 & 0 & 0 & 1 & 1 & 1 \\ 0 & 0 & 1 & 0 & 1 & 0 & 1 \\ 0 & 0 & 0 & 1 & 0 & 1 & 1 \end{pmatrix} = (0, 1, 1, 1, 0, 0, 1).$$

As an exercise, to make sure you understand how to multiply a row vector by a matrix, verify that the calculation above is correct: work out each element in the result long-hand. To get you started, here are the first two elements:

$$\hat{X}_0 = 0 \cdot 1 + 1 \cdot 0 + 1 \cdot 0 + 1 \cdot 0 \quad \text{(mod 2)}$$
$$= 0 \quad \text{(mod 2)}$$
$$\hat{X}_1 = 0 \cdot 0 + 1 \cdot 1 + 1 \cdot 0 + 1 \cdot 0 \quad \text{(mod 2)}$$
$$= 1 \quad \text{(mod 2)}$$

Next we need to translate the decoding step. This demands a closer look at the generating matrix G, considering it as two parts:

1. Consider a matrix of dimension $d \times d$ whose elements are all 0 except those on the main diagonal [12] which are 1. This is called an **identity matrix** [10] and denoted by $\mathcal{I}_d$; for example

$$\mathcal{I}_2 = \begin{pmatrix} 1 & 0 \\ 0 & 1 \end{pmatrix}$$

and

$$\mathcal{I}_4 = \begin{pmatrix} 1 & 0 & 0 & 0 \\ 0 & 1 & 0 & 0 \\ 0 & 0 & 1 & 0 \\ 0 & 0 & 0 & 1 \end{pmatrix}.$$

The first, left-hand 4×4 part of G is an identity matrix of this type, i.e., the left-hand 4×4 sub-matrix is $\mathcal{I}_4$.

2. The second, right-hand 4×3 part of G is less structured; we can call this sub-matrix A for short, i.e.,

$$A = \begin{pmatrix} 1 & 1 & 0 \\ 1 & 1 & 1 \\ 1 & 0 & 1 \\ 0 & 1 & 1 \end{pmatrix}.$$

Using the two parts we can write G as $\mathcal{I}_4 \parallel A$, i.e., G is $\mathcal{I}_4$ with A concatenated onto the right-hand side of it. We now form a new 3×7 **parity check matrix** as

$$H = A^T \parallel I_3,$$

i.e., H is A^T with $\mathcal{I}_3$ concatenated onto the right-hand side of it. In our case this means

$$H = \begin{pmatrix} 1 & 1 & 1 & 0 & 1 & 0 & 0 \\ 1 & 1 & 0 & 1 & 0 & 1 & 0 \\ 0 & 1 & 1 & 1 & 0 & 0 & 1 \end{pmatrix}.$$

The parity check matrix allows us to perform error detection and correction on the codeword $\hat{X}$: we take the codeword and interpret it as a column vector, before computing

$$\mathbf{S} = H \cdot \hat{X}$$

which we call the **syndrome**. As before, all operations on elements are performed modulo 2. If all the elements in **S** are 0 then no errors have occurred; if S is non-zero however, then it tells us where an error occurred just as before. For example, suppose we receive the correct codeword

$$\hat{X} = \begin{pmatrix} 0 \\ 1 \\ 1 \\ 1 \\ 0 \\ 0 \\ 1 \end{pmatrix}.$$

We compute

$$H \cdot \hat{X} = \begin{pmatrix} 1 & 1 & 1 & 0 & 1 & 0 & 0 \\ 1 & 1 & 0 & 1 & 0 & 1 & 0 \\ 0 & 1 & 1 & 1 & 0 & 0 & 1 \end{pmatrix} \cdot \begin{pmatrix} 0 \\ 1 \\ 1 \\ 1 \\ 0 \\ 0 \\ 1 \end{pmatrix} = \begin{pmatrix} 0 \\ 0 \\ 0 \end{pmatrix}$$

and, since the result is zero, deduce that no error occurred. However, if receive the codeword

$$\hat{X}' = \begin{pmatrix} 1 \\ 1 \\ 1 \\ 1 \\ 0 \\ 0 \\ 1 \end{pmatrix}$$

that has an error in the first element we compute

$$H \cdot \hat{X}' = \begin{pmatrix} 1 & 1 & 1 & 0 & 1 & 0 & 0 \\ 1 & 1 & 0 & 1 & 0 & 1 & 0 \\ 0 & 1 & 1 & 1 & 0 & 0 & 1 \end{pmatrix} \cdot \begin{pmatrix} 1 \\ 1 \\ 1 \\ 1 \\ 0 \\ 0 \\ 1 \end{pmatrix} = \begin{pmatrix} 1 \\ 1 \\ 0 \end{pmatrix}.$$

The result we get is non-zero: it is actually equal to the first column vector of the parity check matrix, allowing us to detect *and* correct the error.

As an aside, we can recast the parity code (i.e., the error *detection* scheme) using the same approach. Looking back, the generating and parity check matrices

$$G = \begin{pmatrix} 1 & 0 & 0 & 1 \\ 0 & 1 & 0 & 1 \\ 0 & 0 & 1 & 1 \end{pmatrix}$$

and

$$H = (1, 1, 1, 1)$$

reproduce the same properties. As an exercise, work through the original parity check code example and convince yourself that the syndrome this produces can *detect* errors but not *correct* them.

1.4.5 Generalising the Matrix-Based (7, 4)-Code

We have recast the original $(7, 4)$-code in terms of matrices, but how can we generalise it? That is, how can we use the same theory to construct an arbitrary (n, m)-code? In general, for an (n, m)-code we have

$$G = \mathcal{I}_m \parallel A$$

and

$$H = A^T \parallel \mathcal{I}_{n-m}$$

where we know what $\mathcal{I}_m$ and $\mathcal{I}_{n-m}$ look like, but not the $m \times (n - m)$ matrix A. So the generalisation problem becomes one of trying to find a matrix A which gives us the properties we want, and then a way of interpreting what the syndrome is telling us. This is far from trivial, but at least it gives us somewhere to start: certainly this seems more achievable than imagining what multi-dimensional Venn diagrams would look like!

Research (task #7) The final paragraph leaves an obvious question open: exactly what properties *does* A need to have, and how do we create such a matrix for given values of n and m? Do some research into this issue, and see if you can produce a working (3, 1)-code or larger (15, 11)-code.

References

1. Wikipedia: Coding theory. http://en.wikipedia.org/wiki/Coding_theory
2. Wikipedia: Compact disk. http://en.wikipedia.org/wiki/Compact_disk
3. Wikipedia: Data compression. http://en.wikipedia.org/wiki/Data_compression

4. Wikipedia: Dictionary coder. http://en.wikipedia.org/wiki/Dictionary_coder
5. Wikipedia: Error detection and correction. http://en.wikipedia.org/wiki/Error_correction
6. Wikipedia: Exclusive OR. http://en.wikipedia.org/wiki/XOR
7. Wikipedia: Hamming code. http://en.wikipedia.org/wiki/Hamming_code
8. Wikipedia: Hamming weight. http://en.wikipedia.org/wiki/Hamming_weight
9. Wikipedia: Hubble space telescope. http://en.wikipedia.org/wiki/Hubble_space_telescope
10. Wikipedia: Identity matrix. http://en.wikipedia.org/wiki/Identity_matrix
11. Wikipedia: JPEG. http://en.wikipedia.org/wiki/JPEG
12. Wikipedia: Main diagonal. http://en.wikipedia.org/wiki/Main_diagonal
13. Wikipedia: MODEM. http://en.wikipedia.org/wiki/Modem
14. Wikipedia: Modular arithmetic. http://en.wikipedia.org/wiki/Modular_arithmetic
15. Wikipedia: Parity bit. http://en.wikipedia.org/wiki/Parity_bit
16. Wikipedia: Run-length encoding. http://en.wikipedia.org/wiki/Run-length_encoding
17. Wikipedia: Short Message Service (SMS). http://en.wikipedia.org/wiki/Short_message_service
18. Wikipedia: SMS language. http://en.wikipedia.org/wiki/SMS_language
19. Wikipedia: Venn diagram. http://en.wikipedia.org/wiki/Venn_diagram

Writing and Comparing Algorithms

2

Imagine you are a student at the University of Bristol; lectures for the day are finished, and you fancy a drink to celebrate. How do you get from the Computer Science Department to the Student Union? Easy! Just ask Google Maps:

> http://maps.google.com/?saddr='bristol+bs8+1ub'&daddr='bristol+bs8+1ln'

What comes back is a fancy map plus a list of directions which resemble the following:
1. Start at Bristol, BS8 1UB, UK.
2. Head west on B4051 toward A4018; continue to follow B4051.
3. Continue on A4018.
4. Continue on B3129; go through two roundabouts; destination will be on the left.
5. Finish at Bristol, BS8 1LN, UK.

The directions have some features worth discussing in more detail. Each **line** in the directions represents a static description of some active **step** we should perform while following them. The lines have to be followed, or **processed**, in order: we start at the first step and once that is complete, move on to the next one. If one of the steps is missed out for example, or we start at the third step instead of the first, the directions do not work. The directions are (fairly) unambiguous. It may help to know that the road B4051 is more usually called Park Street, but line #4 is not "go through *some* roundabouts"; we should go through *exactly* two roundabouts. This means it is always clear how to process each line (i.e., exactly what steps to perform): we never become confused because there is not enough information and we do not know what to do.

2.1 Algorithms

As a result of the features described above, our directions at least loosely satisfy the definition of an **algorithm** [1]: they are simply an abstract description of how to solve a problem. Of course in this case the problem is helping someone get from one place to another, but we might just as easily write an algorithm to solve other problems as well.

D. Page, N. Smart, *What Is Computer Science?*,
Undergraduate Topics in Computer Science, DOI 10.1007/978-3-319-04042-4_2,
© Springer International Publishing Switzerland 2014

2.1.1 What Is an Algorithm?

It is unusual to enforce any strict rules about *how* we should write an algorithm down: as long as it makes sense to whoever is reading it, we can use whatever format we want. This often means using **pseudo-code**, literally a "sort of" program [11]. An algorithm can have inputs, which we name, and can provide some outputs; we say the algorithm takes (or is given) some arguments as input, and returns (or produces) a result as output. Based on this, imagine we write the following algorithm:

1 **algorithm** FERMAT-TEST(n) **begin**
2   Choose a random number a between 2 and $n - 1$ inclusive
3   Compute $d = \gcd(a, n)$, the greatest common divisor of a and n
4   If $d \neq 1$ then return **false** as the result
5   Compute $t = a^{n-1} \pmod{n}$
6   If $t = 1$ then return **true** as the result, otherwise return **false**
7 **end**

This looks more formal, but there is no magic going on: the algorithm is simply a list of five lines we can process. Note that we have numbered each of the lines so we can refer to them. In line #1 we name the algorithm FERMAT-TEST and show that it accepts a single argument called n as input; in lines #2 to #6 we list the directions themselves. The lines #4 and #6 are a bit special since they can produce output from the algorithm.

We **invoke** (or use) FERMAT-TEST by giving a concrete value to each of the inputs. For example, if we write

$$\text{FERMAT-TEST}(221)$$

basically what we mean is "follow the algorithm FERMAT-TEST, but each time you see n substitute 221 instead". Like the travel directions, invoking FERMAT-TEST means we perform some active step (or steps) for each line in the algorithm:

Step #1   Choose a random number between 2 and 220 inclusive, e.g., $a = 11$.
Step #2   Compute $d = \gcd(11, 221) = 1$.
Step #3   Since $d = 1$, carry on rather than returning a result.
Step #4   Compute $t = 11^{221-1} \pmod{221} = 81$.
Step #5   Since $t \neq 1$, return **false** as the result.

After step #5 the algorithm **terminates**: from the input 221, we have computed the result **false**. What this result means of course depends on the purpose of the algorithm; the purpose of FERMAT-TEST is certainly less clear than the travel directions we started off with!

FERMAT-TEST is actually quite a famous algorithm [7] due to the French mathematician Pierre de Fermat. The purpose is to tell if n, the input, is a **prime** [12] number or not. Lines #2 to #4 ensure we select an a that is **co-prime** [5] to n; this means a and n have no common factors. If we were to pick an a such that a divided n, then clearly n cannot be prime, so this possibility is ruled out before we carry on. Having computed t, if the result we get after lines #5 to #6 is **false** then n definitely is *not* a prime number; it is composite. On the other hand, if the result is **true** then n *might* be a prime number. The more times we invoke FERMAT-TEST with a given n and get **true** as a result, the more confident we are that n is a prime number. FERMAT-TEST works quite well, except for the so-called **Carmichael numbers** [3] which trick the algorithm: they are composite, but FERMAT-TEST always returns **true**. The smallest Carmichael number is $561 = 3 \cdot 11 \cdot 17$: whatever a it chooses, FERMAT-TEST will always compute $t = 1$ and return **true**.

Try this out for yourself: pick some example values of n, and work through the steps used by FERMAT-TEST to compute a result; you could even use a friend to generate random values of a to make sure you cannot cheat! Using the algorithm, see if you can identify some

1. other Carmichael numbers, or
2. Mersenne primes, which have the special form $n = 2^k - 1$ for an integer value k,

or, get a friend to give you an n (which they *know* is either prime or composite) and try to decide whether or not it is prime.

Implement (task #8)

Different Styles of Structure

There are of course *lots* of ways we can write down the same algorithm. For example, where the inputs and outputs need more explanation (e.g., to explain their type or meaning), it is common to write it in a slightly more verbose but otherwise similar way:

```
1  algorithm FERMAT-TEST begin
       Input: An integer n
       Output: false if n is composite, otherwise true if n is probably prime
2      Choose a random number a between 2 and n − 1 inclusive
3      Compute d = gcd(a, n), the greatest common divisor of a and n
4      If d ≠ 1 then return false as the result
5      Compute t = a^(n−1) (mod n)
6      If t = 1 then return true as the result, otherwise return false
7  end
```

As more of a contrast, Fig. 2.1 shows a *totally* different way to describe the same algorithm. You might find this more natural, or easier to read: this form is called a **flow chart** [9] and can be traced back to the early 1920*s*. Since then, flow charts have become a common way of describing "real life" algorithms such as troubleshooting instructions that tell you what to do when your television breaks down, or for capturing decision making procedures in organisations. The point is, both our written

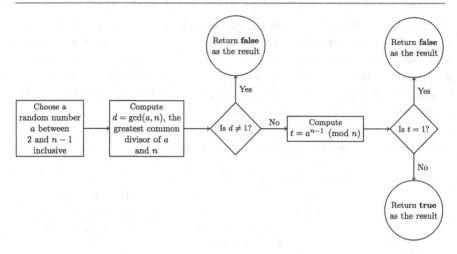

Fig. 2.1 A flow chart description of FERMAT-TEST

and flow chart versions of FERMAT-TEST describe *exactly* the same thing: they are *both* algorithms.

Different Styles of Notation

There is one final, minor issue remaining that we need to be careful about whatever style of algorithm we opt for. As an example, look at the original FERMAT-TEST algorithm again, specifically at lines #3 and #4: both make use of the $=$ (or "equals") symbol. In line #3 we mean "assign the value produced by computing $\gcd(a, n)$ to d" whereas in line #4 we mean "evaluate to **true** if and only if the value d does not equal one". It is reasonable to argue that we might confuse the two meanings. For example, we might mistakenly interpret "compute $t = a^{n-1} \pmod{n}$" as "compute the value **false**" since the value t does not equal $a^{n-1} \pmod{n}$; we have not assigned *any* value to t yet! To prevent this possible ambiguity, Computer Scientists often use

1. the $=$ symbol to mean **equality**, and
2. the $\leftarrow$ symbol to mean **assignment**.

As such, we should really rewrite the algorithm as follows:

```
1 algorithm FERMAT-TEST(n) begin
2     Choose a random number a between 2 and n − 1 inclusive
3     Compute d ← gcd(a, n), the greatest common divisor of a and n
4     If d ≠ 1 then return false as the result
5     Compute t ← a^{n−1} (mod n)
6     If t = 1 then return true as the result, otherwise return false
7 end
```

2.1.2 What Is not an Algorithm?

Algorithms ≠ Functions

It is tempting to treat algorithms like Mathematical functions. After all, invoking an algorithm *looks* like the use of a Mathematical function; writing SIN(90) uses the function SIN to compute a result using the input 90 for example. Strictly speaking, the difference (or at least one difference) comes down to the idea of **state**.

For Mathematical functions, writing something like SIN(x) might give different results depending on x, but once we have chosen an x we get the same result *every* time. For example SIN(90) *always* equals 1 so we are entitled to write SIN(90) = 1, or use 1 whenever we see SIN(90). But algorithms are different: they may depend on the context they are invoked in; there may be some state which effects how an algorithm behaves and hence the result it returns. Another way to say the same thing is that algorithms might have **side effects** which alter the state; in contrast, functions are **pure** in the sense they are totally self contained.

FERMAT-TEST demonstrates this fact neatly: line #2 reads "choose a random number a". Since this can be *any* number (as long as it is co-prime to n), it is perfectly possible we might choose a different one each time we invoke FERMAT-TEST. So the first time we invoke

$$\text{FERMAT-TEST}(221)$$

we might choose $a = 11$ in line #2 as above; we know the result in this case is **false**. However, imagine we invoke the algorithm a second time

$$\text{FERMAT-TEST}(221)$$

and choose $a = 47$ instead. This time, the result is **true**. So we have got a different result with the same input: the context (represented in this case by whatever we are choosing random numbers with) influences what result we get, not just the input.

Algorithms ≠ Programs

It is tempting to treat algorithms like programs. If you have written any programs before, there is a good chance FERMAT-TEST has a similar look and feel. Usually when we talk about a program, we mean something which is intended to be **executed** by a real computer: a word processor, a web-browser, or something like that. This means a program should be written in a "machine readable" form: each step or action required by a program needs to be something a computer can actually do.

Within FERMAT-TEST for example, we are required to compute $a^{n-1} \pmod{n}$ for some a and n. Would most computers know how to do this? Probably not. The computer might know how to do multiplication, and we might be able to explain to it how to do exponentiation using another algorithm, but it is not reasonable that the computer will know how to do the computation itself.

So in contrast to a "machine readable" program, we have written the FERMAT-TEST algorithm in a far less restrictive "human readable" form. Whereas a program relates to a real computer, you can think of an algorithm as relating to some abstract or make believe uber-computer which does not have any similar restrictions. The algorithm needs to be **implemented**, by rewriting it in a programming language, before it is ready for execution by a real computer.

2.2   Algorithms for Multiplication

Imagine you are asked to multiply one number x by another number y. You might perform multiplication in your head without thinking about it, but more formally what does multiplication actually mean? If you met someone from a different planet who does not know what multiplication is, how could you describe to them the steps required to compute $x \cdot y$? Clearly the answer is to write an algorithm that they can follow. As a starting point, notice that multiplication is just repeated addition. So for example

$$x \cdot y = \underbrace{x + x + \cdots + x + x}_{y \text{ copies}},$$

which means if we select $y = 6$ then we obviously have

$$x \cdot 6 = x + x + x + x + x + x.$$

Based on this approach, we can write an algorithm that describes how to multiply x by y. We just need a list of careful directions that someone could follow:

```
1  algorithm MULTIPLY-REPEAT(x, y) begin
2      t ← 0
3      for i from 1 upto y do
4          │ t ← t + x
5      end
6      return t
7  end
```

The basic idea of this algorithm is simple: add together y copies of x, keeping track of the value we have accumulated so far in t. Of course you could argue the algorithm is *much* harder to read and understand because we have replaced this English description with something that looks much more formal. On the other hand, by doing this we have made things more precise. That is, there is no longer any room for someone to misinterpret the description if they know how each **construct** behaves:

- The construct in line #2 is another example of the **assignment** we saw earlier: it assigns a value (on the right) to a name, or variable (on the left). When we write $X \leftarrow Y$, the idea is to set the variable X to a value given by evaluating the expression Y. In this case, the construct $t \leftarrow 0$ sets the variable t to the value 0: every time we evaluate t in some expression after this, we can substitute 0 until t is assigned a new value.

- The construct that starts in line #3 is an example of a **loop**. When we write **for** X **do** Y, the idea is to repeatedly process the block Y for values dictated by X; we say that the construct **iterates** over Y. Our loop is **bounded** because we know how many times we will process Y before we start.

  In this case the block is represented by line #4, and hence $t \leftarrow t + x$ is iterated over for values of i in the range $1 \ldots y$. So basically the loop does the same thing as copying out line #4 a total of y times, i.e.,

$$
\left.
\begin{aligned}
t &\leftarrow t + x \,\} \, i = 1 \\
t &\leftarrow t + x \,\} \, i = 2 \\
&\quad\vdots \\
t &\leftarrow t + x \,\} \, i = y
\end{aligned}
\right\} \; y \text{ copies}
$$

- The construct in line #6 is an example of a **return**. When we write **return** X, the idea is that we evaluate X and return this as the result of the algorithm. In this case, we return the value accumulated in t as the result.

Now that we know the meaning of each line, we can invoke the algorithm and perform the steps required to compute a result. Imagine we select $x = 3$ and $y = 6$ for example; the steps we perform would be something like the following:

Step #1   Assign $t \leftarrow 0$.
Step #2   Assign $t \leftarrow t + x$, i.e., $t \leftarrow 0 + 3 = 3$.
Step #3   Assign $t \leftarrow t + x$, i.e., $t \leftarrow 3 + 3 = 6$.
Step #4   Assign $t \leftarrow t + x$, i.e., $t \leftarrow 6 + 3 = 9$.
Step #5   Assign $t \leftarrow t + x$, i.e., $t \leftarrow 9 + 3 = 12$.
Step #6   Assign $t \leftarrow t + x$, i.e., $t \leftarrow 12 + 3 = 15$.
Step #7   Assign $t \leftarrow t + x$, i.e., $t \leftarrow 15 + 3 = 18$.
Step #8   Return $t = 18$.

After eight steps we reassuringly find the result is $x \cdot y = 18$. The key thing to realise is that fundamentally we are still just following directions: lines in our algorithm might be more formal than "go through two roundabouts", but as long as we know what they mean we can carry out the corresponding steps just as easily.

Another way of looking at what multiplication means is to see that it simply adds another "weight" to the digits that describe y. It might look odd, but imagine we wrote y out as an n-bit binary number, i.e., we write

$$
y = \sum_{i=0}^{n-1} y_i \cdot 2^i
$$

where clearly each $y_i \in 0, 1$. Then, we could write

$$
x \cdot y = x \cdot \sum_{i=0}^{n-1} y_i \cdot 2^i = \sum_{i=0}^{n-1} y_i \cdot x \cdot 2^i.
$$

What we are doing is taking each weighted digit of y, and adding a further weight x to the base which is used to express y in. Again, as an example, selecting $y = 6_{(10)} = 110_{(2)}$ we find that we still get the result we would expect to

$$
\begin{aligned}
y \cdot x &= y_0 \cdot x \cdot 2^0 + y_1 \cdot x \cdot 2^1 + y_2 \cdot x \cdot 2^2 \\
&= 0 \cdot x \cdot 2^0 + 1 \cdot x \cdot 2^1 + 1 \cdot x \cdot 2^2 \\
&= \quad 0 \cdot x \quad + \quad 2 \cdot x \quad + \quad 4 \cdot x \\
&= \quad 6 \cdot x
\end{aligned}
$$

So far so good. Except that this still looks unpleasant to actually compute. For example we keep having to compute those powers of two to weight the terms. Fortunately, a British mathematician called William Horner worked out a scheme to do this more neatly [10]. Sometimes this is termed Horner's rule (or scheme): bracket the thing we started with in such a way that instead of having to compute the powers of two independently we sort of accumulate them as we go. This is best shown by example:

$$
\begin{aligned}
y \cdot x &= y_0 \cdot x + 2 \cdot \big(y_1 \cdot x + 2 \cdot \big(y_2 \cdot x + 2 \cdot (0) \big) \big) \\
&= 0 \cdot x + 2 \cdot \big(1 \cdot x + 2 \cdot \big(1 \cdot x + 2 \cdot (0) \big) \big) \\
&= 0 \cdot x + 2 \cdot \big(1 \cdot x + 2 \cdot \big(1 \cdot x + \quad 0 \big) \big) \\
&= 0 \cdot x + 2 \cdot \big(1 \cdot x + 2 \cdot \big(1 \cdot x \quad \big) \big) \\
&= 0 \cdot x + 2 \cdot \big(1 \cdot x + \quad 2 \cdot x \quad \big) \\
&= 0 \cdot x + 2 \cdot \big(3 \cdot x \quad \big) \\
&= 0 \cdot x + \quad 6 \cdot x \\
&= 6 \cdot x
\end{aligned}
$$

In much the same way as above, we can write an algorithm that describes how to multiply x by y using this approach:

```
1  algorithm MULTIPLY-HORNER(x, y) begin
2      t ← 0
3      for i from |y| − 1 downto 0 do
4          t ← 2 · t
5          if yᵢ = 1 then
6              t ← t + x
7          end
8      end
9      return t
10 end
```

This algorithm again accepts two inputs called x and y, the two numbers we would like to multiply together, and again produces one output that gives us the result $x \cdot y$. This time, the basic idea is to write y in binary, and process it from left-to-right one digit at a time. In terms of the bracketing, we work from inside outward, applying Horner's rule and keeping track of an accumulated value called t:

- The construct in line #2 is another **assignment**. We have already seen what this means: it sets the variable t to the value 0.

- The construct that starts in line #3 is another **loop**; this is a little different from the previous one we saw. The first difference is that the values of i go downward rather than upward: the block, now represented by lines #4 to #7, is iterated over for i in the range $|y| - 1 \ldots 0$. That is fine though, we still just copy out lines #4 to #7 a total of $|y|$ times making sure the right values of i are alongside each copy, i.e.,

$$
\left.\begin{array}{l}
t \leftarrow 2 \cdot t \\
\textbf{if } y_i = 1 \textbf{ then } t \leftarrow t + x
\end{array}\right\} i = |y| - 1
$$

$$\vdots$$

$$
\left.\begin{array}{l}
t \leftarrow 2 \cdot t \\
\textbf{if } y_i = 1 \textbf{ then } t \leftarrow t + x
\end{array}\right\} i = 1 \qquad \left.\rule{0pt}{60pt}\right\} |y| \text{ copies}
$$

$$
\left.\begin{array}{l}
t \leftarrow 2 \cdot t \\
\textbf{if } y_i = 1 \textbf{ then } t \leftarrow t + x
\end{array}\right\} i = 0
$$

The second difference is that the block actually uses i within it. That is fine as well: wherever we see an i, we can substitute the right value for that iteration. For example, the last copy from above becomes

$$
\begin{array}{l}
t \leftarrow 2 \cdot t \\
\textbf{if } y_0 = 1 \textbf{ then } t \leftarrow t + x
\end{array}
$$

after we substitute in the value $i = 0$.
- The construct that start starts on line #5 is an example of a **condition**; it forms part of the block iterated over by the loop. When we write **if** X **then** Y, the idea is that we perform a test: if X evaluates to **true** then we process the block Y, otherwise we skip it. In this case, we test the i-th bit of y: if $y_i = 1$ then we add x to t in line #6, otherwise t remains unchanged.
- The construct in line #9 is another **return**. We have already seen what this means: it returns t as the result.

This algorithm is slightly more complicated than the last one. However, in the same way as before we know what each line means so we can invoke the algorithm and carry out steps in order to compute a result. Imagine we again select $x = 3$ and $y = 6_{(10)} = 110_{(2)}$; the steps we perform would be something like the following:

Step #1   Assign $t \leftarrow 0$.
Step #2   Assign $t \leftarrow 2 \cdot t$, i.e., $t \leftarrow 2 \cdot 0 = 0$.
Step #3   Since $y_2 = 1$, assign $t \leftarrow t + x$, i.e., $t \leftarrow 0 + 3 = 3$.
Step #4   Assign $t \leftarrow 2 \cdot t$, i.e., $t \leftarrow 2 \cdot 3 = 6$.
Step #5   Since $y_1 = 1$, assign $t \leftarrow t + x$, i.e., $t \leftarrow 6 + 3 = 9$.
Step #6   Assign $t \leftarrow 2 \cdot t$, i.e., $t \leftarrow 2 \cdot 9 = 18$.
Step #7   Since $y_0 = 0$, skip the assignment $t \leftarrow t + x$.
Step #8   Return $t = 18$.

The algorithm has clearly computed the result in a different way (i.e., the steps themselves are different), but we still find that $x \cdot y = 18$ as expected.

Although reading and following invocations of *existing* algorithms is a good start, writing your own algorithms is really the only way to get to grips with this topic.

Implement (task #9)

In Chap. 1 we met the HAMMING-WEIGHT function: it counts the number of elements in a binary sequence that are equal to one. Write an algorithm that can compute HAMMING-WEIGHT(x) for a suitable input sequence x; demonstrate how it does so by listing the steps (similar to above) for an example x.

2.3   Algorithms for Exponentiation

So much for multiplication, what about the exponentiation we needed in FERMAT-TEST? It turns out that we can pull the same trick again. In the same was as we wrote multiplication as repeated addition, we can write exponentiation as repeated multiplication:

$$x^y = \underbrace{x \cdot x \cdots \cdots x \cdot x}_{y \text{ copies}}.$$

If we again select $y = 6$ then we obviously have

$$x^6 = x \cdot x \cdot x \cdot x \cdot x \cdot x.$$

The thing to notice is that there is a duality here: where there was an addition in our description of multiplication, that has become a multiplication in our description of exponentiation; where there was a multiplication, this has become an exponentiation. As such, we can adapt the MULTIPLY-REPEAT algorithm as follows:

```
1 algorithm EXPONENTIATE-REPEAT(x, y) begin
2     t ← 1
3     for i from 1 upto y do
4         t ← MULTIPLY-HORNER(t, x)
5     end
6     return t
7 end
```

One purpose of this is to highlight a subtle but fairly obvious fact: we are allowed to invoke one algorithm from within another one. In this case, we needed to multiply t by x in line #4; MULTIPLY-REPEAT and MULTIPLY-HORNER both compute the same result, so we could have used either of them here to do what we wanted. Either way, the idea is that half way through following the steps within the EXPONENTIATE-REPEAT algorithm, we stop for a while and follow steps from MULTIPLY-HORNER instead so as to compute the value we need. Again selecting $x = 3$ and $y = 6$, the steps we perform would be something like the following:

Step #1   Assign $t \leftarrow 1$.

Step #2   Invoke   MULTIPLY-HORNER(t, x),   i.e.,   invoke   MULTIPLY $-$ HORNER$(1, 3)$,

   Step #2.1   Assign $t \leftarrow 0$.
   Step #2.2   Assign $t \leftarrow 2 \cdot t$, i.e., $t \leftarrow 2 \cdot 0 = 0$.
   Step #2.3   Since $y_1 = 1$, assign $t \leftarrow t + x$, i.e., $t \leftarrow 0 + 1 = 1$.
   Step #2.4   Assign $t \leftarrow 2 \cdot t$, i.e., $t \leftarrow 2 \cdot 1 = 2$.
   Step #2.5   Since $y_0 = 1$, assign $t \leftarrow t + x$, i.e., $t \leftarrow 2 + 1 = 3$.
   Step #2.6   Return $t = 3$.
   then assign $t \leftarrow 3$.

Step #3   Invoke   MULTIPLY-HORNER(t, x),   i.e.,   invoke   MULTIPLY $-$ HORNER$(3, 3)$,

   Step #3.1   Assign $t \leftarrow 0$.
   Step #3.2   Assign $t \leftarrow 2 \cdot t$, i.e., $t \leftarrow 2 \cdot 0 = 0$.
   Step #3.3   Since $y_1 = 1$, assign $t \leftarrow t + x$, i.e., $t \leftarrow 0 + 3 = 3$.
   Step #3.4   Assign $t \leftarrow 2 \cdot t$, i.e., $t \leftarrow 2 \cdot 1 = 6$.
   Step #3.5   Since $y_0 = 1$, assign $t \leftarrow t + x$, i.e., $t \leftarrow 6 + 3 = 9$.
   Step #3.6   Return $t = 9$.
   then assign $t \leftarrow 9$.

   $\cdots$

Step #8   Return $t = 729$.

Nothing has changed: we are still just following directions. We need to keep track of which algorithm we are following and ensure the names we give to variables do not get mixed up, but other than that things are not fundamentally more complicated.

Of course, we can also use Horner's rule by replacing all the additions with multiplications, and all multiplications with exponentiations. Using the same example as previously, we would end up with

$$
\begin{aligned}
x^y &= x^{y_0} \cdot \left(x^{y_1} \cdot \left(x^{y_2} \cdot (1)^2 \right)^2 \right)^2 \\
&= x^0 \cdot \left(x^1 \cdot \left(x^1 \cdot (1)^2 \right)^2 \right)^2 \\
&= x^0 \cdot \left(x^1 \cdot \left(x^1 \cdot \quad 1 \quad \right)^2 \right)^2 \\
&= x^0 \cdot \left(x^1 \cdot \left(x^1 \qquad \right)^2 \right)^2 \\
&= x^0 \cdot \left(x^1 \cdot \quad x^2 \qquad \right)^2 \\
&= x^0 \cdot \left(x^3 \qquad \right)^2 \\
&= x^0 \cdot \quad x^6 \\
&= x^6
\end{aligned}
$$

Unsurprisingly, our method for multiplying one number by another has a dual which is able to exponentiate one number by another:

```
1  algorithm EXPONENTIATE-HORNER(x, y) begin
2      t ← 1
3      for i from |y| − 1 downto 0 do
4          t ← MULTIPLY-HORNER(t, t)
5          if yᵢ = 1 then
6              t ← MULTIPLY-HORNER(t, x)
7          end
8      end
9      return t
10 end
```

You should compare EXPONENTIATE-HORNER as given above, line-by-line, with MULTIPLY-HORNER given earlier. Notice that they use the same idea; their structure is the same, we simply changed all the additions to multiplications. EXPONENTIATE-HORNER is often called the **square-and-multiply** algorithm [6] since it performs of a sequence of squaring (line #4) and multiplication (line #6): one squaring is performed for every bit of y whether it is equal to zero or one, and one multiplication for those bits of y which are equal to one.

Research (task #10)

The EXPONENTIATE-HORNER algorithm (so MULTIPLY-HORNER as well, since they are similar) is sometimes described as processing y in a left-to-right order: if you write y in binary, it starts at the left-hand end and finishes at the right-hand end. For instance, we had

$$y = 6_{(10)} = 110_{(2)}$$

and processed $y_2 = 1$ first, then $y_1 = 1$ then finally $y_0 = 0$. There is an alternative version of the algorithm that processes y the other way around, i.e., right-to-left. Do some research into this alternative: write down the algorithm, and convince yourself it will computes the same result using some examples. Can you think why the left-to-right version might be preferred to the right-to-left alternative, or vice versa?

2.4   Computational Complexity

Imagine we have two algorithms that solve the *same* problem, but do so in *different* ways. This should not be hard, because we already have some suitable candidates: given an x and y, MULTIPLY-REPEAT and MULTIPLY-HORNER compute the same result $x \cdot y$ differently. So armed with these, or another example of your choice, here is a question: which one of the algorithms is the "best"? Actually, maybe we should go back a step: what does "best" even *mean*? Fastest? Shortest? Most attractive? All are reasonable measures, but imagine we select the first one and focus on selecting the algorithm which gives us a result in the least time.

Suppose we implemented the algorithms we would like to compare. This would give one way of comparing one against the other, we could simply time how long the corresponding programs take to execute on a computer. There are, however, many factors which might influence how long the execution of each program takes. For example:

- the skill of the programmer who implements the algorithm,
- the programming language used,
- the speed at which the computer can execute programs,
- the input, and
- the algorithm implemented by the program.

We know little or nothing about the first three factors, so have to focus on the latter two. Our goal is to introduce the subject of **computational complexity** [4]. This might sound scary, but is essentially about selectively ignoring detail: via a series of sane simplifications, each focusing on the most important, big picture issues, we can determine the quality of one algorithm compared to another.

2.4.1 Step Counting and Dominant Steps

As a guess at how long an algorithm would take to give a result if it *were* implemented and executed, we could count how many steps it takes. If you think about it, this makes perfect sense: the more steps the algorithm takes, the longer it will take to give result. But this would be quite a boring task if the algorithm had many steps. So the first simplification we make is to focus just on a small set of dominant steps, i.e., those steps we think are the most important. For algorithms that sort things, maybe the number of comparisons is the most important thing to count; for algorithms that process sequences of things, maybe the number of accesses to the sequence is the most important thing to count.

Since we are comparing algorithms that perform multiplication, it makes sense that we are interested mainly in arithmetic operations: the most important thing to count is the number of additions each algorithm uses to compute a result. Table 2.2 shows how many additions each algorithm performs for a range of inputs (ignore the columns marked $f(n)$ and $g(n)$ for now). It only includes a limited sample of inputs, but already we can identify two problems: first, the number of addition depends on y, and, second, it is not clear cut which algorithm uses the least number of additions. That is, sometimes MULTIPLY-REPEAT uses less, sometimes MULTIPLY-HORNER uses less. So in terms of answering our question, we are not really much better off than when we started.

Table 2.1 A table showing values of y and the number of bits in their binary representation

y	$\log_2(y+1)$	$\lceil \log_2(y+1) \rceil$
$1_{(10)} = 1_{(2)}$	1.000	1
$2_{(10)} = 10_{(2)}$	1.584	2
$3_{(10)} = 11_{(2)}$	2.000	2
$4_{(10)} = 100_{(2)}$	2.322	3
$5_{(10)} = 101_{(2)}$	2.585	3
$6_{(10)} = 110_{(2)}$	2.807	3
$7_{(10)} = 111_{(2)}$	3.000	3
$8_{(10)} = 1000_{(2)}$	3.170	4
$\vdots$	$\vdots$	$\vdots$

2.4.2 Problem Size and Step Counting Functions

Usually we would like to make a general judgement about an algorithm which is independent of the input. To do this, we need to make another simplification: instead of thinking about the number of steps for a particular input y, we will shift things to consider a **problem size** n. The basic idea is that we try to write down a function for the number of steps an algorithm takes in terms of n, the problem size; this is a **step counting** function. Once we have such functions, we can forget about the algorithms themselves and simply compare the associated step counting functions with each other.

There is not really a general definition of what the problem size should mean; basically it is just a measure of how hard the problem is. For example, if we have an algorithm that sorts a sequence of numbers, the length of the sequence makes a good problem size: if n is larger, the problem is harder in the sense that the algorithm has to do more work. In our case, suppose we are looking at n-bit numbers: each input x and y has n binary digits. If n is larger, the problem is harder in the sense that the algorithm has to do more work: multiplying together large numbers is harder than multiplying small numbers together. We can describe n in terms of y as

$$n = \lceil \log_2(y+1) \rceil.$$

That is, we add one to y then it takes the logarithm to base two, and then round the result up to the nearest integer (this is called the **ceiling** [8] function); Table 2.1 details some results.

Consider MULTIPLY-REPEAT to start with: if we have n-bit inputs, how many additions will the algorithm perform? Looking at the algorithm again, we can see that the best case is when the inputs are really small: that way, we are clearly going to perform the least additions. The smallest number we can write in n bits is always going to be 0; this means we perform 0 additions. What about the worst case? This would be represented by the largest input we can write using n bits; this is $2^n - 1$. If

Table 2.2 A table showing the number of additions performed by MULTIPLY-REPEAT and MULTIPLY-HORNER, and the values of the associated step counting functions

y	$\lceil \log_2(y+1) \rceil$	MULTIPLY-REPEAT	$f(n) = 2^n - 1$	MULTIPLY-HORNER	$g(n) = 2 \cdot n$
1	1	1	1	2	2
2	2	2	3	3	4
3	2	3	3	4	4
4	3	4	7	4	6
5	3	5	7	5	6
6	3	6	7	5	6
7	3	7	7	6	6
8	4	8	15	5	8
⋮	⋮	⋮	⋮	⋮	⋮

we set $n = 2$ for example, the largest number we can write is three: the next largest number, i.e., four, needs $n = 3$. In the worst case then, we can write the step counting function

$$f(n) = 2^n - 1$$

to describe how many additions we would do. If $n = 2$, we are talking about 2-bit numbers and $f(n) = 3$ indicates that we would do at most three additions.

Now consider MULTIPLY-HORNER. If we have n-bit inputs, the loop in the algorithm iterates n times: we perform one iteration for each bit of the input y. This means we do n additions as a result of line #4. In the best case, all the bits of the input are zero (i.e., each $y_i = 0$) so we *never* process line #6 and do no more additions; in the worst case all the bits are one (i.e., each $y_i = 1$) and we *always* process line #6 and do n more additions. So in the worst case our step counting function will be

$$g(n) = 2 \cdot n.$$

Choosing $n = 2$ again, $g(n) = 4$ indicates that we would do four additions.

Table 2.2 shows the results of the step counting functions along side the actual number of steps performed by the algorithms. Clearly the two are not the same; the key thing to realise is that the actual number of steps is always less than or equal to the step counting function for the corresponding algorithm. This is because we developed each step counting function in relation to the worst case behaviour for a given input size, not the actual behaviour for that specific input.

2.4.3 Ignoring Small Problems and Minor Terms

The next simplification we make is to assume n is always large. In a way, this is obviously sensible: if n were small then nobody cares what algorithm we choose, they will all be fast enough. The main result of making such an assumption is that we can make our step counting functions simpler. For example, we currently have the function

$$f(n) = 2^n - 1.$$

If n is going to be large, who cares about the 1 term? This will be incidental in comparison to the 2^n term. Imagine we select $n = 8$ for example: $2^8 = 256$ and $2^8 - 1 = 255$ are close enough that we may as well just treat them as the same and rewrite the function as

$$f(n) = 2^n.$$

What about the other step counting function? Consider the following *sequence* of step counting functions:

$$\langle 1 \cdot n, 2 \cdot n, 3 \cdot n, 4 \cdot n, 5 \cdot n, 6 \cdot n, \ldots \rangle.$$

Assuming n is positive, if we read the sequence from left-to-right each function is greater than the last one. For example $3 \cdot n$ will *always* be greater than $2 \cdot n$, no matter what n is. This means the number of steps would grow as we read from left-to-right: the associated algorithms would be slower and slower.

The natural end to this sequence is the point where one of the functions is $n \cdot n = n^2$. This is basically saying that n^2 is greater than *all* the functions in our sequence: if we select *any* constant $c < n$, then $c \cdot n$ is going to be less than n^2. As a result, another simplification we can make is to treat any step counting function that looks like $c \cdot n$ as n instead. This means we can rewrite

$$g(n) = 2 \cdot n$$

as

$$g(n) = n.$$

On one hand, this seems mad: an algorithm whose step counting function is $200 \cdot n$ will take 100 times more steps than one whose step counting function is $2 \cdot n$. So how can we rationally treat them as the same? Well, consider running an algorithm on two different computers: one is about ten years old, and one is very modern. The same algorithm will probably run 100 times slower on the old computer than it does on the new one: a ten year old computer is likely to be 100 times slower than a new one. This comparison is nothing to do with the algorithm in the sense that the computers are what makes the difference. So whether we take the step counting function as being $2 \cdot n$ or $100 \cdot n$ does not matter, the constant will eventually be one if we wait for a computer which is fast enough. So in comparing algorithms we always ignore constants terms, thus treat both $2 \cdot n$ and $100 \cdot n$ as the function n.

Actually writing

$$100 \cdot n = n$$

looks a bit odd, so instead we use the **big-O notation** [2] and we write the above non-equation as the equation

$$100 \cdot n = O(n)$$

which basically says that if n is big enough, then the function on the left behaves *at worst* like the function inside the big-O (having ignored any constants). The phrase "at worst" is crucial; we can write $n = O(n^2)$ since n is at worst n^2, but this is slightly lazy since we also know that $n = O(n)$.

2.4.4 Studying the Growth of Functions

Have a look at Fig. 2.2. It plots the growth of a few simple step counting functions as the problem size n grows; actually, it only uses very small values of n because some of the functions fly off the top quite quickly. What we are trying to do is visualise how the functions behave, relating the shape of the plot for a given step counting function to the number of steps taken by the associated algorithm.

1. The plot for $h(n) = 1$ is flat: it does not matter what the problem size is, there is no growth in the function. This is great! No matter how large the problem is, the step counting function says the algorithm will take a constant number of steps.
2. The next plot is for $h(n) = \log_2 n$. Unlike $h(n) = 1$, this function grows as n grows; the larger we make the problem size, the more steps the algorithm takes. On the other hand, $h(n) = \log_2 n$ grows quite slowly. We can see, from the trajectory that the plot is taking, that even for large values of n, $h(n) = \log_2 n$ will not be too large (in comparison to some of the other functions).
3. The plot for $h(n) = n$ is not so great. This time, the growth is constant: if the problems size is n, the algorithm takes n steps. If we compare the trajectory of the function $h(n) = n$ with $h(n) = \log_2 n$, $h(n) = n$ is clearly going to be much larger than $h(n) = \log_2 n$ in the long run.
4. Then things take a turn for the worse. The functions $h(n) = n^2$ and $h(n) = 2^n$ grow *really* quickly compared to the others. The function $h(n) = 2^n$ shows what we call exponential growth: looking at the almost vertical trajectory of $h(n) = 2^n$, it will be *enormous* even for fairly small values of n. So for large values of n, the algorithm will take so many steps to produce a result that it is probably not worth even invoking it!

Just so this hits home, notice that the function $h(n) = n$ is equal to 100 if $n = 100$: if the problem size is 100, the algorithm takes 100 steps. On the other hand, the function $h(n) = 2^n$ is equal to

$$1267650600228229401496703205376$$

if $n = 100$. That is a *lot* of steps!

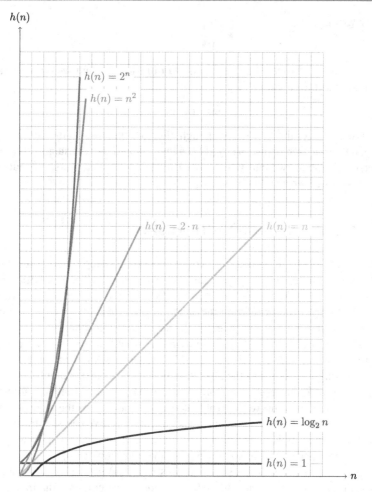

Fig. 2.2 A graph illustrating the growth of several functions as the problem size is increased

Now, if we put all this evidence together we can try to answer our original question: given a problem size n, the number of steps taken by MULTIPLY-REPEAT can approximated by the function $f(n) = 2^n$; for MULTIPLY-HORNER the number of steps is approximated by the function $g(n) = n$. We have seen that f grows so quickly that even with quite small n, it is fair to say it will *always* be larger than g. This implies MULTIPLY-HORNER gives us a result in the least time, and is therefore the "best" algorithm. Putting this into context helps show the value of our analysis: in real computers, 32-bit numbers are common. If we wanted to multiply such numbers together MULTIPLY-REPEAT would take approximately 4294967296 steps in the worst case; if we selected MULTIPLY-HORNER instead, we only need approximately 32 steps. Hopefully it is clear that even though we have made simplifications along the way, they would have to be wrong on a monumental scale to make our selection the incorrect one! So to cut a long story short, computational complexity has allowed us to reason about and compare algorithms in a meaningful, theoretical way: this is a *very* powerful tool *if* used for the right job.

Implement (task #11)

The big-O notation is one of the most important concepts, and also items of Mathematical notation, in Computer Science. It is worth getting used to it now, so consider the following nine examples:

$$2n + 1 = O(n)$$
$$2^n + 3n = O(2^n)$$
$$6n^2 + 3n + 1 = O(6n^2)$$
$$\frac{n}{2} + \log n = O(n)$$
$$2^{n \log n} = O(2^n)$$
$$6n^2 + 3n + 1 = O(n^2 + n)$$
$$(\log n)^3 = O(n)$$
$$(\log n)^3 = O((\log n)^4)$$
$$(\log n)^3 = O((\log n)^3)$$

One of them is wrong, can you work out which one (and the reason why)?

Research (task #12)

In turns out big-O is a short-hand for big-Omicron, if you want to be exact about the Greek symbol used. Within this context, using other Greek symbols allows us make other statements about a function: there is a whole family, including o (or little-O), ω (or little-Omega), Ω (or big-Omega), and Θ (or big-Theta) for instance. Do some research into what these mean, and why we might use them *instead* of big-O in specific situations.

References

1. Wikipedia: Algorithm. http://en.wikipedia.org/wiki/Algorithm
2. Wikipedia: Big-O notation. http://en.wikipedia.org/wiki/Big_O_notation
3. Wikipedia: Carmichael number. http://en.wikipedia.org/wiki/Carmichael_number
4. Wikipedia: Computational complexity theory. http://en.wikipedia.org/wiki/Computational_complexity_theory
5. Wikipedia: Coprime. http://en.wikipedia.org/wiki/Coprime
6. Wikipedia: Exponentiation by squaring. http://en.wikipedia.org/wiki/Exponentiation_by_squaring
7. Wikipedia: Fermat primality test. http://en.wikipedia.org/wiki/Fermat_primality_test

8. Wikipedia: Floor and ceiling functions. http://en.wikipedia.org/wiki/Floor_and_ceiling_functions
9. Wikipedia: Flow chart. http://en.wikipedia.org/wiki/Flowchart
10. Wikipedia: Horner's scheme. http://en.wikipedia.org/wiki/Horner_scheme
11. Wikipedia: Pesudo-code. http://en.wikipedia.org/wiki/Pseudo_code
12. Wikipedia: Prime number. http://en.wikipedia.org/wiki/Prime_number

Playing Hide-and-Seek with Virus Scanners 3

A **computer virus** [5] is a program that attempts to **infect** another **host** file (often another program) by replicating itself (e.g., appending a copy of itself to the host). This is analogous to how Biological viruses attach themselves to host cells. The idea is that when the host file is loaded or executed, the virus is activated: at this point the virus can deploy a **payload** of some kind, which often has malicious intent. Although a definition[1] for computer viruses was yet to be written in 1971, it represents the point in time when instances of programs we retrospectively call viruses started to appear. **Creeper** [7], written by Bob Thomas, is often cited as the first: it targeted PDP [19] computers connected to the **Advanced Research Projects Agency Network (ARPANET)** [3], propagating itself via the telephone system. Once resident it displayed the annoying but otherwise non-destructive message "I'm the creeper, catch me if you can" to users, but seemingly did *not* replicate itself (at least intentionally): once the payload was deployed, it simply moved on to the next computer. Perhaps more (in)famous though, is the 1988 **Morris Worm** [17] written by Robert Morris. Although it again lacked a malign payload, the worm infected computers multiple times, slowing down their normal operation to the point where roughly 10 % of computers connected to the **Internet** [14] were claimed to have been left non-operational.

A rich published history [24] of computer viruses now exists; since much of it is legally dubious, more undoubtedly remains unpublished. Both Creeper and the Morris Worm represented an experimental era in this historical timeline, with honest security researchers exploring what was and was not possible; neither was intentionally malicious, with Creeper being explicitly described as an experimental

---

[1] Strictly speaking, a **virus** is a program that propagates itself from file to file on one computer, but typically requires an external stimulus to propagate between computers (e.g., a user carrying infected files on a USB stick from one computer to another); the requirement for a host file to infect means the virus is typically not a stand-alone program. This contrasts with a **worm**, which propagates from computer to computer itself, acting as a stand-alone program without the need to infect a host file. A specific example might include aspects of both, so a precise classification is often difficult; we largely ignore the issue, using the term virus as an imprecise but convenient catch-all.

D. Page, N. Smart, *What Is Computer Science?*,
Undergraduate Topics in Computer Science, DOI 10.1007/978-3-319-04042-4_3,
© Springer International Publishing Switzerland 2014

self-replicating program. Beyond the technological aspects, the Morris Worm is also notorious because of the subsequent prosecution of Morris and treatment of information, network and computer security as an important emerging threat: governments, rather than just programmers and researchers, started to take notice. Today of course, viruses (and **malware** [16] more generally) have become big business for the wider computer underground. Not content with sending you annoying messages, a modern virus might delete or encrypt your files (holding the owners to ransom, so they must pay before the content can be read again), steal information [15], or even attempt to actively destroy *physical* infrastructure. **Stuxnet** [23], for instance, represents what is widely viewed as a "cyber-weapon" developed and deployed by some (unnamed) government against uranium enrichment plants in Iran.

In many cases therefore, (cyber-)crime increasingly *does* pay. The result is an arms race between the people who write viruses, and the people who write **anti-virus** software. Again drawing on Biology (and the field of virotherapy), the first example of anti-virus was arguably a second virus called **Reaper** written to stamp out the spread of updates to **Creeper** (which, in contrast to the original, *did* replicate themselves). More generally however, before we can disable a virus we need to detect whether a given host file is infected or not. Interestingly we can *prove* this is a good business to be in by showing that it is *impossible* to write a perfect virus detector algorithm. Imagine for a moment we *could* do this: DETECT represents a perfect virus detector, so we are sure $\text{DETECT}(x) = $ **true** whenever x is a virus, and that $\text{DETECT}(x) = $ **false** in all other cases. Now imagine there is a virus called VIRUS. It is clever: it incorporates a *copy* of DETECT, the virus detector algorithm, inside itself. A simple description of how VIRUS works is as follows:

```
1  algorithm VIRUS begin
2      if DETECT(VIRUS) = true then
3          | Behave like a non-virus, i.e., a normal program
4      else
5          | Behave like a virus, i.e., do something "bad"
6      end
7  end
```

So when VIRUS is executed, it checks whether DETECT says it is a virus. If $\text{DETECT}(\text{VIRUS}) = $ **true**, i.e., DETECT thinks VIRUS is a virus, then VIRUS does nothing. Hence, in this case VIRUS *does not* behave like a virus and so DETECT was wrong. If DETECT(VIRUS) returns **false**, i.e., DETECT does not think VIRUS is a virus, then VIRUS does something "bad" such as deleting all your files. In this case VIRUS definitely *does* behave like a virus, and so DETECT is wrong again. Thus, if we assume a perfect virus scanner DETECT exists then we get a contradiction; this means DETECT cannot exist. Although this proof relates to writing perfect anti-virus software, it is in fact a special case of the famous **Halting problem** [10].

Despite the fact that we cannot write perfect anti-virus software, it is still worth looking at how we might at least *try* to detect V; a common tool in this context is a virus **scanner** [2]. Most work in roughly the same way: the idea is that for each virus, one tries to create a unique **signature** that identifies files containing the virus.

The scanner inspects each file in turn, and tries to match the file content with each signature. If there are no matches, then the scanner concludes that there is no virus in the file and moves on to the next one. We can imagine both the signature and the file being sequences of numbers called S and F. There are lots of efficient ways to search F, the easiest of which is to simply take each S and match it up against the content of F one element at a time:

$$
\begin{array}{lll}
F = \langle & \cdots, 6, 5, 2, 1, 4, 0, 3, 5, 2, 1, \cdots \rangle & \\
S = \langle & 3, 5, 2, 1 & \rangle \mapsto \textbf{no match} \\
\langle & 3, 5, 2, 1 & \rangle \mapsto \textbf{no match} \\
\langle & 3, 5, 2, 1 & \rangle \mapsto \textbf{no match} \\
\langle & 3, 5, 2, 1 & \rangle \mapsto \textbf{no match} \\
\langle & 3, 5, 2, 1 & \rangle \mapsto \textbf{no match} \\
\langle & 3, 5, 2, 1 & \rangle \mapsto \textbf{no match} \\
\langle & 3, 5, 2, 1 & \rangle \mapsto \textbf{match} \\
\end{array}
$$

In the i-th step, we compare S against the sub-sequence of F starting at F_i. We continue this process until either we run out of content, or there is a match between S and a particular region of F. In the latter case, we have found an occurrence of S in F and identified the file as containing the virus. This approach relies on the fact that the people who sold you the virus scanner send you a new signature whenever a new virus is detected somewhere; this is basically why you need to update your virus scanner regularly. A given signature might not be perfect, and might sound the alarm for some files that *do not* contain a virus. For example, the signature $\langle 3, 5, 2, 1 \rangle$ might be a valid part of some uninfected data file, but would still cause the scanner to flag it as infected.

In this chapter we will play the part of the bad guy, and imagine we want to write a virus. The goal is to explain how our virus can avoid detection by virus scanners (or at least the one described above), and yet still execute some payload. The approach we use is to have the virus change itself *during* execution so as to fool the virus scanner. This sort of self-modifying program is made possible by the way that modern computers execute programs. So before we start talking about viruses, we will start by looking at what programs are and how computers execute them.

3.1 Computers and Programs

The questions "what is a computer" and "what is computation" are at the core of Computer Science; eminent scholars in the field have spent, and still spend, lots of time thinking about and producing new results in this area. If you pick up a textbook on the subject, the topic of **Turing Machines (TMs)** [25] is often used as a starting point. Alan Turing [1], some might say the father of Computer Science, introduced TMs as a theoretical tool to reason about computers and computation: we still use them for the same tasks today. But TMs and their use are a topic in their own right, and one not quite aligned to what we want here. Specifically, we would like to answer some more concrete, more practical questions instead. So, consider that you probably sit in front of and use a physical (rather than theoretical) computer every day: we would like to know "what is *that* computer" and more importantly "how does *it* compute things"?

3.1.1   A Theoretical Computer

A computer is basically just a machine used to process steps, which we call **instructions**, collected together into **programs**. This should sound familiar: the computer is doing something similar to what *we* do when we step through an algorithm. In a sense, the only thing that makes a computer remarkable is that it **executes** the instructions in a program *much* faster than we can process algorithms, and more or less without error. Just like we can process any reasonably written algorithm, a computer can execute any program. This is a neat feature: we do not need one computer to send emails and a different one to view web-pages, we just need one **general-purpose** computer that can do more or less anything when provided with an appropriate program.

To design a computer, we need to write down an algorithm that describes how to process programs (which are simply algorithms). In a very rough sense, as the user of a computer you "see" the result as the combination of an **operating system** (e.g., UNIX) and a **Central Processing Unit (CPU)** [4], or **processor**, that is the main hardware component within the computer. Basically the processor is the thing that actually executes programs, and the operating systems acts as an assistant by loading the programs from disk, allowing you to select which program to execute and so on. Of course we then need to build the hardware somehow, but we will worry about that later; basically what we want as a starting point is an algorithm for processing algorithms. Here is a first attempt:

1. Write a program as a sequence of instructions called P; start executing the sequence from the first element, i.e., P_0.
2. Fetch the next instruction from the program and call it IR.
3. If $IR = \perp$ (i.e., we have run out of instructions to execute) or if $IR = HALT$ then halt the computer, otherwise execute IR (i.e., perform the operation it specifies).
4. Repeat from line #2.

Look at this a little more closely. The sequence of instructions we call P is a program for the computer; if it makes things easier, think of it as a word processor or web-browser or something. Each element of P is an instruction, and each instruction is taken from an **instruction set** of possibilities that the computer understands. Lines #2 to #4 form a loop. During each iteration we first fetch the next instruction from P. We call the instruction IR because in real computers, it is held in the **Instruction Register (IR)**. Once we have IR to hand, we set about performing whatever operation is specifies; then if we encounter a special instruction called $HALT$ we stop execution, otherwise we carry out the whole loop again.

Hopefully this seems sensible. It should do, because as we have tried to motivate, it more or less models the same thing *you* would do if you were processing the steps of an algorithm. An example makes the whole idea easier to understand: imagine we want to execute a short program that computes $10 + 20$. First we write down the program, e.g.,

$$P = \langle A \leftarrow 10, A \leftarrow A + 20, HALT \rangle,$$

and then process the remaining steps of our algorithm to execute it

Step #1   Fetch $IR = A \leftarrow 10$ from the sequence.
Step #2   Since $IR \neq\perp$ and $IR \neq HALT$, execute $A \leftarrow 10$, i.e., set A to 10.
Step #3   Fetch $IR = A \leftarrow A + 20$ from the sequence.
Step #4   Since $IR \neq\perp$ and $IR \neq HALT$, execute $A \leftarrow A + 20$, i.e., set A to 30.
Step #5   Fetch $IR = HALT$ from the sequence.
Step #6   Since $IR \neq\perp$ but $IR = HALT$, halt the computer.

After which we have the result $10 + 20 = 30$ held in A. Hopefully the underlying point is clear. Specifically, bar the issue with building the hardware itself there is no magic behind the scenes: this *really is* how a computer executes a program.

3.1.2 A Real, Harvard-Style Computer

It turns out that the hardware components we would need to build a computer like the one described above relate well to those you would find in a simple pocket calculator. For example:

A pocket calculator:

- Has an accumulator (i.e., the current value).
- Has some memory (accessed via the $M+$ and MR buttons) that can store values.
- Has some device to perform arithmetic (i.e., to add together numbers).
- Has input and output peripherals (e.g., keypad, LCD screen).
- Responds to simple commands or instructions from the user; for example the user can supply things to perform arithmetic on (i.e., numbers) and commands to perform arithmetic (e.g., do an addition).

A computer:

- Has many accumulators (often called registers).
- Has potentially many levels and large amounts of memory (often called RAM).
- Has an Arithmetic and Logic Unit (ALU) to perform arithmetic.
- Has input and output peripherals (e.g., keyboard, mouse, hard disk, monitor).
- Executes sequences of simple instructions called programs; each instruction consists of some **operands** (i.e., the things to operate on) and an **opcode** (i.e., the operation to perform).

In fact, early computers essentially *were* very large versions of what today we would call a calculator. They were used to perform repetitive computation, such as computing tables of SIN and COS for people to use. Computers of this era typically relied on

1. a paper **tape** [20], where instructions from the program were stored as patterns of holes in the paper, and
2. some **memory**, where data being processed by the computer was stored.

We could expand on both technologies, but their detail is not really that important. Instead we can model them using two sequences called $TAPE$ and MEM. When we write MEM_i, we are accessing the i-th **address** in memory, whereas $TAPE_j$ represents the j-th row on the continuous ream of paper tape.

So imagine we want to build an example computer of this type. We assume it has a tape and a memory as described above, and single **accumulator** called A. Each element of $TAPE$ holds an instruction from the program, while each element of MEM and the accumulator A can hold numbers; to make things simpler, we will write each number using decimal. The computer can understand a limited set of instructions:

- NOP, i.e., do nothing.
- $HALT$, i.e., halt or stop execution.
- $A \leftarrow n$, i.e., load the number n into the accumulator A.
- $MEM_n \leftarrow A$, i.e., store the number in the accumulator A into address n of the memory.
- $A \leftarrow MEM_n$, i.e., load the number from address n in memory into the accumulator A.
- $A \leftarrow A + MEM_n$, i.e., add the number in address n of the memory to the accumulator A and store the result back in the accumulator.
- $A \leftarrow A - MEM_n$, i.e., subtract the number in address n of the memory from the accumulator A and store the result back in the accumulator.
- $A \leftarrow A \oplus MEM_n$, i.e., XOR the number in address n of the memory with the accumulator A and store the result back in the accumulator.

One can view things on the right-hand side of the assignment symbol $\leftarrow$ as being read from, and those on the left-hand side as being written to by an instruction. So for example, an instruction

$$A \leftarrow 10$$

reads the number 10 and writes it into A. This also implies that memory access can be written in the same way; for example

$$MEM_{64} \leftarrow A$$

reads the number in A and writes it into memory at address sixty four.

It is important to notice that a given program for our example computer can *only* include instructions from this instruction set. It simply does not know how to execute any other type. For example, we could not feed it the FERMAT-TEST algorithm from Chap. 2 because it uses operations not included in the instruction set. Even so, we *can* start to write useful programs. Consider a similar example to the one we looked at previously: we want to add together two numbers held in MEM_4 and MEM_5 (where say $MEM_4 = 10$ and $MEM_5 = 20$), and then store the result into MEM_6. The program consists of the four instructions

$$A \leftarrow MEM_4$$
$$A \leftarrow A + MEM_5$$
$$MEM_6 \leftarrow A$$
$$HALT$$

The method used by the computer to execute a program like this is *very* similar to our first attempt above:

1. Encode a program P onto paper tape; load this tape into the tape reader and start the computer.
2. Using the tape reader, fetch the next instruction in the program and call it IR.
3. If $IR = \perp$ (i.e., we have run out of instructions to execute) or if $IR = HALT$ then halt the computer, otherwise execute IR (i.e., perform the operation it specifies).
4. Repeat from line 2.

We can describe each step during execution of the program by detailing the state of the computer, e.g., what values are held by MEM, $TAPE$ and A; Figs. 3.1 and 3.2 do just this. The execution shows that after step #9, the computer halts and we end up with the result of the addition, i.e., 30, stored in MEM_6; not exactly a word processor or web-browser, but quite an achievement by the standards of the 1940s!

It is important to remember that the program is free to alter memory content, but has no means of altering the tape which houses the instructions. That is, once we start the computer, we cannot change the program: our example computer views instructions and the data as fundamentally *different* things. This is now termed a **Harvard architecture** [11] after the **Automatic Sequence Controlled Calculator (ASCC)** designed by Howard Aiken and built by IBM; the installation at Harvard University, delivered in around 1944, was nicknamed the "Mark 1" [12]. The crucial thing to take away is that there is still no magic involved: as shown in Fig. 4.1, the Harvard Mark 1 was a real, physical computer built on *exactly* the principles as above.

3.1.3 A Real, von Neumann-Style Computer

The Harvard style view of computers changed radically when **John von Neumann** [26] documented the concept of a **stored program architecture** in around 1945. The basic idea is that instructions and data are actually the *same* thing. Think about it: what does 1 mean? The meaning of 1 completely depends on the context it is placed in, and how *we* interpret it: if we interpret it as a number it means the integer one, if we interpret it as an instruction it could mean "perform an addition". So basically, as long as we have an encoding from numbers to meaning then we can store *both* instructions and data as numbers in memory. For our purposes, the encoding does not matter too much; imagine we continue to represent everything as decimal numbers:

- $00nnnn$ means NOP.
- $10nnnn$ means $HALT$.
- $20nnnn$ means $A \leftarrow n$.
- $21nnnn$ means $MEM_n \leftarrow A$.
- $22nnnn$ means $A \leftarrow MEM_n$.
- $30nnnn$ means $A \leftarrow A + MEM_n$.
- $31nnnn$ means $A \leftarrow A - MEM_n$.

CPU
state = reset
IR =
A = 0

MEM		TAPE	
Address	Value	Address	Meaning
0	0	0	$A \leftarrow MEM_4$
1	0	1	$A \leftarrow A + MEM_5$
2	0	2	$MEM_6 \leftarrow A$
3	0	3	$HALT$
4	10	4	NOP
5	20	5	NOP
6	0	6	NOP
7	0	7	NOP

(a) Step #1: Load the tape into the tape reader and start the computer.

CPU
state = fetch
IR = $A \leftarrow MEM_4$
A = 0

MEM		TAPE	
Address	Value	Address	Meaning
0	0	0	$A \leftarrow MEM_4$
1	0	1	$A \leftarrow A + MEM_5$
2	0	2	$MEM_6 \leftarrow A$
3	0	3	$HALT$
4	10	4	NOP
5	20	5	NOP
6	0	6	NOP
7	0	7	NOP

(b) Step #2: Fetch the next instruction $IR = A \leftarrow MEM_4$ from the tape.

CPU
state = execute
IR = $A \leftarrow MEM_4$
A = 10

MEM		TAPE	
Address	Value	Address	Meaning
0	0	0	$A \leftarrow MEM_4$
1	0	1	$A \leftarrow A + MEM_5$
2	0	2	$MEM_6 \leftarrow A$
3	0	3	$HALT$
4	10	4	NOP
5	20	5	NOP
6	0	6	NOP
7	0	7	NOP

(c) Step #3: Execute the instruction $A \leftarrow MEM_4$, i.e., set A to $MEM_4 = 10$.

CPU
state = fetch
IR = $A \leftarrow A + MEM_5$
A = 10

MEM		TAPE	
Address	Value	Address	Meaning
0	0	0	$A \leftarrow MEM_4$
1	0	1	$A \leftarrow A + MEM_5$
2	0	2	$MEM_6 \leftarrow A$
3	0	3	$HALT$
4	10	4	NOP
5	20	5	NOP
6	0	6	NOP
7	0	7	NOP

(d) Step #4: Fetch the next instruction $IR = A \leftarrow A + MEM_5$ from the tape.

CPU
state = execute
IR = $A \leftarrow A + MEM_5$
A = 30

MEM		TAPE	
Address	Value	Address	Meaning
0	0	0	$A \leftarrow MEM_4$
1	0	1	$A \leftarrow A + MEM_5$
2	0	2	$MEM_6 \leftarrow A$
3	0	3	$HALT$
4	10	4	NOP
5	20	5	NOP
6	0	6	NOP
7	0	7	NOP

(e) Step #5: Execute the instruction $A \leftarrow A + MEM_5$, i.e., set A to $A + MEM_5 = 30$.

CPU
state = fetch
IR = $MEM_6 \leftarrow A$
A = 30

MEM		TAPE	
Address	Value	Address	Meaning
0	0	0	$A \leftarrow MEM_4$
1	0	1	$A \leftarrow A + MEM_5$
2	0	2	$MEM_6 \leftarrow A$
3	0	3	$HALT$
4	10	4	NOP
5	20	5	NOP
6	0	6	NOP
7	0	7	NOP

(f) Step #6: Fetch the next instruction $IR = MEM_6 \leftarrow A$ from the tape.

Fig. 3.1 Computing the sum $10 + 20$, as executed on a Harvard-style computer

CPU

state = execute
$IR = MEM_6 \leftarrow A$
$A = 30$

MEM		TAPE	
Address	Value	Address	Meaning
0	0	0	$A \leftarrow MEM_4$
1	0	1	$A \leftarrow A + MEM_5$
2	0	2	$MEM_6 \leftarrow A$
3	0	3	$HALT$
4	10	4	NOP
5	20	5	NOP
6	30	6	NOP
7	0	7	NOP

(a) Step #7: Execute the instruction $MEM_6 \leftarrow A$, i.e., set MEM_6 to $A = 30$.

CPU

state = fetch
$IR = HALT$
$A = 30$

MEM		TAPE	
Address	Value	Address	Meaning
0	0	0	$A \leftarrow MEM_4$
1	0	1	$A \leftarrow A + MEM_5$
2	0	2	$MEM_6 \leftarrow A$
3	0	3	$HALT$
4	10	4	NOP
5	20	5	NOP
6	30	6	NOP
7	0	7	NOP

(b) Step #8: Fetch the next instruction $IR = HALT$ from the tape.

CPU

state = execute
$IR = HALT$
$A = 30$

MEM		TAPE	
Address	Value	Address	Meaning
0	0	0	$A \leftarrow MEM_4$
1	0	1	$A \leftarrow A + MEM_5$
2	0	2	$MEM_6 \leftarrow A$
3	0	3	$HALT$
4	10	4	NOP
5	20	5	NOP
6	30	6	NOP
7	0	7	NOP

(c) Step #9: Execute the instruction $HALT$, i.e., stop execution.

Fig. 3.2 Computing the sum $10 + 20$, as executed on a Harvard-style computer

- $32nnnn$ means $A \leftarrow A \oplus MEM_n$.
- $40nnnn$ means $PC \leftarrow n$.
- $41nnnn$ means $PC \leftarrow n$ iff. $A = 0$.
- $42nnnn$ means $PC \leftarrow n$ iff. $A \neq 0$.

The entries on the left-hand side perhaps need some explanation. Take the entry for $20nnnn$: this is a six digit decimal number where the left-most two digits are 2 and 0, and the right-most four can be *any* digits in the range $0, 1, \ldots, 9$. On the right-hand side, we replace $nnnn$ by a single number n so it will be in the range $0, 1, \ldots, 9999$. For example, the decimal number 300005, viewed as an encoded instruction 300005, means $A \leftarrow A + MEM_5$: we match 0005 on the left-hand side of the table, and turn it into 5 on the right-hand side. The 30 part is the **opcode**, and the 0005 part is the **operand**; the 30 part tells the computer what operation to perform, while the 0005 part tells it what to perform the operation on.

So if we store both instructions and data in memory, how do we know which instruction to execute next? Basically, we need an extra accumulator, which we call the **Program Counter (PC)**, to keep track of where to fetch the instruction from: it holds a number just like A does, but the number in PC will be used to keep track of where the next instruction is in memory. With this in mind, we also need to slightly alter the way programs are executed:

Fig. 3.3 The ENIAC installation at the US Army Ballistics Research Laboratory (public domain image, source: US Army Photo http://ftp.arl.army.mil/ftp/historic-computers/gif/eniac5.gif)

1. Encode a program P onto paper tape; load this tape into memory using the tape reader, zero the program counter PC and start the computer.
2. From the address in PC, fetch the next instruction in the program and call it IR.
3. Increment PC so it points to the next instruction.
4. If $IR = \bot$ (i.e., we have run out of instructions to execute), or if $IR = HALT$ then halt the computer, otherwise execute IR (i.e., perform the operation it specifies).
5. Repeat from line 2.

Notice that we have included a new step to update the value of PC (by adding one to it). This is analogous to ensuring we fetch the instruction from the next row of the tape in our previous design. Now reconsider the example program we looked at before, *and* how it is encoded:

$$
\begin{aligned}
A &\leftarrow MEM_4 &&\mapsto 220004 \\
A &\leftarrow A + MEM_5 &&\mapsto 300005 \\
MEM_6 &\leftarrow A &&\mapsto 210006 \\
HALT & &&\mapsto 100000
\end{aligned}
$$

Execution using our new computer proceeds in more or less the same way, except that now it holds both data and instructions in MEM rather than having the instructions on a dedicated tape. As before, one can imagine drawing the state of the computer at each step in the execution; we do this in Figs. 3.6, 3.7, 3.8. Again, after step #13, the computer halts and we end up with the result of the addition, i.e., 30,

Fig. 3.4 Two operators at the ENIAC control panel (public domain image, source: US Army Photo http://ftp.arl.army.mil/ftp/historic-computers/gif/eniac7.gif)

Fig. 3.5 Original caption notes that "replacing a bad [vacuum] tube meant checking among ENIACs 19,000 possibilities"; a daunting task! (public domain image, source: US Army Photo http://ftp.arl.army.mil/ftp/historic-computers/gif/eniac3.gif)

CPU

state	= reset
PC	= 0
IR	=
	=
A	= 0

MEM

Address	Value	Meaning
0	220004	$A \leftarrow MEM_4$
1	300005	$A \leftarrow A + MEM_5$
2	210006	$MEM_6 \leftarrow A$
3	100000	$HALT$
4	10	NOP
5	20	NOP
6	0	NOP
7	0	NOP

(a) Step #1: Load the tape into memory, set $PC = 0$ and start the computer.

CPU

state	= fetch
PC	= 0
IR	= 220004
	=
A	= 0

MEM

Address	Value	Meaning
0	220004	$A \leftarrow MEM_4$
1	300005	$A \leftarrow A + MEM_5$
2	210006	$MEM_6 \leftarrow A$
3	100000	$HALT$
4	10	NOP
5	20	NOP
6	0	NOP
7	0	NOP

(b) Step #2: Fetch the next instruction $IR = 220004$ from $PC = 0$.

CPU

state	= decode
PC	= 1
IR	= 220004
	= $A \leftarrow MEM_4$
A	= 0

MEM

Address	Value	Meaning
0	220004	$A \leftarrow MEM_4$
1	300005	$A \leftarrow A + MEM_5$
2	210006	$MEM_6 \leftarrow A$
3	100000	$HALT$
4	10	NOP
5	20	NOP
6	0	NOP
7	0	NOP

(c) Step #3: Decode $IR = 220004$ into $A \leftarrow MEM_4$, and set PC to $PC + 1 = 1$.

CPU

state	= execute
PC	= 1
IR	= 220004
	= $A \leftarrow MEM_4$
A	= 10

MEM

Address	Value	Meaning
0	220004	$A \leftarrow MEM_4$
1	300005	$A \leftarrow A + MEM_5$
2	210006	$MEM_6 \leftarrow A$
3	100000	$HALT$
4	10	NOP
5	20	NOP
6	0	NOP
7	0	NOP

(d) Step #4: Execute the instruction $A \leftarrow MEM_4$, i.e., set A to $MEM_4 = 10$.

CPU

state	= fetch
PC	= 1
IR	= 300005
	=
A	= 10

MEM

Address	Value	Meaning
0	220004	$A \leftarrow MEM_4$
1	300005	$A \leftarrow A + MEM_5$
2	210006	$MEM_6 \leftarrow A$
3	100000	$HALT$
4	10	NOP
5	20	NOP
6	0	NOP
7	0	NOP

(e) Step #5: Fetch the next instruction $IR = 300005$ from $PC = 1$.

CPU

state	= decode
PC	= 2
IR	= 300005
	= $A \leftarrow A + MEM_5$
A	= 10

MEM

Address	Value	Meaning
0	220004	$A \leftarrow MEM_4$
1	300005	$A \leftarrow A + MEM_5$
2	210006	$MEM_6 \leftarrow A$
3	100000	$HALT$
4	10	NOP
5	20	NOP
6	0	NOP
7	0	NOP

(f) Step #6: Decode $IR = 300005$ into $A \leftarrow A + MEM_5$, and set PC to $PC + 1 = 2$.

Fig. 3.6 Computing the sum $10 + 20$, as executed on a stored program computer

	CPU
state	= execute
PC	= 2
IR	= 300005
	= $A \leftarrow A + MEM_5$
A	= 30

MEM		
Address	Value	Meaning
0	220004	$A \leftarrow MEM_4$
1	300005	$A \leftarrow A + MEM_5$
2	210006	$MEM_6 \leftarrow A$
3	100000	$HALT$
4	10	NOP
5	20	NOP
6	0	NOP
7	0	NOP

(a) Step #7: Execute the instruction $A \leftarrow A + MEM_5$, i.e., set A to $A + MEM_5 = 30$.

	CPU
state	= fetch
PC	= 2
IR	= 210006
	=
A	= 30

MEM		
Address	Value	Meaning
0	220004	$A \leftarrow MEM_4$
1	300005	$A \leftarrow A + MEM_5$
2	210006	$MEM_6 \leftarrow A$
3	100000	$HALT$
4	10	NOP
5	20	NOP
6	0	NOP
7	0	NOP

(b) Step #8: Fetch the next instruction $IR = 210006$ from $PC = 2$.

	CPU
state	= decode
PC	= 3
IR	= 210006
	= $MEM_6 \leftarrow A$
A	= 30

MEM		
Address	Value	Meaning
0	220004	$A \leftarrow MEM_4$
1	300005	$A \leftarrow A + MEM_5$
2	210006	$MEM_6 \leftarrow A$
3	100000	$HALT$
4	10	NOP
5	20	NOP
6	0	NOP
7	0	NOP

(c) Step #9: Decode $IR = 210006$ into $MEM_6 \leftarrow A$, and set PC to $PC + 1 = 3$.

	CPU
state	= execute
PC	= 3
IR	= 210006
	= $MEM_6 \leftarrow A$
A	= 30

MEM		
Address	Value	Meaning
0	220004	$A \leftarrow MEM_4$
1	300005	$A \leftarrow A + MEM_5$
2	210006	$MEM_6 \leftarrow A$
3	100000	$HALT$
4	10	NOP
5	20	NOP
6	30	NOP
7	0	NOP

(d) Step #10: Execute the instruction $MEM_6 \leftarrow A$, i.e., set MEM_6 to $A = 30$.

	CPU
state	= fetch
PC	= 3
IR	= 100000
	=
A	= 30

MEM		
Address	Value	Meaning
0	220004	$A \leftarrow MEM_4$
1	300005	$A \leftarrow A + MEM_5$
2	210006	$MEM_6 \leftarrow A$
3	100000	$HALT$
4	10	NOP
5	20	NOP
6	30	NOP
7	0	NOP

(e) Step #11: Fetch the next instruction $IR = 100000$ from $PC = 3$.

	CPU
state	= decode
PC	= 4
IR	= 100000
	= $HALT$
A	= 30

MEM		
Address	Value	Meaning
0	220004	$A \leftarrow MEM_4$
1	300005	$A \leftarrow A + MEM_5$
2	210006	$MEM_6 \leftarrow A$
3	100000	$HALT$
4	10	NOP
5	20	NOP
6	30	NOP
7	0	NOP

(f) Step #12: Decode $IR = 100000$ into $HALT$, and set PC to $PC + 1 = 4$.

Fig. 3.7 Computing the sum $10 + 20$, as executed on a stored program computer

	CPU
state	= execute
PC	= 4
IR	= 100000
	= HALT
A	= 30

MEM		
Address	Value	Meaning
0	220004	$A \leftarrow MEM_4$
1	300005	$A \leftarrow A + MEM_5$
2	210006	$MEM_6 \leftarrow A$
3	100000	HALT
4	10	NOP
5	20	NOP
6	30	NOP
7	0	NOP

(a) Step #13: Execute the instruction $HALT$, i.e., stop execution.

Fig. 3.8 Computing the sum $10 + 20$, as executed on a stored program computer

stored in MEM_6.

Although reading and following executions of *existing* programs is a good start, writing your own programs is really the only way to get to grips with this topic.

See if you can write a program for the von Neumann computer that evaluates the expression

$$x \cdot (y + z)$$

where x, y and z are stored in memory at addresses of your choice; since the computer has no multiplication instruction, this demands some careful thought! Demonstrate that the program works by listing the steps (similar to above) for example x, y and z.

Implement (task #13)

The current instruction set contains three rough classes of instruction: some perform load and store from and to memory, some perform arithmetic operations, and some perform updates to PC. Depending on what we use the computer for, other instructions might be useful of course: assuming you have a free choice, write the encoding *and* meaning for some other instructions you deem useful.

Why choose *these* instructions in particular? For instance, what might you use them for? There is a limit to how many new instructions we can add: can you explain one reason why?

Research (task #14)

3.2   Harvard Versus von Neumann Computers

With such a simple example program, it might seem as if the two styles of computer are more or less the same, i.e., neither has a massive advantage over the other. For example, they both compute $10 + 20 = 30$ at the end of the day. But, and this is a big but, there are (at least) two subtle and key differences between them.

3.2.1 Beyond Straight-Line Programs

With the Harvard-style design, we were forced to write instructions onto the tape and have them executed in the same order. There was, for example, no mechanism to "skip over" a given instruction or "jump" execution to an instruction based on a result we computed. Clearly this limits the sorts of program we could write. The good news is that the von Neumann-style upgrade removes this restriction by allowing PC to be altered by the program rather than just by the computer. By simply setting the value of PC we can direct execution to *any* instruction; we no longer have to write programs which are **straight-line**.

As a simple example, imagine we alter our example program by replacing the $HALT$ instruction with one that alters the value of PC:

$$
\begin{aligned}
A &\leftarrow MEM_4 & &\mapsto 220004 \\
A &\leftarrow A + MEM_5 & &\mapsto 300005 \\
MEM_6 &\leftarrow A & &\mapsto 210006 \\
PC &\leftarrow 0 & &\mapsto 400000
\end{aligned}
$$

When we execute the last instruction, it sets the value of PC back to zero. Put more simply, it starts executing the program again right from the start. Writing down the steps of execution only, rather than drawing the state at each step, we now get:

Step #1: Load the tape into memory, set $PC = 0$ and start the computer.

Step #2: Fetch the next instruction $IR = 220004$ from $PC = 0$.

Step #3: Decode $IR = 220004$ into $A \leftarrow MEM_4$, and set PC to $PC + 1 = 1$.

Step #4: Execute the instruction $A \leftarrow MEM_4$, i.e., set A to $MEM_4 = 10$.

Step #5: Fetch the next instruction $IR = 300005$ from $PC = 1$.

Step #6: Decode $IR = 300005$ into $A \leftarrow A + MEM_5$, and set PC to $PC + 1 = 2$.

Step #7: Execute the instruction $A \leftarrow A + MEM_5$, i.e., set A to $A + MEM_5 = 30$.

Step #8: Fetch the next instruction $IR = 210006$ from $PC = 2$.

Step #9: Decode $IR = 210006$ into $MEM_6 \leftarrow A$, and set PC to $PC + 1 = 3$.

Step #10: Execute the instruction $MEM_6 \leftarrow A$, i.e., set MEM_6 to $A = 30$.

Step #11: Fetch the next instruction $IR = 400000$ from $PC = 3$.

Step #12: Decode $IR = 400000$ into $PC \leftarrow 0$, and set PC to $PC + 1 = 4$.

Step #13: Execute the instruction $PC \leftarrow 0$, i.e., set PC to 0.

Step #14: Fetch the next instruction $IR = 220004$ from $PC = 0$.

Step #15: Decode $IR = 220004$ into $A \leftarrow MEM_4$, and set PC to $PC + 1 = 1$.

Step #16: Execute the instruction $A \leftarrow MEM_4$, i.e., set A to $MEM_4 = 10$.

Step #17: ...

Clearly the program never finishes in the sense that we never execute a $HALT$ instruction. What we have constructed is an **infinite loop**; in this situation the computer will seem to "freeze" since it ends up executing the same instructions over and

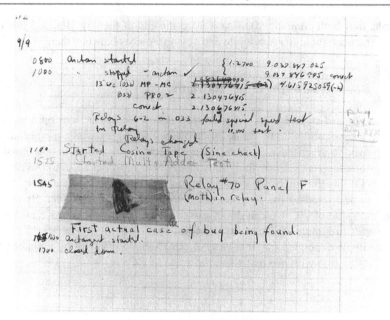

Fig. 3.9 A moth found by operations of the Harvard Mark 2; the "bug" was trapped within the computer and caused it to malfunction (public domain image, source: http://en.wikipedia.org/wiki/File:H96566k.jpg)

over again forever [13].

> Although the occurrence of an infinite loop is normally deemed a problem, can you think of an example where it might be *required*?
>
> **Research (task #15)**
>
> Even so, you might argue it would be useful to detect infinite loops so the computer can be manually halted. How might you approach doing so? For example, what changes to the computer might be necessary? Is your approach *always* guaranteed to work?

3.2.2 Toward Self-Modifying Programs

With the Harvard-style design, we were prevented from altering the tape content after we started execution. Put another way, programming happens strictly *before* program execution. However, with the von Neumann-style design instructions and data are the same thing so we can alter instructions *during* execution just as easily as data.

What does this mean in practise? Imagine we take the example program but introduce a **bug** [22]. A bug is a programming error: it is a mistake in a program that causes it to malfunction, behaving in a different way than we might have intended. The term bug (and **debug** [8], that relates to fixing the mistake) have well-discussed histories; a nice story relates them to a *real* bug (a moth) that famously short-circuited the Harvard Mark 2 computer! The bug here is that instead of storing the addition result in MEM_6, we mistakenly store it in MEM_3:

$$A \leftarrow MEM_4 \qquad \mapsto 220004$$
$$A \leftarrow A + MEM_5 \mapsto 300005$$
$$MEM_3 \leftarrow A \qquad \mapsto 210003$$
$$HALT \qquad\qquad \mapsto 100000$$

Again writing down the steps of execution only, we obtain:

Step #1:   Load the tape into memory, set $PC = 0$ and start the computer.

Step #2:   Fetch the next instruction $IR = 220004$ from $PC = 0$.

Step #3:   Decode $IR = 220004$ into $A \leftarrow MEM_4$, and set PC to $PC + 1 = 1$.

Step #4:   Execute the instruction $A \leftarrow MEM_4$, i.e., set A to $MEM_4 = 10$.

Step #5:   Fetch the next instruction $IR = 300005$ from $PC = 1$.

Step #6:   Decode $IR = 300005$ into $A \leftarrow A + MEM_5$, and set PC to $PC+1 = 2$.

Step #7:   Execute the instruction $A \leftarrow A + MEM_5$, i.e., set A to $A + MEM_5 = 30$.

Step #8:   Fetch the next instruction $IR = 210003$ from $PC = 2$.

Step #9:   Decode $IR = 210003$ into $MEM_3 \leftarrow A$, and set PC to $PC + 1 = 3$.

Step #10:   Execute the instruction $MEM_3 \leftarrow A$, i.e., set MEM_3 to $A = 30$.

Step #11:   Fetch the next instruction $IR = 000030$ from $PC = 3$.

Step #12:   Decode $IR = 000030$ into NOP, and set PC to $PC + 1 = 4$.

Step #13:   Execute the instruction NOP, i.e., do nothing.

Step #14:   Fetch the next instruction $IR = 000010$ from $PC = 4$.

Step #15:   Decode $IR = 000010$ into NOP, and set PC to $PC + 1 = 5$.

Step #16:   Execute the instruction NOP, i.e., do nothing.

Step #17:   . . .

Step #11 is now different: something weird has happened because initially we had a $HALT$ instruction in MEM_3, but when we come to fetch it, it has changed! The reason is obvious if we look a few steps back. In step #10 we execute the instruction which *should* store the result of our addition. But remember the bug: instead of storing the result in MEM_6, we store the result, i.e., 30, in MEM_3. Of course, MEM_3 is part of the program, so as things progress we end up trying to *execute* the number 30 we previously stored. This behaviour is allowed because data and instructions are the same thing now. So we fetch the data value 30 and try to interpret it as an instruction according to our encoding.

To cut a long story short, the program has modified itself [21] by altering instructions relating to the same program as is being executed! In this case, the self-modification can only be a bad thing since without a $HALT$ instruction the computer will never stop executing the program. More than likely it will "crash" somehow [6]. More generally however, the idea is that in other cases we can put self-modification to constructive use, i.e., have a program change instructions so that something useful happens as a result.

3.3   A Self-Modifying Virus

Finally we can talk about our virus which, you will remember, aims to change itself to avoid detection by the virus scanner. Imagine our example computer includes a single instruction that, when executed, causes something bad to happen; maybe the computer self-destructs or something. For the sake of argument, we will say that whenever the computer executes the extra instruction 111111 this represents the payload of our virus. In other words, in our encoding 111111 means **payload**, and when **payload** is executed the virus has won.

It is not too hard to imagine that when we infect a file called F, the virus payload will then appear somewhere within it. If this is the case, the virus scanner can easily detect the virus by using the single element signature $S = \langle 111111 \rangle$ to scan F as we discussed at the beginning of the chapter:

$$
\begin{aligned}
F = \langle \cdots \quad \cdots \qquad \cdots \qquad \cdots \quad 111111 \cdots \rangle, \\
S = \langle \quad 111111 \qquad\qquad\qquad\qquad \rangle \mapsto \textbf{no match} \\
\langle \qquad\quad 111111 \qquad\qquad\quad \rangle \mapsto \textbf{no match} \\
\langle \qquad\qquad\quad 111111 \qquad\quad \rangle \mapsto \textbf{no match} \\
\langle \qquad\qquad\qquad\quad 111111 \quad \rangle \mapsto \quad \textbf{match}
\end{aligned}
$$

With this in mind, the virus writer has to somehow *hide* the virus payload so the virus scanner cannot detect it. To do this, we will use the properties of the XOR (short for "exclusive-or") function [9] we met in Chap. 1.

3.3.1   Using XOR to Mask Numbers

XOR can be used to mask (or hide) the value of a number. Imagine we have a bit x and we do not want anyone to know it; select a bit k and compute $y = x \oplus k$. If we give y to someone, can they tell us what x is? Well, if $y = 0$ then that could have been produced by us having $x = 0$ and selecting $k = 0$ *or* having $x = 1$ and selecting $k = 1$ because

$$
y = 0 = x \oplus k = \begin{cases} 0 \oplus 0 & \text{if } x = 0 \text{ and } k = 0 \\ 1 \oplus 1 & \text{if } x = 1 \text{ and } k = 1 \end{cases}
$$

Similarly, if $y = 1$ then that could have been produced by us having $x = 0$ and selecting $k = 1$ or having $x = 1$ and selecting $k = 0$ because

$$
y = 1 = x \oplus k = \begin{cases} 0 \oplus 1 & \text{if } x = 0 \text{ and } k = 1 \\ 1 \oplus 0 & \text{if } x = 1 \text{ and } k = 0 \end{cases}
$$

The point is, if we give someone y they can not tell us x for sure unless they also know k. Since we know k, we can easily tell what x is since $y \oplus k = x \oplus k \oplus k = x$. You can think of this as a limited form of encryption, except we call k the mask (rather than the key) and say x has been masked by k to produce y.

The problem is that XOR is a Boolean function: the inputs and output have to be either 0 or 1. To apply it to the decimal numbers in MEM, we first apply what we learnt in Chap. 1 to convert between decimal and binary. For example

$$310000_{(10)} = 01001011101011110000_{(2)}$$
$$329975_{(10)} = 01010000100011110111_{(2)}$$

Now we can compute

$$01001011101011110000_{(2)} \oplus 01010000100011110111_{(2)}$$
$$= 00011011001000000111_{(2)}$$
$$= 111111_{(10)}$$

simply by applying XOR to the corresponding bits. Likewise, since

$$111111_{(10)} = 00011011001000000111_{(2)}$$
$$329975_{(10)} = 01010000100011110111_{(2)}$$

we can compute

$$00011011001000000111_{(2)} \oplus 01010000100011110111_{(2)}$$
$$= 01001011101011110000_{(2)}$$
$$= 310000_{(10)}$$

More simply, in terms of our example above we start with $x = 310000$ and select $k = 329975$. Then, if we compute $x \oplus k = 310000 \oplus 329975$ we get $y = 111111$. We know k, so if we compute $y \oplus k = 111111 \oplus 329975$ then we get back $x = 310000$.

3.3.2   A Virus that Masks the Payload

Now for the clever part: notice that

- 310000 corresponds to the encoded instruction 310000 which means $A \leftarrow A - MEM_0$,
- 329975 corresponds to the encoded instruction 329975 which means $A \leftarrow A \oplus MEM_{9975}$, and
- 111111 corresponds to the encoded instruction 111111 which means **payload**.

So basically

$$111111 = 310000 \oplus 329975$$

means we can build the **payload** instruction by simply applying $\oplus$ to two innocent looking instructions. Our strategy for hiding the virus payload should now be obvious: we mask the payload instruction within F which we load into memory and start executing. While the program is executing, we unmask the payload instruction using self-modification, and then execute it. There is a fancy name for viruses like this: they are called polymorphic [18]. The first time a virus was seen using the technique was around 1990 when a virus called **1260** (referring to the length) was discovered.

Confused? Understanding why it works might be a puzzle, but either way the end result is the following program and the corresponding encoding:

$$
\begin{array}{ll}
A \leftarrow MEM_3 & \mapsto 220003 \\
A \leftarrow A \oplus MEM_5 & \mapsto 320005 \\
MEM_3 \leftarrow A & \mapsto 210003 \\
A \leftarrow A - MEM_0 & \mapsto 310000 \\
HALT & \mapsto 100000 \\
A \leftarrow A \oplus MEM_{9975} & \mapsto 329975
\end{array}
$$

Just by eye-balling the encoded program we can see that the virus payload does not appear, so if we use the virus scanner on it we fail to detect a virus:

$$
\begin{array}{lll}
F = \langle \cdots 220003 \; 320005 \; 210003 \; 310000 \; 100000 \; 329975 \cdots \rangle, \\
S = \langle \quad 111111 & \rangle \mapsto \textbf{no match} \\
\quad\langle \qquad\quad 111111 & \rangle \mapsto \textbf{no match} \\
\quad\langle \qquad\qquad\quad 111111 & \rangle \mapsto \textbf{no match} \\
\quad\langle \qquad\qquad\qquad\quad 111111 & \rangle \mapsto \textbf{no match} \\
\quad\langle \qquad\qquad\qquad\qquad\quad 111111 & \rangle \mapsto \textbf{no match} \\
\quad\langle \qquad\qquad\qquad\qquad\qquad\quad 111111 & \rangle \mapsto \textbf{no match}
\end{array}
$$

But so what? If the program does not contain the virus payload, nothing bad can happen right?! Unfortunately not. Have a look at what happens when we execute the program:

Step #1: Load the tape into memory, set $PC = 0$ and start the computer.

Step #2: Fetch the next instruction $IR = 220003$ from $PC = 0$.

Step #3: Decode $IR = 220003$ into $A \leftarrow MEM_3$, and set PC to $PC + 1 = 1$.

Step #4: Execute the instruction $A \leftarrow MEM_3$, i.e., set A to $MEM_3 = 310000$.

Step #5: Fetch the next instruction $IR = 320005$ from $PC = 1$.

Step #6: Decode $IR = 320005$ into $A \leftarrow A \oplus MEM_5$, and set PC to $PC + 1 = 2$.

Step #7: Execute the instruction $A \leftarrow A \oplus MEM_5$, i.e., set A to $A \oplus MEM_5 = 111111$.

Step #8: Fetch the next instruction $IR = 210003$ from $PC = 2$.

Step #9: Decode $IR = 210003$ into $MEM_3 \leftarrow A$, and set PC to $PC + 1 = 3$.

Step #10: Execute the instruction $MEM_3 \leftarrow A$, i.e., set MEM_3 to $A = 111111$.

Step #11: Fetch the next instruction $IR = 111111$ from $PC = 3$.

Step #12: Decode $IR = 111111$ into **payload**, and set PC to $PC + 1 = 4$.

Step #13: Execute the instruction **payload**, i.e., do something bad.

Step #14: ...

Step #13 executes **payload** somehow, so the virus payload has been triggered even though it did not appear in F. Look at what happens step-by-step:

- Step #4 loads the masked virus payload, which looks like a $A \leftarrow A - MEM_0$ instruction, from MEM_3 and into A.
- Step #7 unmasks it using an XOR instruction that applies the mask value k stored in MEM_5 just like we saw above.

- At this point we have $A = 111111$ which is then stored back into MEM_3 by step #10.
- Step #13 executes the unmasked instruction from MEM_3, at which point the payload is triggered and the virus wins.

3.3.3   Preventing the Virus Without a Virus Scanner

The obvious question is, if the virus scanner we have does not work in this case then what *can* we do to stop the virus? In reality, this is quite an open question. On real computers we still do not have a definitive, general solution against viruses and malware. However, in the particular case of *our* virus we can think of a few possibilities:

- We could monitor the program during execution and prevent the virus payload being executed. So, for example, execution of *every* instruction would have to include an extra step saying "if IR is the virus payload then stop execution". But of course in reality there is not just one instruction that does something bad: more usually a subtle combination of many instructions will represent the payload, so this approach would not work. It also has the drawback of reducing the speed at which we can execute *all* programs, which might be quite unpopular.
- We could try to be more clever at coming up with the signature that identifies this sort of virus. We cannot use the masked payload 310000 because that is a valid instruction which basically *any* program might include! We cannot use the mask 329975 because this could be anything: the virus is free to choose any mask it wants (although obviously this alters the masked payload). One option could be to try and identify the pattern of self-modifying code. For example, if the virus scanner knew the meaning of instructions it could perhaps analyse the program and work out what is really going on. Clearly this means the virus scanner needs to be much more sophisticated and depends on the fact that writing similar code in a different way is not possible.
- We could alter the computer so that writing self-modifying programs is impossible. Modern computers include a scheme which roughly works by adding an extra "tag" to each element of MEM. If the tag is 0, this indicates that the element can be written to but *not* executed as an instruction; if the flag is 1, this means the element can be executed as an instruction but *not* written to. In terms of our example virus, this would mean the memory looks like:

MEM			
Address	Tag	Value	Meaning
0	1	220003	$A \leftarrow MEM_3$
1	1	320005	$A \leftarrow A \oplus MEM_5$
2	1	210003	$MEM_3 \leftarrow A$
3	1	310000	$A \leftarrow A - MEM_0$
4	1	100000	$HALT$
5	0	329975	$A \leftarrow A \oplus MEM_{9975}$

So basically, we could not execute the virus because MEM_3 could not be written to once the program was loaded. Put another way, the instruction $MEM_3 \leftarrow A$ would cause the computer to halt due to a violation of the rules. The drawback is that there *are* reasonable uses for self-modifying programs; by implementing this solution we prevent those from being executed as well. Plus, we have to make our memory, and the mechanism that accesses it, more complicated and therefore more costly.

The current instruction set includes instructions to load from and store into *fixed* addresses. For instance $MEM_n \leftarrow A$ stores A at the address n which is fixed when we write the program. For computers such as ENIAC, self-modifying programs were often used in a positive way to extend this ability to *variable* addresses; put simply, this allows access to MEM_i for some i chosen during execution.

Imagine a sequence of numbers $X = \langle X_0, X_1, \ldots, X_{m-1} \rangle$ is stored at a known address in memory, and we want to compute the sum

$$\sum_{i=0}^{i<m} X_i.$$

Implement (task #16)

If the sequence has 10 elements and starts at address 100, say, one way to do this would be

$$A \leftarrow \quad\;\; MEM_{100+0}$$
$$A \leftarrow A + MEM_{100+1}$$
$$\vdots$$
$$A \leftarrow A + MEM_{100+9}$$

where clearly $100 + 1 = 101$ is fixed, so we can write an appropriate instruction.

But what if m is *really* large, or only known once the program starts to execute? In these cases, we might prefer to write a loop: based on an m also stored in memory somewhere (at address 99 say), use the concept of self-modifying programs to compute the same result by looping through each i (like the loop in Chap. 2) and hence accumulating each X_i.

References

1.   Wikipedia Alan Turing. http://en.wikipedia.org/wiki/Alan_Turing
2.   Wikipedia: Anti-virus software. http://en.wikipedia.org/wiki/Antivirus_software

3. Wikipedia: ARPANET. http://en.wikipedia.org/wiki/ARPANET
4. Wikipedia: Central Processing Unit (CPU). http://en.wikipedia.org/wiki/Central_processing_unit
5. Wikipedia: Computer virus. http://en.wikipedia.org/wiki/Computer_virus
6. Wikipedia: Crash. http://en.wikipedia.org/wiki/Crash_(computing)
7. Wikipedia: Creeper. http://en.wikipedia.org/wiki/Creeper_(program)
8. Wikipedia: Debugging. http://en.wikipedia.org/wiki/Debugging
9. Wikipedia: Exclusive OR. http://en.wikipedia.org/wiki/XOR
10. Wikipedia: Halting problem. http://en.wikipedia.org/wiki/Halting_problem
11. Wikipedia: Harvard architecture. http://en.wikipedia.org/wiki/Harvard_architecture
12. Wikipedia: Harvard Mark I. http://en.wikipedia.org/wiki/Harvard_Mark_I
13. Wikipedia: Infinite loop. http://en.wikipedia.org/wiki/Infinite_loop
14. Wikipedia: Internet. http://en.wikipedia.org/wiki/Internet
15. Wikipedia: Keystroke logging. http://en.wikipedia.org/wiki/Keystroke_logging
16. Wikipedia: Malware. http://en.wikipedia.org/wiki/Malware
17. Wikipedia: Morris worm. http://en.wikipedia.org/wiki/Morris_worm
18. Wikipedia: Polymorphic code. http://en.wikipedia.org/wiki/Polymorphic_code
19. Wikipedia: Programmed Data Processor (PDP). http://en.wikipedia.org/wiki/Programmed_Data_Processor
20. Wikipedia: Punched tape. http://en.wikipedia.org/wiki/Punched_tape
21. Wikipedia: Self-modifying code. http://en.wikipedia.org/wiki/Self-modifying_code
22. Wikipedia: Software bug. http://en.wikipedia.org/wiki/Software_bug
23. Wikipedia: Stuxnet. http://en.wikipedia.org/wiki/Stuxnet
24. Wikipedia: Timeline of computer viruses and worms. http://en.wikipedia.org/wiki/Timeline_of_computer_viruses_and_worms
25. Wikipedia: Turing machine. http://en.wikipedia.org/wiki/Turing_machine
26. Wikipedia: von Neumann architecture. http://en.wikipedia.org/wiki/Von_Neumann_architecture

How Long Is a Piece of String?

4

Recall that in Chap. 3 we described how computers only understand a fixed set of instructions that can operate only on fixed types of operand; at the lowest level, instructions typically only operate on operands which are numbers. So, for example, most computers understand how to add together numbers: in this case we would say that a number is a **native** type of data. However, it is not common for a computer to understand types of data more complicated than this. For example a computer does not have a native understanding of emails; there is no instruction that tells it to "search for the text X in the email Y". In order to write a program that deals with non-native types of data like this, we need to decide on a representation for it using a **data structure**.

The design of data structures and the algorithms that perform operations on them is a fundamental subject that underpins almost every aspect of Computer Science. Essentially, a data structure allows us to look at numbers and interpret them as something else. Sometimes the data structure is simply a description of how numbers should be arranged so we can interpret them correctly; sometimes we add extra information or **meta-data** which allows us to inspect and alter the data structure. Interested in computer graphics? You need data structures (e.g., representations of images, or points in 3D space) and algorithms to operate on them (e.g., change the colour of an image, or rotate a 3D scene). Interested in computer networks? You need data structures (e.g., representations of connectivity between computers on the network) and algorithms to operate on them (e.g., find a path from computer X to computer Y). Interested in computer security? You need data structures (e.g., representations of very large numbers) and algorithms to operate on them (e.g., add together X and Y modulo Z). In all cases, efficiency is key: if we use a more efficient data structure, we might reduce the time taken to perform a given operation, or the amount of memory required to store the data.

Our focus here is on **strings**. The term string crops up in a lot of places, but generically means a sequence of things. For example, we string together a sequence of words to make a sentence, protein is made from a string of many amino acids and so on. In Computer Science, a string is a sequence of **characters** and one of the most fundamental data structures after the native types of data which a computer

D. Page, N. Smart, *What Is Computer Science?*,
Undergraduate Topics in Computer Science, DOI 10.1007/978-3-319-04042-4_4,
© Springer International Publishing Switzerland 2014

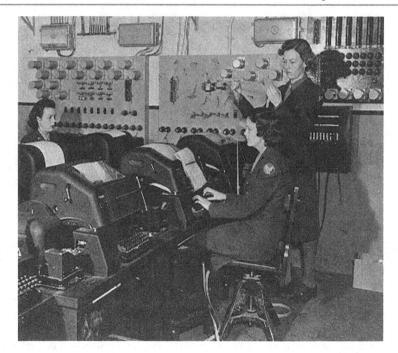

Fig. 4.1 A teletype machine being used by UK-based Royal Air Force (RAF) operators during WW2 (public domain image, source: http://en.wikipedia.org/wiki/File:WACsOperateTeletype.jpg)

can operate on. If you think about it, an email is just a string of characters, the files created by a word processor could be thought of as similar strings, the messages a computer displays so it can communicate with the user are also strings, and so on. The aim is to show that even with something that seems so simple, there are *many* options for useful data structures and that our choice has a *major* impact on the algorithms used to manipulate them.

4.1   String Data Structures

As we saw in Chap. 3, the memory of a computer is where it stores data in the long term. The computer loads the data into an accumulator to operate on it, and stores the result back in memory afterwards. We modelled memory using a sequence called MEM and stored decimal numbers in each element. Since MEM is large, it is convenient to avoid writing out the whole sequence. To allow this, we will write the addresses of elements above the elements themselves. For example, imagine we have

$$i \ = \ \dots, \quad 3, \quad 4, \quad 5, \quad 6, \quad 7, \dots$$
$$MEM = \langle \dots, 104, 101, 108, 108, 111, \dots \rangle$$

Table 4.1 A table describing the printable ASCII character set

y ORD(x)	CHR(y) x	y ORD(x)	CHR(y) x	y ORD(x)	CHR(y) x	y ORD(x)	CHR(y) x
0	NUL	1	SOH	2	STX	3	ETX
4	EOT	5	ENQ	6	ACK	7	BEL
8	BS	9	HT	10	LF	11	VT
12	FF	13	CR	14	SO	15	SI
16	DLE	17	DC1	18	DC2	19	DC3
20	DC4	21	NAK	22	SYN	23	ETB
24	CAN	25	EM	26	SUB	27	ESC
28	FS	29	GS	30	RS	31	US
32	SPC	33	!	34	"	35	#
36	$	37	%	38	&	39	'
40	(	41	)	42	*	43	+
44	,	45	-	46	.	47	/
48	0	49	1	50	2	51	3
52	4	53	5	54	6	55	7
56	8	57	9	58	:	59	;
60	<	61	=	62	>	63	?
64	@	65	A	66	B	67	C
68	D	69	E	70	F	71	G
72	H	73	I	74	J	75	K
76	L	77	M	78	N	79	O
80	P	81	Q	82	R	83	S
84	T	85	U	86	V	87	W
88	X	89	Y	90	Z	91	[
92	\	93	]	94	^	95	_
96	`	97	a	98	b	99	c
100	d	101	e	102	f	103	g
104	h	105	i	106	j	107	k
108	l	109	m	110	n	111	o
112	p	113	q	114	r	115	s
116	t	117	u	118	v	119	w
120	x	121	y	122	z	123	{
124	|	125	}	126	~	127	DEL

If MEM has n elements in total, we have missed out the elements at addresses $0 \ldots 2$ and those at addresses $8 \ldots n - 1$. We are only interested in addresses #3, #4, #5, #6 and #7 which have the values 104, 101, 108, 108 and 111. Our goal is to represent strings within MEM but to do this, we need to solve two problems: first how to represent characters, and second how to represent strings.

4.1.1   Problem #1: Representing Characters

The first problem is that MEM can only store numbers, and the computer it exists within can only really process numbers. To allow it to deal with characters, we need some way to represent them numerically. Basically we just need to translate from one to the other. More specifically, we need two functions: $\text{ORD}(x)$ which takes a character x and gives us back the corresponding numerical representation, and $\text{CHR}(y)$ which takes a numerical representation y and gives back the corresponding character. But how should the functions work? Fortunately, people have thought about this problem for us and provided standards we can use. One of the oldest is the **American Standard Code for Information Interchange (ASCII)** [1], pronounced "ass key".

ASCII has a rich history, but was developed to permit communication between early teleprinter devices. These were like a combination of a typewriter and a telephone, and were able to communicate text to each other before innovations such as the fax machine. Later, but long before monitors and graphics cards existed, similar devices allowed users to send input to early computers and receive output from them. Table 4.1 shows the 128-entry ASCII table which tells us how characters are represented as numbers. Of the entries, 95 are printable characters we can instantly recognise (including SPC which is short for "space"). There are also 33 others which represent non-printable control characters: originally, these would have been used to control the teleprinter rather than to have it print something. For example, the CR and LF characters (short for "carriage return" and "line feed") would combine to move the print head onto the next line; we still use these characters to mark the end of lines in text files. Other control characters also play a role in modern computers. For example, the BEL (short for "bell") characters play a "ding" sound when printed to most UNIX terminals, we have keyboards with keys that relate to DEL and ESC (short for "delete" and "escape") and so on.

Implement (task #17)

You can test this out by issuing the command

```
echo -e '\x07'
```

in a BASH terminal. It asks `echo` to display the ASCII character $07_{(16)} = 7_{(10)} = BEL$ on the terminal, which *should* mean a sound is produced (or perhaps a visual indicator if the sound is disabled). The $-e$ option is quite important, because it means that $\x07$ is interpreted as an ASCII code rather than a normal string. Try this with some other examples. For instance, what would you expect

```
echo -e 'hello\x08world'
```

to produce?

Since there are 128 entries in the table, ASCII characters can be and are represented by bytes as 8-bit numbers. However, notice that $2^7 = 128$ and $2^8 = 256$ so in fact we *could* represent 256 characters: essentially one of the bits is not used by the ASCII encoding. Specific computer systems sometimes use the unused bit to permit use of an "extended" ASCII table with 256 entries; the extra characters in this table can be used for some special purpose. For example, foreign language characters are often defined in this range (e.g., é or ø). However, the original use of the unused bit was as an error detection mechanism: more specifically, it represents the parity bit from the even parity code in Chap. 1.

Another use for extended ASCII characters is **ASCII art** [2], popular in an era when plain text was the *only* viable display medium. Examples archived at

http://www.textfiles.com/

were often used by **Bulletin Board Systems (BBSs)** [4], which used the telephone system and MODEMs to form an early form of computer network: text was used almost exclusively to compensate for the relatively slow speed of data transfer. An excellent documentary at

http://www.bbsdocumentary.com/

chronicles the technology and personalities involved.
There are now various ASCII art editors online, such as

http://www.asciigraffiti.com/

Forget GIMP, which we used in Chap. 1, or other modern image manipulation software: take a trip into the past, and see how hard it is to draw images using text!

Given the table, we can see, for example, that CHR(104) = 'h', i.e., if we see the number 104 then this represents the character 'h'. Conversely we have that ORD('h') = 104. Although in a sense any consistent translation between characters and numbers like this would do, ASCII has some useful properties. Look specifically at the alphabetic characters:

- Imagine we want to test if one character x is alphabetically before some other y. The way the ASCII translation is specified, we can simply compare their numeric representation. If we find ORD(x) < ORD(y) then the character x is before the character y in the alphabet. For example 'a' is before 'c' because

$$\text{ORD('a')} = 97 < 99 = \text{ORD('c')}.$$

- Imagine we want to convert a character x from lower-case into upper-case. The lower-case characters are represented numerically as the contiguous range $97 \ldots 122$; the upper-case characters as the contiguous range $65 \ldots 90$. So we can covert from lower-case into upper-case simply by subtracting 32. For example

$$\text{CHR}\big(\text{ORD}(\text{`a'}) - 32\big) = \text{`A'}.$$

Armed with the ASCII table and the new translation method, we can read new meaning into the contents of MEM. As well as writing the addresses of elements above the elements, we can write the ASCII translation of each element (i.e., the character that each numeric element represents) below this, on an extra line. For example:

$$
\begin{array}{rl}
i & = \ldots, \quad 3, \quad 4, \quad 5, \quad 6, \quad 7, \ldots \\
MEM & = \langle \ldots, 104, 101, 108, 108, 111, \ldots \rangle \\
\text{CHR}(MEM_i) = & \ldots, \text{ `h', `e', `l', `l', `o',} \ldots
\end{array}
$$

We can now see that addresses $3 \ldots 7$ hold the string "hello" if we interpret the memory content as ASCII characters. Just to show that this really *is* how things work, consider this short experiment using BASH:

```
bash$ cat > A.txt
hello
bash$ cat A.txt
hello
bash$ cat A.txt | od -Ad -tu1 | cut -c 9-
104 101 108 108 111  10

bash$
```

First we create a file called A.txt by typing the characters 'h', 'e', 'l', 'l' and 'o' followed by return (which you cannot see). The second use of cat prints the file to the terminal as ASCII characters as one might expect. However, using the od command we can inspect the numerical representation. In particular using the option -t with format u1 instructs od to format the content as a sequence of unsigned decimal integers in the range $0 \ldots 255$. As a result we see a total of six numbers, namely 104, 101, 108, 108 and 111 representing characters 'h', 'e', 'l', 'l' and 'o' as in MEM, and the number 10 which represents the character LF (which occurs as a result of our pressing return after "hello" when creating A.txt).

4.1.2   Problem #2: Representing Strings

The second problem is that so far we do not really have a way to know how long a string is, i.e., how many characters it contains. What we have been doing is looking at the memory content

$$
\begin{array}{rl}
i & = \ldots, \quad 3, \quad 4, \quad 5, \quad 6, \quad 7, \ldots \\
MEM & = \langle \ldots, 104, 101, 108, 108, 111, \ldots \rangle \\
\text{CHR}(MEM_i) = & \ldots, \text{ `h', `e', `l', `l', `o',} \ldots
\end{array}
$$

then seeing the characters 'h', 'e', 'l', 'l' and 'o' and assuming that they are the string "hello". But how do we know the length of the string starting at address #3? It could be possible that addresses higher than #7 hold more characters so that we actually have a longer string than we thought. For example, maybe $MEM_8 = 46$ which means there is a full stop character there:

$$
\begin{aligned}
i \quad &= \quad \ldots, \quad 3, \quad 4, \quad 5, \quad 6, \quad 7, \quad 8, \ldots \\
MEM \quad &= \langle \ldots, 104, 101, 108, 108, 111, 46, \ldots \rangle \\
\text{CHR}(MEM_i) &= \quad \ldots, \text{'h'}, \text{'e'}, \text{'l'}, \text{'l'}, \text{'o'}, \text{'.'}, \ldots
\end{aligned}
$$

How do we know if the full stop is actually *part* of the string starting at address #3, or if it is just some unrelated value which is there by chance? That is, how do we know we really mean the five character string "hello" rather than the six character string "hello."?

Given some address x which tells us where in memory a string starts, our goal is to add structure to the data so we know the length (and therefore what the intended content is). One way is to form a data structure by embedding some extra information in MEM to tell us how long the string is; there are at least two schemes we could consider:

1. We could embed the string length, which is a number, as the first element:

$$
\begin{aligned}
i \quad &= \quad \ldots, \quad 3, \quad 4, \quad 5, \quad 6, \quad 7, \quad 8, \ldots \\
MEM \quad &= \langle \ldots, \quad 5, 104, 101, 108, 108, 111, \ldots \rangle \\
\text{CHR}(MEM_i) &= \quad \ldots, ENQ, \text{'h'}, \text{'e'}, \text{'l'}, \text{'l'}, \text{'o'}, \ldots
\end{aligned}
$$

We still have a string starting at address #3 but instead of interpreting the first element as a character, we interpret it as the length of the string. Since $MEM_3 = 5$ we know this string has five characters in it, and that they will be in addresses $4 \ldots 8$.

2. We could embed a character, which will mark the end of the string, as the last element:

$$
\begin{aligned}
i \quad &= \quad \ldots, \quad 3, \quad 4, \quad 5, \quad 6, \quad 7, \quad 8, \ldots \\
MEM \quad &= \langle \ldots, 104, 101, 108, 108, 111, \quad 0, \ldots \rangle \\
\text{CHR}(MEM_i) &= \quad \ldots, \text{'h'}, \text{'e'}, \text{'l'}, \text{'l'}, \text{'o'}, NUL, \ldots
\end{aligned}
$$

Again we have a string starting at address #3, but now we can be sure where it ends because $MEM_8 = 0$. This is not a character as such, but the end of string marker or **terminator** which enables us to determine that the length is $8 - 3 = 5$ characters.

The reason these two schemes are interesting is because they are adopted by the Pascal [6] and C [5] programming languages respectively; because they do not really have good names[1] we will refer to them as the P-string and C-string schemes. No, there is no G-string or equivalent before you ask.

Neither the P-string or C-string scheme is right or wrong, but *do* give particular advantages and disadvantages in each case:

---

[1]The second option is sometimes termed ASCIIZ which sort of reads as "zero-terminated ASCII".

P-string:

- The string is represented using one more element than the content suggests; if there are n characters, we need $n + 1$ elements because one is used to store the length.
- Since the length needs to fit into one element of MEM, there is an upper limit on the lengths of string we can represent. We can remove this restriction by using more elements, but things become more tricky and we use more space.
- We have direct access to the length of the string, since we simply have to load it from the first element.

C-string:

- The string is represented using one more element than the content suggests; if there are n characters, we need $n + 1$ elements because one is used to store the NUL terminator.
- The actual string content cannot contain a NUL character, otherwise we would interpret this as the terminator, i.e., the end of the string. Although NUL is not printable, the fact we cannot use it can be a disadvantage in some circumstances.
- There is no real restriction on the string length, but we do not have direct access to that length. To find the length of a string, we need to search for the NUL terminator.

Research (task #19) These are just two data structures that could be used to represent strings. Still more exist: can you think of at least one more possibility? Explain how this third data structure works using an example, and contrast it with the C-string and P-string approaches by constructing a list of advantages and disadvantages.

4.2   String Algorithms

The idea of introducing these two data structures is to demonstrate some more algorithms; unlike the algorithms in Chap. 2 that computed an arithmetic result, these ones operate on and manipulate instances of the string data structures. The real goal is to point out something subtle about the algorithms and data structures involved, but it will take a while to get there.

Keep in mind that we can reuse the ideas we developed in Chap. 2 to compare algorithms against each other. In this case, a good definition of the problem size n is the length of the strings are dealing with.

4.2.1   `strlen`: Finding the Length of a String

About the most simple task one might think of in the context of strings is computing their length. Given a string starting at address x, the idea is to return the number of characters in that string. The C programming language includes a standard function called `strlen` which represents an implementation of this idea.

1 **algorithm** P-STRING-LENGTH(x) **begin**
2 | **return** MEM_x
3 **end**

(a) P-string version

1 **algorithm** C-STRING-LENGTH(x) **begin**
2 | $i \leftarrow 0$
3 | **while** $MEM_{x+i} \neq 0$ **do**
4 | | $i \leftarrow i + 1$
5 | **end**
6 | **return** i
7 **end**

(b) C-string version

Fig. 4.2 Algorithms to compute the length of a string at address x, represented using a P-string (left-hand side) or C-string (right-hand side) data structure

P-String Version

The P-string version is shown in Fig. 4.2a. Imagine the memory content is initially

$$
\begin{aligned}
i &= \ldots, \quad 3, \quad 4, \quad 5, \quad 6, \quad 7, \quad 8, \ldots \\
MEM &= \langle \ldots, \quad 5, 104, 101, 108, 108, 111, \ldots \rangle \\
\text{CHR}(MEM_i) &= \ldots, ENQ, \text{'h'}, \text{'e'}, \text{'l'}, \text{'l'}, \text{'o'}, \ldots
\end{aligned}
$$

and we invoke the algorithm using P-STRING-LENGTH(3). The only input is the string address, so in this case we want to find the length of a string at address 3; the corresponding steps performed by the algorithm are as follows:

Step #1   Return $MEM_3 = 5$.

This could not be simpler! Remember the string length is embedded as the first element, so the algorithm computes the required length in one step by simply loading it. Because of this, the algorithm *always* takes just one step; describing it using big-O notation we say it is $O(1)$ because no matter what the input size is, it takes a constant number of steps to give us a result.

C-String Version

The C-string version is shown in Fig. 4.2b. Imagine the memory content is initially

$$
\begin{aligned}
i &= \ldots, \quad 3, \quad 4, \quad 5, \quad 6, \quad 7, \quad \quad 8, \ldots \\
MEM &= \langle \ldots, 104, 101, 108, 108, 111, \quad 0, \ldots \rangle \\
\text{CHR}(MEM_i) &= \ldots, \text{'h'}, \text{'e'}, \text{'l'}, \text{'l'}, \text{'o'}, NUL, \ldots
\end{aligned}
$$

which is just the C-string version of the P-string one we used above. If we invoke the algorithm with C-STRING-LENGTH(3) in a similar way, the corresponding steps performed by the algorithm are now:

Step #1   Assign $i \leftarrow 0$.
Step #2   Since $MEM_{3+0} \neq 0$, assign $i \leftarrow i + 1$, i.e., $i \leftarrow 1$.
Step #3   Since $MEM_{3+1} \neq 0$, assign $i \leftarrow i + 1$, i.e., $i \leftarrow 2$.
Step #4   Since $MEM_{3+2} \neq 0$, assign $i \leftarrow i + 1$, i.e., $i \leftarrow 3$.
Step #5   Since $MEM_{3+3} \neq 0$, assign $i \leftarrow i + 1$, i.e., $i \leftarrow 4$.
Step #6   Since $MEM_{3+4} \neq 0$, assign $i \leftarrow i + 1$, i.e., $i \leftarrow 5$.
Step #7   Return $i = 5$.

This time things are a bit more complicated. So what is going on? We have used a slightly different loop construct than in Chap. 2 for this algorithm. When we write **while** X **do** Y, the idea is that we repeatedly process the block Y until X evaluates to **false**. So we perform a test: if X evaluates to **true** then we process the block Y, and then start again, otherwise we do not bother and exit the loop. This sort of loop is **unbounded** because we do not know how many times we will process Y before we start.

Here, the test X is "have we found the string terminator". We keep adding one to a counter called i until $MEM_{x+i} = 0$ at which point we know that i should give the length of the string. So how many steps does the algorithm take? The answer is that if we add one to i for each character in the string, then we must take at least n steps for an n-character string. Using big-O notation we say it is $O(n)$.

So the P-string approach is much better when we want to compute the length of a string: an algorithm which has complexity $O(1)$ will always be better than one which has complexity $O(n)$, assuming n is large enough. In this case we do not even need n to be large since for *all* strings the P-string method will be better: there is only one string for which the two methods will take exactly the same number of steps. As an exercise, can you work out which string this is?

4.2.2   `toupper`: Converting a String to Upper-Case

Computing the length of a string *accesses* the string content but does not *alter* it. The next task we look at is altering the string starting at address x so that the content consists of upper-case characters only: we take each lower-case character in the string and convert it into the upper-case equivalent. The C programming language does not include a standard function which represents quite this idea, but it does have a function called `toupper` that turns lower-case characters (rather than strings) into the upper-case equivalent.

P-String Version
The P-string version is shown in Fig. 4.3a. Imagine the memory content is initially

$$
\begin{aligned}
i &= \ldots, \quad\quad 3, \quad 4, \quad 5, \quad 6, \quad 7, \quad 8, \ldots \\
MEM &= \langle \ldots, \quad\quad 5, 104, 101, 108, 108, 111, \ldots \rangle \\
\text{CHR}(MEM_i) &= \quad \ldots, ENQ, \text{'h'}, \text{'e'}, \text{'l'}, \text{'l'}, \text{'o'}, \ldots
\end{aligned}
$$

and we invoke the algorithm using P-STRING-TOUPPER(3). The only input is the string address, so in this case we want to convert the string at address 3 into upper-

```
 1  algorithm P-STRING-TOUPPER(x) begin
 2      n ← P-STRING-LENGTH(x)
 3      for i from 0 upto n − 1 do
 4          t ← MEM_{x+1+i}
 5          if 97 ≤ t ≤ 122 then
 6              MEM_{x+1+i} ← t − 32
 7          end
 8      end
 9      return
10  end
```

(a) P-string version

```
 1  algorithm C-STRING-TOUPPER(x) begin
 2      n ← C-STRING-LENGTH(x)
 3      for i from 0 upto n − 1 do
 4          t ← MEM_{x+i}
 5          if 97 ≤ t ≤ 122 then
 6              MEM_{x+i} ← t − 32
 7          end
 8      end
 9      return
10  end
```

(b) C-string version

Fig. 4.3 Algorithms to convert a string at address x, represented using a P-string (left-hand side) or C-string (right-hand side) data structure, into upper-case

case. The corresponding steps performed by the algorithm are

Step # 1   Assign $n = $ P-STRING-LENGTH$(3) = 5$.
Step # 2   Assign $t = MEM_{3+1+0} = 104$.
Step # 3   Since $97 \leq t \leq 122$, store the result, i.e., $MEM_{3+1+0} = 104 - 32 = 72$.
Step # 4   Assign $t = MEM_{3+1+1} = 101$.
Step # 5   Since $97 \leq t \leq 122$, store the result, i.e., $MEM_{3+1+1} = 101 - 32 = 69$.
Step # 6   Assign $t = MEM_{3+1+2} = 108$.
Step # 7   Since $97 \leq t \leq 122$, store the result, i.e., $MEM_{3+1+2} = 108 - 32 = 76$.
Step # 8   Assign $t = MEM_{3+1+3} = 108$.
Step # 9   Since $97 \leq t \leq 122$, store the result, i.e., $MEM_{3+1+3} = 108 - 32 = 76$.
Step #10   Assign $t = MEM_{3+1+4} = 111$.
Step #11   Since $97 \leq t \leq 122$, store the result, i.e., $MEM_{3+1+4} = 111 - 32 = 79$.
Step #12   Return.

Of course this time the algorithm actually stores new content in memory rather than just reading existing content from it; after the algorithm has finished, the content is described by:

$$
\begin{aligned}
i &= \ldots, & 3, & 4, & 5, & 6, & 7, & 8, \ldots \\
MEM &= \langle \ldots, & 5, & 72, & 69, & 76, & 76, & 79, \ldots \rangle \\
\text{CHR}(MEM_i) &= \quad \ldots, & ENQ, & \text{`H'}, & \text{`E'}, & \text{`L'}, & \text{`L'}, & \text{`O'}, \ldots
\end{aligned}
$$

How did it end up this way? In the example where we were finding the length of a string, the complication was a new type of loop to deal with; here the complication is that by invoking P-STRING-TOUPPER, we invoke P-STRING-LENGTH as well during the first step. From then on, it is fairly easy to see what is going on. We perform a series of loads from memory to retrieve the "current" character at MEM_{x+1+i}, and if the character we load is in the range $97 \ldots 122$ (i.e., it is a lower-case character) we subtract 32 from it and store it back at the same place.

Working out how to express this in big-O notation is not hard. The main loop in lines #3 to #8 clearly takes $2 \cdot n$ steps since, for each character, we need one step to load it and one step to test and assign it if applicable. But to be fair, we *also* need to include the number of steps that it took to compute the string length via P-STRING-LENGTH. In a sense we just add the number of steps together, so informally we might write $O(1) + O(n) = O(1 + n)$. Of course $O(n)$ dominates $O(1)$ so using the same sort of simplification we did in Chap. 2, this turns into $O(n)$.

C-String Version

The C-string version is shown in Fig. 4.3b. Imagine the memory content is initially

$$
\begin{aligned}
i &= \ldots, & 3, & 4, & 5, & 6, & 7, & 8, \ldots \\
MEM &= \langle \ldots, & 104, & 101, & 108, & 108, & 111, & 0, \ldots \rangle \\
\text{CHR}(MEM_i) &= \quad \ldots, & \text{`h'}, & \text{`e'}, & \text{`l'}, & \text{`l'}, & \text{`o'}, & NUL, \ldots
\end{aligned}
$$

which, again, is just the C-string version of the P-string one we used above. If we invoke the algorithm with C-STRING-TOUPPER(3) again, the corresponding steps performed by the algorithm are

Step # 1   Assign $n = $ C-STRING-LENGTH(3) $= 5$.
Step # 2   Assign $t = MEM_{3+0} = 104$.
Step # 3   Since $97 \le t \le 122$, store the result, i.e., $MEM_{3+0} = 104 - 32 = 72$.
Step # 4   Assign $t = MEM_{3+1} = 101$.
Step # 5   Since $97 \le t \le 122$, store the result, i.e., $MEM_{3+1} = 101 - 32 = 69$.
Step # 6   Assign $t = MEM_{3+2} = 108$.
Step # 7   Since $97 \le t \le 122$, store the result, i.e., $MEM_{3+2} = 108 - 32 = 76$.
Step # 8   Assign $t = MEM_{3+3} = 108$.
Step # 9   Since $97 \le t \le 122$, store the result, i.e., $MEM_{3+3} = 108 - 32 = 76$.
Step #10   Assign $t = MEM_{3+4} = 111$.
Step #11   Since $97 \le t \le 122$, store the result, i.e., $MEM_{3+4} = 111 - 32 = 79$.
Step #12   Return.

which alter the memory content to read

$$
\begin{array}{llllllll}
i & = & \dots, & 3, & 4, & 5, & 6, & 7, & 8, \dots \\
MEM & = \langle \dots, & & 72, & 69, & 76, & 76, & 79, & 0, \dots \rangle \\
\text{CHR}(MEM_i) = & \dots, & \text{`H'}, & \text{`E'}, & \text{`L'}, & \text{`L'}, & \text{`O'}, & NUL, \dots
\end{array}
$$

afterwards. In the example where we were finding the length of a string, the steps taken by the two algorithms were radically different; here they are more similar. They are more or less the same in fact, bar the first step which obviously needs to use C-STRING-LENGTH instead of P-STRING-LENGTH. Since C-STRING-LENGTH takes $O(n)$ steps, the function C-STRING-TOUPPER takes $O(n) + O(n) = O(2 \cdot n)$ steps. The constant can be ignored if we again tolerate the simplifications described in Chap. 2, and we end up with $O(n)$.

4.2.3 `strcmp`: Testing if One String Is the Same as Another

Next we look at the task of string comparison, or string matching. The idea is that we take two strings, one starting at address x and one at address y, and try to determine whether they are the same or not. The C programming language includes a standard function called `strcmp` which represents an implementation of this idea.

P-string version

The P-string version is shown in Fig. 4.4a. Imagine the memory content is initially

$$
\begin{array}{llllllll}
i & = & \dots, & 3, & 4, & 5, & 6, & 7, & 8, \\
MEM & = \langle \dots, & & 5, & 104, & 101, & 108, & 108, & 111, & \rangle \\
\text{CHR}(MEM_i) = & \dots, & ENQ, & \text{`h'}, & \text{`e'}, & \text{`l'}, & \text{`l'}, & \text{`o'}, \\
i & = & & 9, & 10, & 11, & 12, & 13, & 14, \dots \\
MEM & = \langle & & 5, & 104, & 101, & 76, & 76, & 111, \dots \rangle \\
\text{CHR}(MEM_i) = & & ENQ, & \text{`h'}, & \text{`e'}, & \text{`L'}, & \text{`L'}, & \text{`o'}, \dots
\end{array}
$$

Notice that we have got some more content: in fact *so* much more we have now split the memory content onto two lines. This is, in part, because this algorithm takes two arguments representing the addresses of the strings we want to compare. Using P-STRING-MATCH$(3, 9)$ to invoke the algorithm means we want to compare the strings at addresses 3 and 9, with the corresponding steps performed as follows:

Step #1   Assign $n = $ P-STRING-LENGTH$(3) = 5$.
Step #2   Assign $m = $ P-STRING-LENGTH$(9) = 5$.
Step #3   Since $n = m$, continue.
Step #4   Since $MEM_{3+1+0} = MEM_{9+1+0} = 104$, continue.
Step #5   Since $MEM_{3+1+1} = MEM_{9+1+1} = 101$, continue.
Step #6   Since $MEM_{3+1+2} \neq MEM_{9+1+2}$, return **false**.

The strings are *similar*, but not the *same*. In particular, the 'l' characters in the string at address #3 (i.e., the characters at addresses #6 and #7) are lower-case, but those in the string at address #9 (i.e., the characters at addresses #12 and #13) are upper-case. This is reflected in the fact that the algorithm returned **false**.

```
1 algorithm P-STRING-MATCH(x, y) begin
2    n ← P-STRING-LENGTH(x)
3    m ← P-STRING-LENGTH(y)
4    if n ≠ m then
5       return false
6    end
7    for i from 0 upto n − 1 do
8       if MEM_{x+1+i} ≠ MEM_{y+1+i} then
9          return false
10      end
11   end
12   return true
13 end
```

(a) P-string version

```
1 algorithm C-STRING-MATCH(x, y) begin
2    n ← C-STRING-LENGTH(x)
3    m ← C-STRING-LENGTH(y)
4    if n ≠ m then
5       return false
6    end
7    for i from 0 upto n − 1 do
8       if MEM_{x+i} ≠ MEM_{y+i} then
9          return false
10      end
11   end
12   return true
13 end
```

(b) C-string version

Fig. 4.4 Algorithms to match one string at address x against another at address y, both represented using a P-string (left-hand side) or C-string (right-hand side) data structure

To understand the reason it gives the right answer we need to take a closer look at what happens at each step. The first thing that happens is a condition, namely if the number of characters in the first string is not the same as the number of characters in the second string then the strings cannot be the same, and the algorithm returns **false** as the result. But that does not happen here, since both strings have five characters in them so we carry on, and proceed to check each character. To do this, we use a loop which iterates over a block for values of i in the range $0 \ldots n − 1$. By this point we know $n = m$ so there is no danger of the i-th character of either string being "out of bounds" (i.e., beyond their actual length). For each value of i, we test the i-th characters of the two strings against each other. If they are not equal, then clearly the two strings are not equal and we can return **false** as the result. For $i = 0$

and $i = 1$, the characters in both strings are 'h' and 'e' so the algorithm continues. When we hit $i = 3$, however, the characters are 'l' and 'L' which are *not* equal; the algorithm notices this, concludes that the strings do not match, then returns **false** as the result. If, on the other hand, it had got all the way through the strings and found that they *all* matched it would return **true** instead.

As you might have expected, there is an extra complication here. The number of steps the algorithm takes depends on the strings themselves, i.e., their content and length, but it is not too hard to describe the number of steps in big-O notation. The two invocations of P-STRING-LENGTH take $O(1) + O(1)$ steps which is still $O(1)$, and then in the worst case we have to test all n characters of the strings so the main loop takes $O(n)$. The total number of steps is therefore $O(1) + O(n)$ which simplifies to $O(n)$.

C-String Version

The C-string version is shown in Fig. 4.4b. Imagine the memory content is initially

$$
\begin{array}{llllllll}
i & = & \ldots, & 3, & 4, & 5, & 6, & 7, & 8, \\
MEM & = \langle \ldots, & 104, & 101, & 108, & 108, & 111, & 0, & \rangle \\
\mathrm{CHR}(MEM_i) = & \ldots, & \text{'h'}, & \text{'e'}, & \text{'l'}, & \text{'l'}, & \text{'o'}, & NUL, \\
i & = & 9, & 10, & 11, & 12, & 13, & 14, \ldots \\
MEM & = \langle & 104, & 101, & 76, & 76, & 111, & 0, \ldots \rangle \\
\mathrm{CHR}(MEM_i) = & & \text{'h'}, & \text{'e'}, & \text{'L'}, & \text{'L'}, & \text{'o'}, & NUL, \ldots
\end{array}
$$

which, again, is just the C-string version of the P-string one we used above. Invoking the algorithm with C-STRING-MATCH(3, 9) gives basically the same steps as last time, namely

Step # 1 Assign $n = $ C-STRING-LENGTH(3) $= 5$.
Step # 2 Assign $m = $ C-STRING-LENGTH(9) $= 5$.
Step # 3 Since $n = m$, continue.
Step # 4 Since $MEM_{3+0} = MEM_{9+0} = 104$, continue.
Step # 5 Since $MEM_{3+1} = MEM_{9+1} = 101$, continue.
Step # 6 Since $MEM_{3+2} \neq MEM_{9+2}$, return **false**.

This time we use C-STRING-LENGTH instead of P-STRING-LENGTH, but the result is still **false** as you would expect. The two initial invocations of C-STRING-LENGTH plus the main algorithm take a grand total of $O(n) + O(n) + O(n) = O(3 \cdot n)$ steps, but of course we again ignore the constant and simplify this to $O(n)$.

4.2.4 `strcat`: Concatenating Two Strings Together

The final task we look at is the key one we have been building up to, as you might have guessed. The idea is to take one string (the source string) starting at address y and concatenate it with, or join it onto, another one (the target string) starting at address x; the source string remains unaltered.

1 **algorithm** P-STRING-CONCAT(x, y) **begin**
2      $n \leftarrow$ P-STRING-LENGTH(x)
3      $m \leftarrow$ P-STRING-LENGTH(y)
4   **for** i **from** 0 **upto** $m - 1$ **do**
5        $MEM_{x+1+i+n} \leftarrow MEM_{y+1+i}$
6   **end**
7      $MEM_x \leftarrow n + m$
8   **return**
9 **end**

(a) P-string version

1 **algorithm** C-STRING-CONCAT(x, y) **begin**
2      $n \leftarrow$ C-STRING-LENGTH(x)
3      $m \leftarrow$ C-STRING-LENGTH(y)
4   **for** i **from** 0 **upto** $m - 1$ **do**
5        $MEM_{x+i+n} \leftarrow MEM_{y+i}$
6   **end**
7      $MEM_{x+n+m} \leftarrow 0$
8   **return**
9 **end**

(b) C-string version

Fig. 4.5 Algorithms to concatenate (i.e., join) one string at address y onto the end of another at address x, both represented using a P-string (left-hand side) or C-string (right-hand side) data structure

P-String Version

The P-string version is shown in Fig. 4.5a. Imagine the memory content is initially

$$
\begin{array}{rlcccccc}
i & = \ldots, & 3, & 4, & 5, & 6, & 7, & 8, \\
MEM & = \langle \ldots, & 5, & 104, & 101, & 108, & 108, & 111, & \rangle \\
\text{CHR}(MEM_i) = & \ldots, ENQ, & \text{'h'}, & \text{'e'}, & \text{'l'}, & \text{'l'}, & \text{'o'}, \\
i & = & 9, & 10, & 11, & 12, & 13, & 14, \ldots \\
MEM & = \langle & 5, & 104, & 101, & 108, & 108, & 111, \ldots \rangle \\
\text{CHR}(MEM_i) = & ENQ, & \text{'h'}, & \text{'e'}, & \text{'l'}, & \text{'l'}, & \text{'o'}, \ldots
\end{array}
$$

and we invoke the algorithm using P-STRING-CONCAT(9, 3). This means we specify that the target string starts at address #9, and the source string starts at address #3; both strings are initially "hello". The algorithm itself is quite simple. Basically, after computing the lengths of the source and target string, it uses a loop to copy each character of the source string to the corresponding address *after* the target string ends. In short, the character at address $y + 1 + i$ in the source string is copied to address $x + 1 + i + n$ in the target string. The steps performed by the algorithm in this case are

Step # 1   Assign $n =$ P-STRING-LENGTH(9) $= 5$.
Step # 2   Assign $m =$ P-STRING-LENGTH(3) $= 5$.

Step # 3   Assign $MEM_{9+1+0+5} = MEM_{3+1+0} = 104$.
Step # 4   Assign $MEM_{9+1+1+5} = MEM_{3+1+1} = 101$.
Step # 5   Assign $MEM_{9+1+2+5} = MEM_{3+1+2} = 108$.
Step # 6   Assign $MEM_{9+1+3+5} = MEM_{3+1+3} = 108$.
Step # 7   Assign $MEM_{9+1+4+5} = MEM_{3+1+4} = 111$.
Step # 8   Assign $MEM_9 = 5 + 5 = 10$.
Step # 9   Return.

Which alter the memory content to read

$$
\begin{array}{llllllll}
i & = \ldots, & 3, & 4, & 5, & 6, & 7, & 8, \\
MEM & = \langle \ldots, & 5, & 104, & 101, & 108, & 108, & 111, & \rangle \\
\text{CHR}(MEM_i) = & \ldots, ENQ, & \text{‘h’}, & \text{‘e’}, & \text{‘l’}, & \text{‘l’}, & \text{‘o’}, \\
i & = & 9, & 10, & 11, & 12, & 13, & 14, \\
MEM & = \langle & 10, & 104, & 101, & 108, & 108, & 111, & \rangle \\
\text{CHR}(MEM_i) = & & LF, & \text{‘h’}, & \text{‘e’}, & \text{‘l’}, & \text{‘l’}, & \text{‘o’}, \\
i & = & 15, & 16, & 17, & 18, & 19, & \ldots \\
MEM & = \langle & 104, & 101, & 108, & 108, & 111, & \ldots \rangle \\
\text{CHR}(MEM_i) = & & \text{‘h’}, & \text{‘e’}, & \text{‘l’}, & \text{‘l’}, & \text{‘o’}, & \ldots
\end{array}
$$

We have split the content across three lines now to make it fit, but the point is that if you check the addresses and the content you find that the source string at address #3 is still "hello" but the target string at address #9 is now "hellohello", i.e., the original source and target joined together.

In terms of a big-O description of P-STRING-CONCAT, the two invocations of P-STRING-LENGTH take $O(1) + O(1)$ steps which is still $O(1)$, and then we perform n steps inside the loop that copies the characters. This gives a total of $O(1) + O(1) + O(n)$ which of course we simplify to $O(n)$.

C-String Version

The C-string version is shown in Fig. 4.5b. Imagine the memory content is initially

$$
\begin{array}{llllllll}
i & = \ldots, & 3, & 4, & 5, & 6, & 7, & 8, \\
MEM & = \langle \ldots, & 104, & 101, & 108, & 108, & 111 & 0, & \rangle \\
\text{CHR}(MEM_i) = & \ldots, & \text{‘h’}, & \text{‘e’}, & \text{‘l’}, & \text{‘l’}, & \text{‘o’} & NUL, \\
i & = & 9, & 10, & 11, & 12, & 13, & 14, \ldots \\
MEM & = \langle & 104, & 101, & 108, & 108, & 111, & 0, \ldots \rangle \\
\text{CHR}(MEM_i) = & & \text{‘h’}, & \text{‘e’}, & \text{‘l’}, & \text{‘l’}, & \text{‘o’}, & NUL, \ldots
\end{array}
$$

which, again, is just the C-string version of the P-string one we used above. Invoking the algorithm with C-STRING-CONCAT(9, 3) gives basically the same steps as last time, i.e.,

Step # 1   Assign $n = $ C-STRING-LENGTH(9) $= 5$.
Step # 2   Assign $m = $ C-STRING-LENGTH(3) $= 5$.
Step # 3   Assign $MEM_{9+0+5} = MEM_3 + 0 = 104$.
Step # 4   Assign $MEM_{9+1+5} = MEM_3 + 1 = 101$.
Step # 5   Assign $MEM_{9+2+5} = MEM_3 + 2 = 108$.

Step # 6   Assign $MEM_{9+3+5} = MEM3 + 3 = 108$.
Step # 7   Assign $MEM_{9+4+5} = MEM3 + 4 = 111$.
Step # 8   Assign $MEM_1 9 = 0$.
Step # 9   Return.

The only real difference is the last step, which instead of setting the length of the target string to $n+m$, i.e., the sum of the lengths of the source and target, it "moves" the terminator character to the correct position at the new end of the target. The memory content is altered to read

$$
\begin{array}{rlcccccc}
i & = \dots, & 3, & 4, & 5, & 6, & 7, & 8, \\
MEM & = \langle \dots, & 104, & 101, & 108, & 108, & 111 & 0, & \rangle \\
\text{CHR}(MEM_i) = & \dots, & \text{`h'}, & \text{`e'}, & \text{`l'}, & \text{`l'}, & \text{`o'} & NUL, \\
i & = & 9, & 10, & 11, & 12, & 13, & 14, \\
MEM & = \langle & 104, & 101, & 108, & 108, & 111, & 104, & \rangle \\
\text{CHR}(MEM_i) = & & \text{`h'}, & \text{`e'}, & \text{`l'}, & \text{`l'}, & \text{`o'}, & \text{`h'}, \\
i & = & 15, & 16, & 17, & 18, & 19, & \dots \\
MEM & = \langle & 101, & 108, & 108, & 111, & 0, & \dots \rangle \\
\text{CHR}(MEM_i) = & & \text{`e'}, & \text{`l'}, & \text{`l'}, & \text{`o'}, & NUL, & \dots
\end{array}
$$

so that again we find the source string at address #3 is still "hello" but the target string at address #9 is now "hellohello", i.e., the original source and target joined together. Again, the big-O notation for C-STRING-CONCAT is simple. We end up with $O(n) + O(n) + O(n)$ which we simplify to $O(n)$.

You can probably think of *lots* of other useful operations we could perform on a string, but two examples are described below. In each case, your challenge is to write two algorithms that apply the operation using the C-string and P-string data structures respectively.

Implement (task #20)

1. C has a standard function called strchr that takes a character c and the address of a string x as input: the function returns how far the first instance of the character is (i.e., the offset) from the start of the string. For example, if the character is 'l' and the string is "hello" we expect the result to be 2: the first instance of 'l' is 2 characters from the start of "hello".

   What happens if the character does not occur in the string: what useful value could the algorithm return in this case?

2. C has no standard function called strrev, but imagine it takes the address of a string x as input and reverses the order of the characters. For example, the string "hello" would become "olleh".

4.2.5   Problem #3: Repeated Concatenation

After all that, here is the problem that justifies what we have been doing. Have a look again at the last task of concatenating strings together and imagine we try to concatenate m strings together, accumulating the result in the string at address x. Using P-STRING-CONCAT as an example, we would end up with something like this:

$$\text{P-STRING-CONCAT}(x, \text{``foo''}) \mapsto x = \text{``foo''}$$
$$\text{P-STRING-CONCAT}(x, \text{``bar''}) \mapsto x = \text{``foobar''}$$
$$\text{P-STRING-CONCAT}(x, \text{``baz''}) \mapsto x = \text{``foobarbaz''}$$

That is, after the first invocation we would have appended "foo" to the empty string to get "foo", and after the second we would have appended "bar" to "foo" to get "foobar" and so on.

The thing to notice is that x gets longer and longer, but each string we concatenate to it remains short (say n characters). So how does this alter the number of steps taken by each invocation of P-STRING-CONCAT? Well, the number of steps in the main loop is determined by the number of characters in the source string, so this does not change. What about the number of steps required *before* the main loop to compute the length of the strings? P-STRING-LENGTH is $O(1)$, so no matter how long x is it will take a constant number of steps to give us a result. Even if we invoke P-STRING-LENGTH m times like this, the end result is still $O(n)$.

What about the C-string alternative? Again starting off with x as the empty string, we would get the same result, i.e.,

$$\text{C-STRING-CONCAT}(x, \text{``foo''}) \mapsto x = \text{``foo''}$$
$$\text{C-STRING-CONCAT}(x, \text{``bar''}) \mapsto x = \text{``foobar''}$$
$$\text{C-STRING-CONCAT}(x, \text{``baz''}) \mapsto x = \text{``foobarbaz''}$$

but now the behaviour is a bit different. Of course, the number of steps is still determined by the number of characters in the source string and this still does not change. But now, as x gets longer and longer C-STRING-LENGTH takes more and more steps to give us a result. Remember, it is $O(n)$ and n is getting larger and larger with each invocation. This might not look that bad, because if we invoke C-STRING-CONCAT four times then the total number of steps will be

$$O(n) + O(2n) + O(3n) + O(4n) = O(10n),$$

but we simplify this by ignoring the constants to get $O(n)$. But what happens if we invoke C-STRING-CONCAT m times? Now we get the sum

$$O(n) + O(2n) + \cdots + O(m \cdot n) = O\left(\left(\sum_{i=1}^{m} i\right) \cdot n\right)$$

which simplifies first to

$$O\big((m \cdot (m+1)/2) \cdot n\big)$$

because $\sum_{i=1}^{m} i = m(m+1)/2$ and then to

$$O(n \cdot m^2)$$

because $O(m(m+1)/2) = O(m^2)$. So the upshot is that if we invoke C-STRING-CONCAT m times like this, the end result is more like $O(m^2)$, since now we treat the value n as the constant. Yikes! Remember Chap. 2? $O(m^2)$ is *bad*. An eloquent analogy of this problem is offered by famed writer and programmer Joel Spolsky [8]:

> *Shlemiel gets a job as a street painter, painting the dotted lines down the middle of the road. On the first day he takes a can of paint out to the road and finishes 300 yards of the road. "That's pretty good!" says his boss, "you're a fast worker!" and pays him a kopeck. The next day Shlemiel only gets 150 yards done. "Well, that's not nearly as good as yesterday, but you're still a fast worker. 150 yards is respectable," and pays him a kopeck. The next day Shlemiel paints 30 yards of the road. "Only 30!" shouts his boss. "That's unacceptable! On the first day you did ten times that much work! What's going on?" "I can't help it," says Shlemiel. "Every day I get farther and farther away from the paint can!"*

The C-string `strcat` algorithm *is* poor old Shlemiel in this analogy: each time we try to concatenate one of our m strings, we need to place it further and further away from the end of the start of x.

Hopefully you can appreciate the problem now that we have spelled it out in such gruesome detail, but why does it *matter*? In short, understanding problems like this highlights the fact that C hides low-level detail of the data structure from us; this is even more true of languages such as Java. On one hand the abstraction this offers is great news because we do not have to worry about the data structure so much: the programming language takes care of it all for us automatically. But on the other hand, *only* by understanding low-level details can one hope to write efficient high-level programs! This is an issue that, in the opinion of many people, plagues modern Computer Science. We have built great tools to abstract away detail so we can construct wondrous hardware and software artefacts, but without an understanding of the fundamentals, one is *always* at a disadvantage.

C is not a bad language, and the C-string data structure is not the wrong choice: remember each of the C-string and P-string approaches have advantages and disadvantages. Therefore, it is interesting to look at the reason *why* the designers of C, Brian Kernighan and Dennis Ritchie, chose C-string rather than the P-string alternative in the 1970s. Two historical drivers are important. First, memory was at a real premium at the time C was developed; when dealing with large strings, the advantage of having a single string terminator character rather than a larger length field is tangible. It might seem amazing now, but saving even an extra byte of memory here and there could have been important then. Second, the PDP [7] range of computers used as early development platforms for C already used C-string type strings, and had some instructions that could deal with such strings quite efficiently. Hindsight is a wonderful thing; maybe they would have made a different choice looking back, maybe not. But it should be clear that by understanding low-level details, one at least has the opportunity to learn from the benefit of hindsight, and potentially to design better data structures and algorithms as a result. After all, data structures get *much* more complicated than strings so the cost of not understanding the details is potentially *much* greater as well.

Lots of instruction sets include instructions that were once useful, but now seem slightly odd; these legacy instructions often remain to ensure **backward compatibility**, i.e., to make sure old programs still work.

The x86 instruction set used by Intel includes support for something called **Binary Coded Decimal (BCD)** [3]. Find out about the instructions available for BCD; what do you think the original motivation for including them was? Why do you think they are or are not still useful now?

References

1. Wikipedia: ASCII. http://en.wikipedia.org/wiki/ASCII
2. Wikipedia: ASCII art. http://en.wikipedia.org/wiki/ASCII_art
3. Wikipedia: Binary Coded Decimal (BCD). http://en.wikipedia.org/wiki/Binary-coded_decimal
4. Wikipedia: Bulletin Board System (BBS). http://en.wikipedia.org/wiki/Bulletin_board_system
5. Wikipedia: C. http://en.wikipedia.org/wiki/C_(programming_language)
6. Wikipedia: Pascal. http://en.wikipedia.org/wiki/Pascal_(programming_language)
7. Wikipedia: Programmed Data Processor (PDP). http://en.wikipedia.org/wiki/Programmed_Data_Processor
8. Wikipedia: "Schlemiel the painter's" algorithm. http://en.wikipedia.org/wiki/Schlemiel_the_painter's_Algorithm

Demystifying Web-Search: the Mathematics of PageRank

5

Ask yourself a question: other **web-search** engines [39] exist of course, but how often do you use Google via

https://www.google.com/

to search for something? In fact, if you have a Google account the answer is available at

https://history.google.com/

unless you turned this feature off. For me it was around 100 times a day, although interestingly it changes a lot depending on what day it is. Another one: how often does the set of results produced *fail* to include what you were searching for? This is harder to answer precisely, but my guess would be not *that* often overall. Even accepting that it might fail sometimes, if you stop to think about it this is really amazing: versus only a generation ago, it seems fair to say that the ability to access so much information with such ease and accuracy has changed the world we live in fundamentally.

Although online advertising underpins the Google business model (a large proportion of income stemming from the **AdWords** [2] and **AdSense** [1] systems), from a technology perspective their web-search system remains a core interest. To support it, Google store and process a *lot* of information (some estimates cite upward of 50 billion web-sites alone, on top of which they deal with images etc.) and deal with a *lot* of **search queries** (40 % of the current 7 billion world population make use of the Internet, so if each of them perform 100 Google searches a day we are potentially talking about a huge volume of queries at any given point in time). This means they clearly need a *lot* of computing power to keep pace with demand. Beyond this however, and given all the challenges involved, how are they able to provide such high-*quality* results?

A full answer is obviously quite complicated, and has also changed over time to meet new challenges and capitalise on new opportunities. Even so, the central concepts depend on applying fundamental Computer Science to solve real, practical challenges; better still, they can be explained using Mathematical techniques you

D. Page, N. Smart, *What Is Computer Science?*,
Undergraduate Topics in Computer Science, DOI 10.1007/978-3-319-04042-4_5,
© Springer International Publishing Switzerland 2014

are already (somewhat) familiar with. These concepts represent our focus in this chapter: our aim is to explain how Google produces results for your search queries, using graph theory and probability theory behind the scenes.[1]

5.1   PageRank: the Essence of Google Web-Search

5.1.1   What Actually *Is* Web-Search?

First, a recap of things you probably already know. The **World Wide Web (WWW)** [41] (or **web**) was conceived in a 1989 proposal by Tim Berners-Lee: the idea was to develop a universal mechanism to view (and edit) documents, with embedded connections that would facilitate browsing through them. Overviewing the rich body of previous and related work is beyond our scope, but the proposal basically aimed to implement what was an established concept called **hypertext** [13]; one famous example[2] is the so-called "mother of all demos" in 1969 by Doug Engelbart [32], which included use of the first mouse to navigate hypertext documents in NLS [22]. This aim was achieved when Berners-Lee and a group of collaborators eventually developed

1. the **HTML** [14] language for describing document content, which we now know as **web-pages**, and the embedded **hyperlinks** [11],
2. the **HTTP** [15] protocol used to communicate such content to and from client (or **web-browser**) and **web-server** software, plus
3. the first actual implementations of such software that could be used to form a working system.

The result was advertised[3] to the Internet at large in 1991, and the rest, as they say, is history: various aspects of the original system have matured and improved, but either way it now represents a ubiquitous presence in modern life.

If you think of the web as a massive database of information stored within web-pages, **web-search** can be described as an information retrieval problem [17]: given the database of web-pages, represented by a set V, we want to find the sub-set $R \subset V$ so each $x \in R$ matches a **search query** q. Exactly what constitutes a match depends on the type of search queries allowed [40] of course, so deciding whether a given web-page matches or not is a challenge in itself. To make things simple however, imagine q is just a single word: R might then be the set of web-pages which contain it somewhere.

---

[1] The chapter assumes you have at least *some* exposure to these topics, and focuses on explaining how they are used. However, we include a number of fairly lengthy introductions in case you need a refresher or even a place to start learning about them from scratch.

[2] A copy of the video is preserved at http://www.dougengelbart.org/firsts/dougs-1968-demo.html.

[3] A copy of the post is preserved at http://groups.google.com/groups?selm=6487%40cernvax.cern.ch.

5.1.2 Web-Search Before Google

Depending on how old you are, the birth of the web in 1991 might already seem like a long time ago. But systems for web-search *did* already exist between then and 1998, when Google was founded as a company. Understanding of this history is important, because it explains the technical context into which Google web-search was born a few years earlier (based on a 1996 research project at Stanford University): like most good products it solved a problem, so by understanding the problem means we can better appreciate the solution.

Web-Directories

Once a significant number of web-pages were available, the most obvious way to locate one of interest was initially a **web-directory** [36]. Probably the first example, dated roughly 1992, was a list[4] of web-server maintained by Tim Berners-Lee at CERN (when there were few enough to do so easily); contemporary examples include the **WWW Virtual Library** [42], also started by Berners-Lee, at

http://www.vlib.org/

and the **Open Directory Project (ODP)** [24] at

http://www.dmoz.org/

The basic idea is to classify web-pages within a giant table of contents. Much like the table of contents in a book is divided into chapters and/or sections, the web-directory is arranged into a hierarchy of categories with all web-pages about a given topic listed under the same category. Imagine some user wants to find web-pages related to some topic q. To do so, they start at the top, least specific level of the hierarchy and move level-by-level through more specific categories until they get to a set R of matches for q. Imagine $q =$ "star wars" for instance: using ODP, they might navigate through

"Top" $\rightarrow$ "Arts" $\rightarrow$ "Movies" $\rightarrow$ "Titles" $\rightarrow$ "S" $\rightarrow$ "Star Wars Movies"

until eventually finding (lots of) relevant matches.

Web-Search Engines

A **web-search engine** (or **search engine**) offers a different way to resolve search queries, basically forming R by testing q against every web-page on behalf of the user. This avoids the need to maintain the hierarchy of categories, and also automates the process so that users no longer need to manually control the search.

A lot of web-search engines have existed, and their history is interesting as a topic in itself. Although it oversimplifies the range of approaches employed somewhat, we can think of them as using three stages:

---

[4] A copy of the web-page is preserved at http://www.w3.org/History/19921103-hypertext/hypertext/DataSources/WWW/Servers.html.

1. **web-crawling** [35],
2. **web-indexing** [38], then
3. search query resolution.

The first and second stages automatically collect and summarise information about web-pages, using the content to form a **web-index** used by the third stage to produce a set of results. The volume of information and relative lack of storage capacity initially limited the information collected to specific features of a web-pages (e.g., within so-called **meta tags** [20], or headings and titles), but this was quickly expanded to full-text search (meaning search of any web-page content).

Think of it like this: the index of a book is basically a map from words (usually those deemed important in some sense), to pages on which they appear. The index is prepared before the book is printed by analysing the content of each pagem, then if you want to know which page includes word x, you look-up x in the index and it tells you. The concept of web-indexing is exactly the same, except we want a mapping from words to *web*-pages. Now, we want to know which web-pages match the search query q, so we look-up q in the web-index and use the associated web-pages as R.

The system as a whole operates in two phases [23]: preparation of the web-index is performed **offline** (meaning before anyone uses the system), while search query resolution is performed **online** (meaning during use of the system). It is important the web-index *can* be prepared offline, because the web-crawling process will take a long time for the entire web. By **pre-computing** [26] it before anyone uses the system, the actual searches queries can still be resolved quickly because the bulk of the work has already been completed.

5.1.3   Web-Search After Google

Arguably, a good web-directory will produce high-quality results provided users can navigate the hierarchy to resolve their query. Why? Ignoring the issue of deciding on a category for web-page x, a quality control system decides whether or not x is good enough to include at all: this decision might be resolved in two parts, by a submitter first suggesting the web-page then an editor making a final decision about inclusion. You could think of this as roughly analogous to them voting for the web-page. However, there are a number of problems, including

- the actual decisions may be subjective and/or hard to articulate precisely, so it is hard to deal with issues such as bias,
- it is difficult to cope with many web-pages, since the workload involved in doing so is relatively high, and
- it sort of assumes the web-pages stay the same, because otherwise the process would have to be repeated again and again, which of course further adds to the workload.

You could also argue that web-search engines solve some of these problems through automation, since the workload can be borne by a computer rather than a human. However, it also seems fair to say they just shift rather than solve the underlying problem: the maintainer of a given web-search engine has an easier task than for a web-directory, but now the *user* is faced with the challenge of enforcing quality control. *They* must filter the good results from potentially lots of bad ones.

PageRank [25] is, roughly speaking, the solution employed by Google. Although it represents an important aspect of their producing such high-quality results, and therefore the success of the company, the concept itself is very easy to grasp: instead of *humans* voting for web-pages, the web-pages will vote for *each other*. Think of each link from web-page x to y as a vote, in the sense that x indicates y has something important (or at least relevant) on it: y is deemed important if many other web-pages link to it, and even more so if those web-pages are themselves important. By considering the *structure* of the web (i.e., the links between web-pages) alongside their content, a PageRank-based web-search engine can solve the quality control problem: it allows us to automatically sort the results, and display the good, important ones before the bad, unimportant ones.

Strictly speaking, PageRank is just a component within the wider Google web-search system: the term may be used to describe either the measure of importance assigned to each web-page, or the algorithm used to compute such values. So given our intuition about what it is, how does it work? This is really three questions in one. In reality, we need to answer the following:

1. how do we collect information to inform our analysis of web-page importance, which is basically the same web-crawling challenge that any other web-search engine faces,
2. how do we formalise the concept of importance, so we can compute actual PageRank values for each web-page, and,
3. once we have those values, how do we use them while resolving a given search query?

These questions are addressed, in order, by the following sections.

5.2   Using Graph Theory to Model and Explore the Web

As already discussed, the goal of web-crawling is to automatically collect and summarise information about web-pages: we want a computer to do this rather than a human because there are a *lot* of web-pages to process. The idea is to develop an algorithm that controls the web-crawler software, i.e., determines exactly *how* it automatically browses the web. This task can be made a lot easier by using **graph theory**, including various existing algorithms, as a starting point: we model the *real* web as a directed graph

$$G = (V, E)$$

called the **web-graph** [37]: each vertex $v \in V$ represents a web-page, and each edge $(u, v) \in E$ represents a link from web-page u to web-page v. A (very small) example is illustrated by Fig. 5.3, which includes $n = 6$ web-pages identified by URLs such as a.html, and links such as from a.html to d.html. This might not *seem* like

---

An aside: a quick introduction to graphs and graph theory

In **graph theory** [9], a **graph** [8] is used to describe a set of abstract objects and relationships between them. Formally, we specify a graph using two sets:
1. The set V is called the set of **vertices** (or **nodes**): these are basically labels that identify the abstract objects we are interested in.
2. The set E is called the set of **edges**: each edge is a pair of vertices from V, i.e., (u, v) where $u, v \in V$, which specify a relationship between the associated objects.

As a result, we often write $G = (V, E)$ to show that a particular graph G is specified by particular sets V and E. Consider an example where

$$V = \{a, b, c, d\} \qquad E = \big\{(a, b), (b, d), (d, c), (d, d), (c, a), (c, b)\big\}$$

From this, we can see there are four vertices labelled a, b, c and d; there are six edges between them in total, meaning for example that a and b are connected and so on. We often visualise the structure of a graph by drawing each of the vertices, and linking them with lines to depict the edges.

Beyond this general definition, several particular types of graph are useful:

Undirected versus directed edges   In a directed graph, edges still connect vertices, but their order matters. For example, (u, v) is an edge from u to v (but not from v to u) whereas (v, u) is an edge from v to u (but not from u to v). It is common to visualise this using an arrow head on the edge.

Unweighted versus weighted edges   In a weighted graph, we associated an extra **weight** with each of the edges: a edge between some u and v would look like (u, v, w) where w is the weight, which is usually just a number.

There are numerous properties we can define given some graph G, but an important one is the **degree** of a given vertex $u \in V$: given two functions

$$\text{into}(u) = \big\{v \mid v \in V, (v, u) \in E\big\}$$
$$\text{from}(u) = \big\{v \mid v \in V, (u, v) \in E\big\}$$

that produce the set of all vertices v where there is an edge from v to u or u to v respectively, the degree of u is $\deg(u) = |\text{from}(u) \cup \text{into}(u)|$ meaning the total number of edges that connect it to any other vertex.

   A **path** is a sequence of edges in E which connect a sequence of vertices in V: in a sense, it connects the first vertex in the sequence to the last vertex by moving along the intermediate edges. Within our example, the path $P = \langle (a, b), (b, d), (d, c) \rangle$ connects a to c, for instance; a path like this with no repeated vertices is deemed to be **simple**.

---

a massive step; the web-graph is certainly a natural, and fairly obvious way to model the real web. Crucially though, this added formalism allows us to develop and reason about algorithms that process the web-graph.

5.2.1   Graph Traversal

Given a graph $G = (V, E)$ as input, **graph traversal** [10] is fairly simple problem to explain: starting at some vertex s, the goal is simply to move along edges until all are vertices have been visited. If you translate "vertex" into "web-page" and "visit" into "extract and summarise the content", this should seem reasonably close to what we want.

Algorithms 5.1a and 5.1b detail two classic ways to solve this problem, called **Breadth-First Search (BFS)** [3] and **Depth-First Search (DFS)** [7] respectively.[5] Each algorithm starts at s, and then visits vertices one at a time by traversing edges from those already visited. To keep track of this process, a sequence Q of vertices yet to visit (called the worklist), and a set D of vertices already visited are maintained. The intuition is as follows:

- The loop in lines #3 to #12 processes vertices until the worklist is empty; line #4 removes the first vertex u from Q and then processes it.
- The loop in lines #5 to #9 process each edge (u, v) from u to some other vertex v: if v has not been visited already (i.e., $v \notin D$), then it is added to both Q and D. Checking D first is important, because it allows **cycles** [5] to be avoided.
- Finally, line #11 visits vertex u, processing it in whatever way is appropriate.

Given a worklist $Q = \langle Q_0, Q_1, \ldots, Q_{n-1} \rangle$, one or two of the steps might need some more detailed explanation:

- In line #7 of Algorithm 5.1a, where we need to *append* v to Q, we update Q to be $Q \parallel \langle v \rangle = \langle Q_0, Q_1, \ldots, Q_{n-1}, v \rangle$ so that v becomes the new last element.
- In line #7 of Algorithm 5.1b, where we need to *prepend* v to Q, we update Q to be $\langle v \rangle \parallel Q = \langle v, Q_0, Q_1, \ldots, Q_{n-1} \rangle$ so that v becomes the new first element.
- In line #4 of either algorithm, where we need to remove the first element from Q, we just take Q_0 (i.e., the first element) as u then update Q to be $\langle Q_1, \ldots, Q_{n-1} \rangle$ (i.e., all the other elements).

Beyond this, the behaviour of both algorithms is better explained with an example. Using a **tree** [34], a special type of undirected graph in which any two vertices are connected by one simple path, means their differing behaviours are easier to explain: consider a 7-vertex tree described formally via

$$V = \{a, b, c, d, e, f, g\}$$
$$E = \big\{(a, b), (a, c), (b, d), (b, e), (c, f), (c, g)\big\}$$

or visually in Fig. 5.2. If we invoke the BFS algorithm using a (the so-called **root** of the tree) as a starting point, it proceeds as follows:

Step #1   Set $Q = \langle a \rangle$ and $D = \{a\}$.
Step #2   Since $|Q| \neq 0$, perform the next loop iteration for $v \in \{b, c\}$.

---

[5] Why *search*? This terminology relates to how BFS and DFS are often used, namely to search for a target vertex within the graph: once the target vertex v is visited, the traversal usually stops rather than continuing to visit all vertices.

```
 1  algorithm BFS(V, E, s) begin
 2  │   Q ← ⟨s⟩, D ← {s}
 3  │   while |Q| ≠ 0 do
 4  │   │   Remove first element u from Q
 5  │   │   foreach v such that (u, v) ∈ E do
 6  │   │   │   if v ∉ D then
 7  │   │   │   │   Append v to Q
 8  │   │   │   │   Add v to D
 9  │   │   │   end
10  │   │   end
11  │   │   Visit and process u
12  │   end
13  │   return
14  end
```

(a) An algorithm for Breadth-First Search (BFS)

```
 1  algorithm DFS(V, E, s) begin
 2  │   Q ← ⟨s⟩, D ← {s}
 3  │   while |Q| ≠ 0 do
 4  │   │   Remove first element u from Q
 5  │   │   foreach v such that (u, v) ∈ E do
 6  │   │   │   if v ∉ D then
 7  │   │   │   │   Prepend v to Q
 8  │   │   │   │   Add v to D
 9  │   │   │   end
10  │   │   end
11  │   │   Visit and process u
12  │   end
13  │   return
14  end
```

(b) An algorithm for Depth-First Search (DFS)

Fig. 5.1 Two approaches to traversal of vertices in a graph

Fig. 5.2 A simple 7-vertex tree used to explain the behaviour of BFS and DFS algorithms

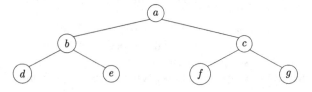

Step #2.1   Set $u = a$ and $Q = \langle \rangle$.
Step #2.2   Since $b \notin D$, set $Q = \langle b \rangle$ and $D = \{a, b\}$.
Step #2.3   Since $c \notin D$, set $Q = \langle b, c \rangle$ and $D = \{a, b, c\}$.

Step #2.4   Visit a.

Step #3   Since $|Q| \neq 0$, perform the next loop iteration for $v \in \{d, e\}$.

    Step #3.1   Set $u = b$ and $Q = \langle c \rangle$.

    Step #3.2   Since $d \notin D$, set $Q = \langle c, d \rangle$ and $D = \{a, b, c, d\}$.

    Step #3.3   Since $e \notin D$, set $Q = \langle c, d, e \rangle$ and $D = \{a, b, c, d, e\}$.

    Step #3.4   Visit b.

Step #4   Since $|Q| \neq 0$, perform the next loop iteration for $v \in \{f, g\}$.

    Step #4.1   Set $u = c$ and $Q = \langle d, e \rangle$.

    Step #4.2   Since $f \notin D$, set $Q = \langle d, e, f \rangle$ and $D = \{a, b, c, d, e, f\}$.

    Step #4.3   Since $g \notin D$, set $Q = \langle d, e, f, g \rangle$ and $D = \{a, b, c, d, e, f, g\}$.

    Step #4.4   Visit c.

Step #5   Since $|Q| \neq 0$, perform the next loop iteration for $v \in \emptyset$.

    Step #5.1   Set $u = d$ and $Q = \langle e, f, g \rangle$.

    Step #5.2   Visit c.

Step #6   Since $|Q| \neq 0$, perform the next loop iteration for $v \in \emptyset$.

    Step #6.1   Set $u = e$ and $Q = \langle f, g \rangle$.

    Step #6.2   Visit e.

Step #7   Since $|Q| \neq 0$, perform the next loop iteration for $v \in \emptyset$.

    Step #7.1   Set $u = f$ and $Q = \langle g \rangle$.

    Step #7.2   Visit f.

Step #8   Since $|Q| \neq 0$, perform the next loop iteration for $v \in \emptyset$.

    Step #8.1   Set $u = g$ and $Q = \langle \rangle$.

    Step #8.2   Visit g.

Step #9   Since $|Q| = 0$, stop the loop.

Step #10   Return.

Doing the same with the DFS algorithm produces a different behaviour:

Step #1   Set $Q = \langle a \rangle$ and $D = \{a\}$.

Step #2   Since $|Q| \neq 0$, perform the next loop iteration for $v \in \{b, c\}$.

    Step #2.1   Set $u = a$ and $Q = \langle \rangle$.

    Step #2.2   Since $b \notin D$, set $Q = \langle b \rangle$ and $D = \{a, b\}$.

    Step #2.3   Since $c \notin D$, set $Q = \langle c, b \rangle$ and $D = \{a, b, c\}$.

    Step #2.4   Visit a.

Step #3   Since $|Q| \neq 0$, perform the next loop iteration for $v \in \{f, g\}$.

    Step #3.1   Set $u = c$ and $Q = \langle b \rangle$.

    Step #3.2   Since $f \notin D$, set $Q = \langle f, b \rangle$ and $D = \{a, b, c, f\}$.

    Step #3.3   Since $g \notin D$, set $Q = \langle g, f, b \rangle$ and $D = \{a, b, c, f, g\}$.

    Step #3.4   Visit c.

Step #4   Since $|Q| \neq 0$, perform the next loop iteration for $v \in \emptyset$.

    Step #4.1   Set $u = g$ and $Q = \langle f, b \rangle$.

    Step #4.2   Visit c.

Step #5   Since $|Q| \neq 0$, perform the next loop iteration for $v \in \emptyset$.

    Step #5.1   Set $u = f$ and $Q = \langle b \rangle$.

    Step #5.2   Visit f.

Step #6   Since $|Q| \neq 0$, perform the next loop iteration for $v \in \{d, e\}$.

    Step #6.1   Set $u = b$ and $Q = \langle \rangle$.

Step #6.2   Since $d \notin D$, set $Q = \langle d \rangle$ and $D = \{a, b, c, f, g, d\}$.
Step #6.3   Since $e \notin D$, set $Q = \langle e, d \rangle$ and $D = \{a, b, c, f, g, d, e\}$.
Step #6.4   Visit c.
Step #7   Since $|Q| \neq 0$, perform the next loop iteration for $v \in \emptyset$.
Step #7.1   Set $u = e$ and $Q = \langle d \rangle$.
Step #7.2   Visit e.
Step #8   Since $|Q| \neq 0$, perform the next loop iteration for $v \in \emptyset$.
Step #8.1   Set $u = d$ and $Q = \langle \rangle$.
Step #8.2   Visit d.
Step #9   Since $|Q| = 0$, stop the loop.
Step #10   Return.

To summarise, both BFS and DFS satisfy the goal of visiting all vertices but differ in the order they do so. You can think of this tree as three levels, where the top level contains a, the middle level contains b and c, and the bottom level contains d, e, f and g. BFS visits each vertex in the current level before moving onto a lower level; the order of traversal is

$$\langle a, b, c, d, e, f, g \rangle$$

which sort of moves across the tree then down. DFS on the other hand visits each vertex in the lower level before the current one; the order of traversal is therefore

$$\langle a, c, g, f, b, e, d \rangle,$$

which moves down the tree then across.

Using a tree is just a way to make the behaviours easier to explain however: we can of course invoke the same algorithms on a more general graph. If we take the web-graph in Fig. 5.3 for example, the order BFS visits the web-pages is

$$\langle \mathtt{a.html}, \mathtt{c.html}, \mathtt{d.html}, \mathtt{b.html}, \mathtt{e.html}, \mathtt{f.html} \rangle,$$

whereas for DFS this changes to

$$\langle \mathtt{a.html}, \mathtt{d.html}, \mathtt{f.html}, \mathtt{e.html}, \mathtt{b.html}, \mathtt{c.html} \rangle.$$

Both BFS or DFS traverse the web-graph, so provided they act in the right way when visiting each web-page they (*more or less*) solve the original problem of automatically browsing the web.

Research (task #22)   In BFS and DFS, the way v is added to the worklist Q in line #7 is the central difference; formally, Q is used as a **queue** in BFS and as a **stack** in DFS. Find out more about these data structures.

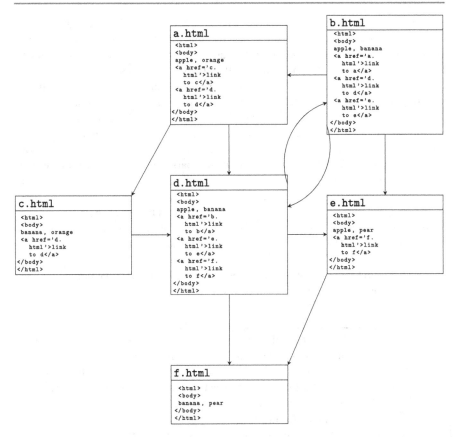

Fig. 5.3 A simple, concrete web-graph that captures the link structure between, and content of each web-page; each of the $n = 6$ highly artificial web-pages is a short HTML file, which in combination provide structure (i.e., links between the web-pages) and content (i.e., some words, in this case names of fruit)

Research (task #23) By using a so-called `robots.txt` file [29], a web-server can signal that certain web-pages should be ignored by a web-crawler. Find out about this mechanism: when and why do you think it makes sense to use it?

5.2.2   Graph Exploration

"*More or less* solves" is a hint: a subtle problem exists with using standard graph traversal. Remember that the web-crawler does not have access to the web-graph as input. The whole point is to automatically browse the web and collect information about web-pages, so if we already have the web-graph there would be no point!

Really solving this problem means translating BFS or DFS into **graph exploration** algorithms, but fortunately the difference is minor. Obviously we cannot have G as an input to the algorithm any longer; in a sense, the web-graph is now an output from exploration, not the input to traversal. As a result, line #5 cannot check for edges $(u, v) \in E$ because E is unknown. Instead, we need to take u and discover edges from it to other, potentially unknown web-pages. The form of web-pages makes this easy: HTML is a **mark-up language** [19], meaning as well as the actual content we see, each web-page contains extra information (the so-called mark-up). This mark-up will includes specifications of which web-page a given link is to, so if we parse the web-page content for `a.html` in Fig. 5.3 for example, we might extract the edges (a.html, c.html) and (a.html, d.html) from the links `<a href='c.html'>link to c</a>` and `<a href='d.html'>link to d</a>` which are embedded in it.

So the idea is that we invoke the web-crawler on a starting point, for example a Top Level Domain (TLD) [33] such as $s = $ www.bbc.co.uk, and let it explore links from there to construct G. Once finished (e.g., when it runs out of web-pages to explore) we might invoke it on *another* starting point and merge together the results (e.g., to increase the chance of visiting every web-page), or just use G as is for whatever purpose we had in mind.

Implement (task #24)

In line #11 of Algorithms 5.1a and 5.1b, we need to visit and process a web-page u. What this actually means depends on the task at hand of course: for some web-search engines this could just mean extracting and summarising the content of u, noting that `a.html` contains the words "apple" and "orange" for instance.

Since PageRank needs the actual web-graph structure (i.e., the links between web-pages) as input, the processing basically needs to form and eventually return $G = (V, E)$ by collecting the vertices and edges. Write an graph exploration algorithm to do this, using either Algorithms 5.1a or 5.1b as a basis; demonstrate how it works using the web-graph in Fig. 5.3.

5.3   Using Probability Theory to Model Web-Browsing

Section 5.2 showed a suitable web-crawler can automatically generate a web-graph $G = (V, E)$ for us, where the edges in E capture the link structure required to reason about each web-page $x \in V$. The example in Fig. 5.3 is quite detailed however: once we have G, it is easier to consider Fig. 5.4a instead. This is the same graph (e.g., `a.html` is just renamed a) but any unnecessary detail such as the web-page content is removed.

Given a G as input, our next challenge is computation of a PageRank value for each web-page. So where do we start? As stated, this challenge is enormously vague:

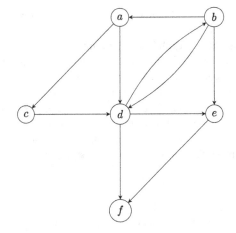

(a) Before processing to deal with sink web-page f.

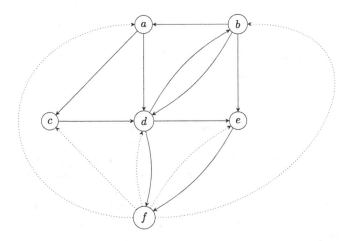

(b) After processing to deal with sink web-page f; artificially added
links from f shown as dashed lines.

Fig. 5.4 Two simple, abstract web-graphs (derived from Fig. 5.3) that capture the link structure
between, but *not* content of each web-page

we lack a formal definition of *what* we should compute, *how* we should try to compute it, or even what the correct answer looks like! To make reasoning about the
problem easier, Google use the following model: imagine the web is comprised of
n web-pages, which a user browses indefinitely. At each step, this user randomly
causes one of two events to occur:

1. with probability $1 - p$, a random web-page is loaded from anywhere on the web
   (i.e., it thinks of a random web-page and types the URL into the web-browser
   address bar), or

2. with probability p, it clicks on and hence follows a random link on the current web-page to some other web-page.

This is called the **random surfer model**, and amounts to performing a **random walk** [28] on the web-graph. Although this might not be how people *really* behave, it allows us to translate the vague English description into something more concrete: assuming we accept the random surfer model, the PageRank of a web-page is equivalent to the probability of visiting it. Think about it: if web-page x is more important then there will be more links to it, and as a result the probability is higher that at some point the random surfer visits x by following such a link (plus the probability it visits it at random of course). We can stress this by keeping in mind

$$\text{``the PageRank of } x\text{''} \equiv \Pr[x]$$

where the right-hand side means the probability that web-page x is visited; this in turn is equivalent to the number of votes accumulated by x if you prefer the voting analogy. It also allows a sanity check later when we come to compute the actual values: since we are dealing with probabilities, the sum of $\Pr[x]$ for all $x \in V$ should be 1.

This all becomes more concrete still by capturing the description as a formula:

$$\Pr[x] = \underbrace{\frac{1-p}{n}}_{\substack{\text{term representing} \\ \text{random web-page}}} + p \cdot \underbrace{\left(\sum_{y \in \text{into}(x)} \frac{\Pr[y]}{|\text{from}(y)|} \right)}_{\substack{\text{term representing} \\ \text{random link}}}$$

There are two terms because there are two events possible within the random surfer model; each term computes the associated probability, which we then add together because we want the probability of either one event or the other occurring as the result. Although they might *look* cryptic, both terms are just translations of the English description of random surfer behaviour into Mathematics. For the first term, this is easy to see: if there are n web-pages in total and we load a random one with probability $1 - p$ then we end up on x with a probability of $\frac{1-p}{n}$. The second is more difficult however. The term itself is p multiplied by

$$\sum_{y \in \text{into}(x)} \frac{\Pr[y]}{|\text{from}(y)|}$$

or, in English, the probability of this event occurring multiplied by the combined probabilities of arriving at x having followed a link from another web-page y. Think about it again using the voting analogy: a web-page y has a number of votes to cast (i.e., $\Pr[y]$), so gives each web-page x that it links to a number of votes in proportion to the total number of links it contains (i.e., divides $\Pr[y]$ by the number of outgoing links from y, namely $|\text{from}(y)|$). We are interested in x of course, so the summation basically deals with all web-pages y that link to x (i.e., all $y \in \text{into}(x)$), forming the sum of their votes cast for x per the above. This means two things:

1. if y has many votes to cast, the number given to x will be larger (since the numerator $\Pr[y]$ will be larger) than if it had few, and

2. if y votes for fewer web-pages by linking to them, the proportion given to x will be larger (since the denominator $|from(y)|$ will be smaller) than if it votes for many.

By replacing votes with probabilities we get the desired result: there is a higher probability the random surfer visits x by following a link if other web-pages link to it, and even more so if those web-pages have a high probability of being visited themselves.

Although PageRank is probably the most famous, other similar examples exist within a family of related techniques. Two such examples are

- the **impact factor** [16] used to gauge how important an academic publication is, and
- the **Hyperlink-Induced Topic Search (HITS)** algorithm [12] that deals with web-page ranking.

It is often important to see how techniques relate or build on each other: do some research into the above, and compare them with PageRank in terms of their approach, features and so on.

Research (task #25)

5.3.1   Sanitising the Web-Graph to Avoid a Subtle Problems

Two special types of web-page can occur in a web-graph, namely

1. **source web-pages**, which have no incoming links (i.e., $into(x) = \emptyset$) so will never be *visited* by following links, and
2. **sink web-pages**, which have no outgoing links (i.e., $from(x) = \emptyset$) so will never be *exited* by following links.

For the first case, the only potential problem might be that our web-crawler fails to visit it. In terms of computing PageRank values, there is no issue: it is just deemed unimportant according to the PageRank metric, due to the lack of links to it. The second case *is* problematic however. There are two ways to think about why this is the case:

1. The random surfer model says one of two events will occur: either the random surfer loads a random web-page or follows a random link. If the random surfer visits a sink web-page however, the first event cannot occur because there are no links to follow. Intuitively this is a problem because it means the probabilistic model of behaviour we rely on breaks down for sink web-pages.
2. In the corresponding formula, each web-page can be seen as voting for others by distributing the votes allocated to it via the links it contains. A sink web-page votes for no other web-page however, even though they *might* vote for it. Numerically this is a problem because a sink web-page accumulates votes like a sort of black hole. That is, votes flow in but never comes out again; this skews the results produced for non-sink web-pages because there is a fixed number of votes in total.

As a result, it is common to treat sink nodes differently. Various ways to do this have been proposed, but the easiest to justify is as follows: for each sink web-page x identified, we add an artificial edge of the form (x, y) to every other vertex $y \in V$. By doing so, the random surfer is happy again because either event can occur once it visits x; it also ensures fairness to non-sink web-pages, because the PageRank accumulated by x is now shared evenly among all other web-pages.

Consider Fig. 5.4a: web-page f satisfies the criteria for being a sink, since from$(f) = \emptyset$. To cope, we might amend the web-graph to produce Fig. 5.4b where the dashed edges have been added artificially; these ensure f is linked to every other web-page, in this case a, b, c, d and e. We use this altered web-graph rather than the original from here on.

The "link sink web-page x to all other web-pages" strategy described is not the *only* option: various other strategies have also been proposed. Find out about at least one other strategy, then compare and contrast each option using a list of advantages and disadvantages.

Write an algorithm that takes a web-graph as input, and applies a strategy (whether the one described, or discovered in Task 26) for dealing with sink web-pages; the output should be the amended web-graph ready for use during computation of PageRank values.

If you consider the *real* web rather than the examples presented, the value of n is large and hence many web-pages will be identified as sinks. If you implement the strategy described for dealing with them *exactly*, a problem starts to emerge. What do you think this problem could be, and, with reference to your algorithm in Task 27 for instance, how could it be avoided?

5.3.2 A Mathematical Approach to Computing PageRank

Rewriting the Formula to Avoid Cycles

Now armed with a web-graph *and* a formula to compute Pr$[x]$ for each web-page, you could be forgiven for thinking that we are done. There is a subtle but important problem lucking behind the scenes however. Look again at

$$\Pr[x] = \frac{1-p}{n} + p \cdot \left(\sum_{y \in \text{into}(x)} \frac{\Pr[y]}{|\text{from}(y)|} \right),$$

An aside: root finding with the iterative Newton-Raphson method

A good example to illustrate the concept of using iterative methods is the Newton-Raphson [21] method for computing the **roots** of a function δ, i.e., an x such that

$$\delta(x) = 0.$$

If you think about the case of finding the square root of an integer y, this amounts to finding an x such that $x^2 = y$ meaning $\delta(x) = x^2 - y = 0$. Skipping a lot of theory that explains why, we do so using the relationship

$$x_{i+1} = x_i - \frac{\delta(x_i)}{\delta'(x_i)}$$

where δ' is the derivative of δ; here, since $\delta(x) = x^2 - y = 0$, we know $\delta'(x) = 2 \cdot x$. The important thing is that the left-hand side shows how to compute the $(i+1)$-th element in a sequence of progressively more accurate solutions, given the i-th such element on the right-hand side. For example, imagine we have $y = 4321$ and want to compute $x = \sqrt{y}$. First we make a guess at x, say $x_0 = 100$, and then iterate use of the recurrence to produce the following sequence:

$$x_1 = x_0 - \frac{\delta(x_0)}{\delta'(x_0)} = 100.000 - \frac{5679.000}{200.000} = 71.605$$

$$x_2 = x_1 - \frac{\delta(x_1)}{\delta'(x_1)} = 71.605 - \frac{806.276}{143.210} = 65.974$$

$$x_3 = x_2 - \frac{\delta(x_2)}{\delta'(x_2)} = 65.974 - \frac{31.697}{131.949} = 65.734$$

$$x_4 = x_3 - \frac{\delta(x_3)}{\delta'(x_3)} = 65.734 - \frac{0.057}{131.468} = 65.734$$

$$x_5 = x_4 - \frac{\delta(x_4)}{\delta'(x_4)} = 65.734 - \frac{0.000}{131.468} = 65.734$$

$$\vdots \qquad \vdots \qquad \vdots$$

Eventually, the changes in our solution get very small and we can say they **converge**. We need a **termination criteria** to detect this, but in our example this is easy since we can check whether $\text{abs}(x_i^2 - y)$ is small enough to consider that x_i as correct: here we might say that because

$$\text{abs}(65.734^2 - 4321) = \text{abs}(4320.958 - 4321) = 0.041$$

is small enough, $x = x_5 = 65.734 \simeq \sqrt{4321}$ is an acceptable solution.

keeping in mind the goal is to compute the left-hand side. How? There is no hidden trick: to get the left-hand side, we just evaluate the right-hand side as with any equality. But the right-hand side includes $\Pr[y]$, so how do we compute this? Use the formula again! Now we have a chicken-and-egg style problem: we cannot compute $\Pr[x]$ until we already know $\Pr[y]$ for all $y \in V$, which is then a cyclic argument (*literally*, because the problem stems from cycles in the web-graph).

Fortunately, we can resolve this using some slightly more advanced probability theory. The basic idea is that the random surfer model implicitly includes a notion of time: the random surfer browses web-pages indefinitely, but it does so step-by-step. Instead of thinking of $\Pr[x]$, as we have done so far, we make an alteration by letting $\Pr[x^{(t)}]$ denote the probability that the random surfer visits web-page x in step (or at time) t. If we count the steps as starting at $t = 0$, then

$$\Pr[a^{(0)}] = \Pr[b^{(0)}] = \Pr[c^{(0)}] = \Pr[d^{(0)}] = \Pr[e^{(0)}] = \Pr[f^{(0)}] = \frac{1}{6}.$$

Hopefully this makes sense: we have to start *somewhere*, and since there are $n = 6$ web-pages then each one has probability $\frac{1}{n} = \frac{1}{6}$ of being the starting point. What now? Well, at step $t = 1$ one or other of the events occurs and the random surfer visits another web-page. Imagine the random surfer starts by visiting web-page b at step $t = 0$ for example; what is the probability it visits web-page d at step $t + 1$? We can answer this by looking at how probable the two events are in this case:

1. It might visit d with probability $1 - p$, by loading the web-page at random. There is a $\frac{1}{n}$ probability of visiting any specific web-page of the n in total, so a $\frac{1}{6}$ probability of visiting d. This means a $\frac{1-p}{6}$ probability overall.
2. It might visit d with probability p, by following a random link. There are $|\text{from}(y)|$ links from any given web-page y, so $|\text{from}(b)| = |\{a, d, e\}| = 3$ from b specifically. Only one of those links is to d though, so the probability of following that one specifically is $\frac{1}{3}$. This means a $\frac{p}{3}$ probability overall.

Putting this together, we can write

$$\Pr[d^{(t+1)} \mid b^{(t)}] = \frac{1-p}{6} + \frac{p}{3}$$

where the left-hand side means the probability of visiting web-page d in step $t + 1$ having visited web-page b in step t; this is an example of **conditional probability** [4].

Of course this is only one way we might visit d. To be complete, we need to take into account that we could follow a link from *any* web-page to it. We can follow the same reasoning as above, and find the following:

$$\Pr[d^{(t+1)} \mid a^{(t)}] = \frac{1-p}{6} + \frac{p}{2}$$

$$\Pr[d^{(t+1)} \mid b^{(t)}] = \frac{1-p}{6} + \frac{p}{3}$$

$$\Pr[d^{(t+1)} \mid c^{(t)}] = \frac{1-p}{6} + \frac{p}{1}$$

$$\Pr[d^{(t+1)} \mid d^{(t)}] = \frac{1-p}{6} + 0$$

$$\Pr[d^{(t+1)} \mid e^{(t)}] = \frac{1-p}{6} + 0$$

$$\Pr[d^{(t+1)} \mid f^{(t)}] = \frac{1-p}{6} + \frac{p}{5}$$

What we want though, is what is the probability of visiting web-page d in step $t+1$ outright *not* as part of some condition. All this means is we combine all possible ways of visiting d per the above. Keeping in mind that the sum of $\Pr[y^{(t)}]$ for all $y \in V$ must be 1 since these are probabilities, we end up with the following:

$$\Pr[d^{(t+1)}] = \Pr[d^{(t+1)} \mid a^{(t)}] \cdot \Pr[a^{(t)}] + \Pr[d^{(t+1)} \mid b^{(t)}] \cdot \Pr[b^{(t)}]$$
$$+ \Pr[d^{(t+1)} \mid c^{(t)}] \cdot \Pr[c^{(t)}] + \Pr[d^{(t+1)} \mid d^{(t)}] \cdot \Pr[d^{(t)}]$$
$$+ \Pr[d^{(t+1)} \mid e^{(t)}] \cdot \Pr[e^{(t)}] + \Pr[d^{(t+1)} \mid f^{(t)}] \cdot \Pr[f^{(t)}]$$

$$= \left(\frac{1-p}{6} + \frac{p}{2}\right) \cdot \Pr[a^{(t)}] + \left(\frac{1-p}{6} + \frac{p}{3}\right) \cdot \Pr[b^{(t)}]$$
$$+ \left(\frac{1-p}{6} + \frac{p}{1}\right) \cdot \Pr[c^{(t)}] + \left(\frac{1-p}{6} + 0\right) \cdot \Pr[d^{(t)}]$$
$$+ \left(\frac{1-p}{6} + 0\right) \cdot \Pr[e^{(t)}] + \left(\frac{1-p}{6} + \frac{p}{5}\right) \cdot \Pr[f^{(t)}]$$

$$= \frac{1-p}{6} + p \cdot \left(\frac{\Pr[a^{(t)}]}{2} + \frac{\Pr[b^{(t)}]}{3} + \frac{\Pr[c^{(t)}]}{1} + \frac{\Pr[f^{(t)}]}{5}\right)$$

Each term on the right-hand side multiplies the probability of visiting some web-page x in step $t+1$ having visited another one y at step t, i.e.,

$$\Pr[x^{(t+1)} \mid y^{(t)}],$$

with the probability of actually having visited y at step t, i.e.,

$$\Pr[y^{(t)}].$$

All such terms are added together, because we want to know the probability of any one of them occurring. Doing a similar thing for each web-page, we end up with

$$\Pr[a^{(t+1)}] = \frac{1-p}{6} + p \cdot \left(\frac{\Pr[b^{(t)}]}{3} + \frac{\Pr[f^{(t)}]}{5}\right)$$

$$\Pr[b^{(t+1)}] = \frac{1-p}{6} + p \cdot \left(\frac{\Pr[d^{(t)}]}{3} + \frac{\Pr[f^{(t)}]}{5}\right)$$

$$\Pr[c^{(t+1)}] = \frac{1-p}{6} + p \cdot \left(\frac{\Pr[a^{(t)}]}{2} + \frac{\Pr[f^{(t)}]}{5}\right)$$

$$\Pr\left[d^{(t+1)}\right] = \frac{1-p}{6} + p \cdot \left(\frac{\Pr[a^{(t)}]}{2} + \frac{\Pr[b^{(t)}]}{3} + \frac{\Pr[c^{(t)}]}{1} + \frac{\Pr[f^{(t)}]}{5}\right)$$

$$\Pr\left[e^{(t+1)}\right] = \frac{1-p}{6} + p \cdot \left(\frac{\Pr[b^{(t)}]}{3} + \frac{\Pr[d^{(t)}]}{3} + \frac{\Pr[f^{(t)}]}{5}\right)$$

$$\Pr\left[f^{(t+1)}\right] = \frac{1-p}{6} + p \cdot \left(\frac{\Pr[d^{(t)}]}{3} + \frac{\Pr[e^{(t)}]}{1}\right)$$

or, generalising this for *any* given web-page x,

$$\Pr\left[x^{(t+1)}\right] = \frac{1-p}{n} + p \cdot \left(\sum_{y \in \text{into}(x)} \frac{\Pr[y^{(t)}]}{|\text{from}(y)|}\right).$$

Unsurprisingly, this looks a like the formula we started with. The crucial difference is that on the left-hand side we now refer to step $t+1$ (values relating to which are unknown), whereas on the right-hand side we *only* refer to step t (values relating to which we know). That might not *seem* like a big difference, but is solves our chicken-and-egg problem: finally, we can compute actual PageRank values.

Using an Iterative Method to Compute Results

To do so, we draw on use of **iterative methods** [18] elsewhere in Mathematics. The underlying idea is that instead of computing a solution directly, we compute a sequence of approximate solutions each of which is more accurate (i.e., closer to the real solution) than the last: we start with an approximation x_0, then use a function δ to iteratively compute

$$x_{i+1} = \delta(x_i)$$

forming the next, $(i+1)$-th approximation from the last, i-th one. At some i-th step the process will converge, meaning x_i is then accurate enough to accept as the solution. This general description should seem similar to what we developed above. Remember that we want to compute

$$\Pr\left[x^{(t+1)}\right] = \frac{1-p}{n} + p \cdot \left(\sum_{y \in \text{into}(x)} \frac{\Pr[y^{(t)}]}{|\text{from}(y)|}\right),$$

so, following the above, δ is basically just the PageRank formula with a right-hand side relating to the last, t-th approximation and a left-hand side relating to the next, $(t+1)$-th approximation. To adopt the same approach however, we need to resolve one minor difference: in the general description we are only interested in one x, whereas we want a solution for each web-pages in the web-graph, i.e., all $x \in V$ or n solutions in total. To cope, we combine all n formula into one using the matrix form of what is then a system of n **linear equations** [31]:

$$
\begin{pmatrix} \Pr[a^{(t+1)}] \\ \Pr[b^{(t+1)}] \\ \Pr[c^{(t+1)}] \\ \Pr[d^{(t+1)}] \\ \Pr[e^{(t+1)}] \\ \Pr[f^{(t+1)}] \end{pmatrix} = \left(\frac{1-p}{n} \right) \cdot \begin{pmatrix} 1 \\ 1 \\ 1 \\ 1 \\ 1 \\ 1 \end{pmatrix} + p \cdot \begin{pmatrix} 0 & \frac{1}{3} & 0 & 0 & 0 & \frac{1}{5} \\ 0 & 0 & 0 & \frac{1}{3} & 0 & \frac{1}{5} \\ \frac{1}{2} & 0 & 0 & 0 & 0 & \frac{1}{5} \\ \frac{1}{2} & \frac{1}{3} & 1 & 0 & 0 & \frac{1}{5} \\ 0 & \frac{1}{3} & 0 & \frac{1}{3} & 0 & \frac{1}{5} \\ 0 & 0 & 0 & \frac{1}{3} & 1 & 0 \end{pmatrix} \cdot \begin{pmatrix} \Pr[a^{(t)}] \\ \Pr[b^{(t)}] \\ \Pr[c^{(t)}] \\ \Pr[d^{(t)}] \\ \Pr[e^{(t)}] \\ \Pr[f^{(t)}] \end{pmatrix}
$$

This could be simplified into

$$
\mathbf{x}^{(t+1)} = \delta\left(\mathbf{x}^{(t)}\right) = \mathbf{b} + A \cdot \mathbf{x}^{(t)}
$$

where $\mathbf{x}$ is now a column vector capturing the PageRank values for *all* web-pages rather than just one, while A and $\mathbf{b}$ are a constant column vector and a matrix respectively (the latter of which is derived from link structure in the web-graph). We already informally decided that an appropriate initial approximation would be

$$
\mathbf{x}^{(0)} = \begin{pmatrix} \frac{1}{n} \\ \frac{1}{n} \\ \vdots \\ \frac{1}{n} \end{pmatrix}
$$

i.e., an n-element column vector whose elements are all $\frac{1}{n}$. So, using this we can proceed to iteratively compute

$$
\begin{aligned}
\mathbf{x}^{(1)} &= \delta\left(\mathbf{x}^{(0)}\right) = \mathbf{b} + A \cdot \mathbf{x}^{(0)} \\
\mathbf{x}^{(2)} &= \delta\left(\mathbf{x}^{(1)}\right) = \mathbf{b} + A \cdot \mathbf{x}^{(1)} \\
&= \mathbf{b} + A \cdot \left(\mathbf{b} + A \cdot \mathbf{x}^{(0)}\right) \\
&= \mathbf{b} + A \cdot \mathbf{b} + A^2 \mathbf{x}^{(0)}
\end{aligned}
$$

$$
\vdots \qquad \vdots
$$

$$
\mathbf{x}^{(t+1)} = \delta\left(\mathbf{x}^{(t)}\right) = \left(\sum_{i=0}^{t-1} A^i \right) \cdot \mathbf{b} + A^t \cdot \mathbf{x}^{(0)}
$$

until at some t-th step the process converges, meaning $\mathbf{x}^{(t)}$ is then accurate enough to accept as the solution.

Challenge (task #29)   If you consider the *real* web rather than the examples presented, the value of n is large and hence the value of $\Pr[x]$ for any given x will be very small; numerical precision [27] becomes a problem. How can this problem be resolved?

Selecting the Probability p

The only remaining question is what value we should choose for p, the probability which controls the random surfer model: a larger p means there is a higher probability the random surfer opts to follow a random link, whereas a smaller p means a higher probability it loads a random web-page. It is quite important to find a balance, because taken to an extreme,

- if p is *too* large then the random surfer might never encounter poorly connected web-pages at all (since it is less likely to load them at random), whereas
- if p is *too* small then we sort of ignore the web-graph structure (since it is less likely to follow any given link), which of course contradicts the original aim.

A little more formally, p also influences how quickly the iterative method will arrive at a solution: a larger p places more emphasis on following links, meaning their influence will spread[6] more quickly, and vice versa. In their original research paper describing a prototype **Google** web-search system, Sergey Brin and Larry Page quote $p = 0.85$; it is less clear what **Google** use now, but we will stick with this as a reasonable guess.

Concrete PageRank Values for the Example Web-Graph

Now, *finally*, we can actually compute the PageRank values themselves. Recall that we now have a formula

$$\mathbf{x}^{(t+1)} = \delta\big(\mathbf{x}^{(t)}\big) = \mathbf{b} + A \cdot \mathbf{x}^{(t)}$$

which allows an iterative method of computing a solution; each part of the formula is now specified, in the sense that our example web-graph shown in Fig. 5.4b tells us that $n = 6$ and

$$A = \begin{pmatrix} 0 & \frac{1}{3} & 0 & 0 & 0 & \frac{1}{5} \\ 0 & 0 & 0 & \frac{1}{3} & 0 & \frac{1}{5} \\ \frac{1}{2} & 0 & 0 & 0 & 0 & \frac{1}{5} \\ \frac{1}{2} & \frac{1}{3} & 1 & 0 & 0 & \frac{1}{5} \\ 0 & \frac{1}{3} & 0 & \frac{1}{3} & 0 & \frac{1}{5} \\ 0 & 0 & 0 & \frac{1}{3} & 1 & 0 \end{pmatrix}.$$

Likewise, we know that

$$\mathbf{b} = \begin{pmatrix} \frac{1}{40} \\ \frac{1}{40} \\ \frac{1}{40} \\ \frac{1}{40} \\ \frac{1}{40} \\ \frac{1}{40} \end{pmatrix}$$

---

[6]This also explains why in various descriptions, including the original research paper, p is termed a **damping factor** (or **damping ratio**); this term stems from description of a similar feature of physical systems [6].

and

$$
\mathbf{x}^{(0)} = \begin{pmatrix} \frac{1}{6} \\ \frac{1}{6} \\ \frac{1}{6} \\ \vdots \\ \frac{1}{6} \end{pmatrix}.
$$

We therefore produce the following sequence of approximate but concrete solutions:

	$\mathbf{x}^{(0)}$	$\mathbf{x}^{(1)}$	$\mathbf{x}^{(2)}$	$\mathbf{x}^{(3)}$	$\mathbf{x}^{(4)}$	$\mathbf{x}^{(5)}$	
$\Pr[a^{(t)}]$	0.166	0.101	0.090	0.108	0.104	0.104	···
$\Pr[b^{(t)}]$	0.166	0.101	0.150	0.133	0.133	0.134	···
$\Pr[c^{(t)}]$	0.166	0.124	0.104	0.104	0.113	0.110	···
$\Pr[d^{(t)}]$	0.166	0.313	0.238	0.235	0.239	0.244	···
$\Pr[e^{(t)}]$	0.166	0.148	0.179	0.176	0.171	0.171	···
$\Pr[f^{(t)}]$	0.166	0.214	0.239	0.244	0.241	0.238	···

We could continue of course, but the values in iteration 4 versus those in iteration 5 already show little change. Using this as a termination criteria, we take $\mathbf{x}^{(5)}$ as our solution: these are the probabilities the random surfer will visit each web-page in our web-graph. For instance, it visits a with probability 0.104, i.e., about 10 percent of the time.

Implement (task #30) The results presented above relate to Fig. 5.4b, i.e., the web-graph that has been amended to cope with any sink web-pages (in this case just f). Try to
1. reproduce these results yourself, then
2. do the same thing with Fig. 5.4a, the original web-graph. Compare the results with each other: what do you notice, and how do you explain each identifiable difference?

5.4   Putting It All Together: Using PageRank to Produce Web-Search Results

As noted, PageRank is only one component in the Google web-search system: it forms part of the final stage outlined in Sect. 5.1.2 by ranking (or sorting) the set of results produced for some search query. To wrap-up and meet the challenge of explaining how the system works, it makes sense to look at how and where PageRank fits in. To start with, in the offline phase, we
1. use a web-crawler to build a web-graph and summary of content for each web-page, then
2. compute PageRank values for each web-page in the web-graph.

For our limited example, the outcome of this phase can be summarised as follows

$$
\begin{array}{ll}
\{\text{"apple", "orange"}\} \in a & \Pr[a] = 0.104 \\
\{\text{"apple", "banana"}\} \in b & \Pr[b] = 0.134 \\
\{\text{"banana", "orange"}\} \in c & \Pr[c] = 0.110 \\
\{\text{"apple", "banana"}\} \in d & \Pr[d] = 0.244 \\
\{\text{"apple", "pear"}\} \in e & \Pr[e] = 0.171 \\
\{\text{"banana", "pear"}\} \in f & \Pr[f] = 0.238
\end{array}
$$

in the sense that web-page a is viewed as containing content relating to the words "apple" and "orange", and has a PageRank of 0.104. Now, imagine a user gives us a search query q during the online phase. We need to

1. match web-pages with the query in order to build R, an initial set of results, then
2. take the web-pages in R, and sort them according to their PageRank values to produce the results actually presented for the user.

The first step depends a lot on the type of queries we want to allow, but given the simple form of content our web-pages house, imagine a simple form of query that is just a single word: we want the set of results to give us the web-pages which are most relevant, ranked by their PageRank-decided importance. Consider the following for example:

- If $q = $ "orange", the initial set of results is $R = \{a, c\}$. Given

$$
\begin{array}{l}
\Pr[a] = 0.104 \\
\Pr[c] = 0.110
\end{array}
$$

the results are displayed with web-page c first, then a.

- If $q = $ "apple", the initial set of results is $R = \{a, b, d, e\}$. Given

$$
\begin{array}{l}
\Pr[a] = 0.104 \\
\Pr[b] = 0.134 \\
\Pr[d] = 0.244 \\
\Pr[e] = 0.171
\end{array}
$$

the results are displayed with web-page d first, then e, b and finally a.

Even with such simple web-pages and queries, you see the PageRank concept in action. For instance, a, b, d and e are all relevant for the query "apple". Both a and b have links to d: each link source can be viewed as attesting to the importance of the link target, meaning d ends up with a (relatively) high PageRank value and is displayed first.

Search Engine Optimisation (SEO) [30] is the art of designing web-pages so they appear in web-search results more often and/or with a higher ranking than normal; this might be used in a marketing strategy, where the overall goal is that users visit the web-page more often.

Various acceptable and unacceptable SEO methods exist: do some research into both sides of this arms race, i.e.,

1. how web-page owners might try to inflate their PageRank and hence get ranked higher in a set of results, and
2. how Google identify and eliminate unfair SEO practices which skew their results and, arguably, devalue PageRank.

Given a small example, it is hard to see the value PageRank gives in general. There are two related take-away points from this chapter. First, once n grows large enough, a huge number of web-pages will always be deemed relevant for any given query. Put another way, without PageRank we would almost be back to square one: there would be so many web-pages like a, b and e that match, without PageRank to help us we would be tasked with picking out d by hand. Second, given the benefit PageRank provides, you may have previously thought of it as complex or even magic in some way (if you knew it existed at all). In reality however, we have explained more or less the entire thing by taking a 2-step strategy:

1. model various problems in a way we can more easily understand and reason about, and
2. apply fundamental but fairly simple Mathematics (i.e., probability and graph theory, and iterative methods) and Computer Science (i.e., algorithms) to produce solutions.

Although the techniques themselves might not be applicable to all problems, the general strategy *is*. This makes PageRank a great example, and advert, for Computer Science as a whole.

References

1.   Wikipedia: AdSense. https://en.wikipedia.org/wiki/AdSense
2.   Wikipedia: AdWords. http://en.wikipedia.org/wiki/AdWords
3.   Wikipedia: Breadth-first search. https://en.wikipedia.org/wiki/Breadth-first_search
4.   Wikipedia: Conditional probability. http://en.wikipedia.org/wiki/Conditional_probability
5.   Wikipedia: Cycle. http://en.wikipedia.org/wiki/Cycle_(graph_theory)
6.   Wikipedia: Damping ratio. http://en.wikipedia.org/wiki/Damping_ratio
7.   Wikipedia: Depth-first search. http://en.wikipedia.org/wiki/Depth-first_search
8.   Wikipedia: Graph. http://en.wikipedia.org/wiki/Graph_(mathematics)
9.   Wikipedia: Graph theory. http://en.wikipedia.org/wiki/Graph_theory
10.   Wikipedia: Graph traversal. http://en.wikipedia.org/wiki/Graph_traversal
11.   Wikipedia: Hyperlink. http://en.wikipedia.org/wiki/Hyperlink
12.   Wikipedia: Hyperlink-Induced Topic Search (HITS). http://en.wikipedia.org/wiki/HITS_algorithm

13. Wikipedia: Hypertext. http://en.wikipedia.org/wiki/Hypertext
14. Wikipedia: HyperText Mark-up Language (HTML). http://en.wikipedia.org/wiki/HTML
15. Wikipedia: HyperText Transfer Protocol (HTTP). http://en.wikipedia.org/wiki/Hypertext_Transfer_Protocol
16. Wikipedia: Impact factor. http://en.wikipedia.org/wiki/Impact_factor
17. Wikipedia: Information retrieval. http://en.wikipedia.org/wiki/Information_retrieval
18. Wikipedia: Iterative method. http://en.wikipedia.org/wiki/Iterative_method
19. Wikipedia: Mark-up language. http://en.wikipedia.org/wiki/Markup_language
20. Wikipedia: Meta element. http://en.wikipedia.org/wiki/Meta_element
21. Wikipedia: Newton-Raphson method. https://en.wikipedia.org/wiki/Newton's_method
22. Wikipedia: On-Line System (NLS). http://en.wikipedia.org/wiki/NLS_(computer_system)
23. Wikipedia: Online and offline. http://en.wikipedia.org/wiki/Online_and_offline
24. Wikipedia: Open Directory Project (ODP). http://en.wikipedia.org/wiki/Open_Directory_Project
25. Wikipedia: PageRank. http://en.wikipedia.org/wiki/PageRank
26. Wikipedia: Pre-computation. http://en.wikipedia.org/wiki/Precomputation
27. Wikipedia: Precision. http://en.wikipedia.org/wiki/Precision_(computer_science)
28. Wikipedia: Random walk. http://en.wikipedia.org/wiki/Random_walk
29. Wikipedia: Robots exclusion standard. http://en.wikipedia.org/wiki/Robots_Exclusion_Standard
30. Wikipedia: Search engine optimization. http://en.wikipedia.org/wiki/Search_engine_optimization
31. Wikipedia: System of linear equations. https://en.wikipedia.org/wiki/System_of_linear_equations
32. Wikipedia: The mother of all demos. http://en.wikipedia.org/wiki/The_Mother_of_All_Demos
33. Wikipedia: Top Level Domain (TLD). http://en.wikipedia.org/wiki/Top-level_domain
34. Wikipedia: Tree. https://en.wikipedia.org/wiki/Tree_(graph_theory)
35. Wikipedia: Web-crawler. http://en.wikipedia.org/wiki/Web_crawler
36. Wikipedia: Web-directory. http://en.wikipedia.org/wiki/Web_directory
37. Wikipedia: Web-graph. http://en.wikipedia.org/wiki/Webgraph
38. Wikipedia: Web indexing. http://en.wikipedia.org/wiki/Web_indexing
39. Wikipedia: Web-search engine. http://en.wikipedia.org/wiki/Web_search_engine
40. Wikipedia: Web-search query. http://en.wikipedia.org/wiki/Web_search_query
41. Wikipedia: World Wide Web. http://en.wikipedia.org/wiki/World_Wide_Web
42. Wikipedia: World Wide Web Virtual Library (WWWVL). http://en.wikipedia.org/wiki/World_Wide_Web_Virtual_Library

Part II
Examples from Information Security

Using Short Programs to Make and Break Historical Ciphers

6

It might seem hard to imagine, but in early 1587 Mary Stewart (or Mary Queen of Scots) [6] was sitting in a jail cell, most likely cursing the subject of **cryptography**. Around a year or so beforehand, Mary was imprisoned in Chartley Hall as a result of her increasingly tense relationship with the then Queen, Elizabeth I. Having been placed under close observation, Mary was only able to communicate with her allies using messages smuggled in and out of the jail inside beer barrels. However, to prevent the messages being used against her should they be discovered, Mary used a system of encoding that substituted characters and common words with a variety of symbols. This gave Mary enough confidence that, while still in jail, she instigated a plot to overthrow Elizabeth: what we now know as the **Babington Plot** is named after her chief conspirator, Anthony Babington. Unbeknown to them, messages sent between Mary and Babington were being intercepted by a double agent, then analysed by an espionage team established by Sir Francis Walsingham. The messages were processed by Thomas Phelippes, who carefully copied their content before resealing and sending them to their intended recipient. Phelippes eventually worked out the encoding system used, and the plot was uncovered when Phelippes took a real message from Mary and added a forged postscript that asked Babington for the names of the conspirators. The resulting proof of conspiracy led to the arrest of Babington and subsequent execution of Mary.

Historical significance aside, the same underlying issue in this story has reoccurred again and again. In 2006, for instance, the famed Mafia boss Bernardo Provenzano was captured for much the same reason as Mary Stewart was executed. Provenzano's encoded notes, including orders to his henchmen and so on, were decoded by police who were then able to capture him. The issue, basically, is that while both Stewart *and* Provenzano clearly understood the need for secrecy, they lacked the range of formal techniques offered by modern cryptography.

Almost all terms used above can be translated into a modern setting. We still talk about encoding messages, but now call this **encryption**, a technique that is used to ensure the secrecy of messages. An unencrypted message is called a **plaintext**, whereas an encrypted message is called a **ciphertext**. In the context of Mary Stewart, a plaintext was formed from characters of the English alphabet while a ci-

D. Page, N. Smart, *What Is Computer Science?*,
Undergraduate Topics in Computer Science, DOI 10.1007/978-3-319-04042-4_6,
© Springer International Publishing Switzerland 2014

phertext was formed from an alphabet of abstract symbols. We still use the term alphabet to describe the symbols used to form plaintext and ciphertext, but they are more likely to be sequences of bits or bytes that can be processed by a computer. Put another way, we still think about a **sender** and a **receiver** who are communicating messages, but the message is more likely to be an electronic file communicated over a network such as the Internet than written on paper. As a result, either the sender and/or receiver might also be a computer rather than a human. Finally, interception and attempted decryption of messages also has an analogy in communication as we use it today. We call the party trying to do this an **attacker** or **adversary**, while the art of trying to decrypt a message that should be kept secret would be termed **cryptanalysis**. Whereas the encoding methods used by Stewart and Provenzano were eventually **broken** via cryptanalysis of some sort, the design of modern encryption schemes is intended to resist even the most capable attacker.

As with any topic that has evolved in this way, study of basic techniques can still offer insight into modern practise. Our aim here is to look at two types of historical **cipher** (i.e., methods of encryption) in a very practical way. In each case we describe how the cipher works, how it can be broken via cryptanalysis, and how both aspects can be reproduced using single-line (or at least very short) BASH commands.

6.1   Shift Ciphers

Apparently, Julius Caesar knew about cryptography. Chronicling the life of the Roman leader in *De Vita Caesarum, Divus Iulius*, Suetonius wrote:

> *If he had anything confidential to say, he wrote it in cipher, that is, by so changing the order of the letters of the alphabet, that not a word could be made out. If anyone wishes to decipher these, and get at their meaning, he must substitute the fourth letter of the alphabet, namely D, for A, and so with the others.*

This should sound familiar: Caesar was doing something similar to Mary Stewart in the sense that he was translating characters in a plaintext message into other characters to form a ciphertext message. We use the name **shift cipher** [2] to describe the method of translation used by Caesar. ROT13 [10], a modern day equivalent of the same method, is still used to hide solutions to puzzles in newspapers and so on.

6.1.1   Encryption and Decryption

3-Place Shifts
We can describe the method used by Caesar using two functions

$$
\text{ENC}(x) = \begin{cases}
\text{'d'} & \text{if } x = \text{'a'} \\
\text{'e'} & \text{if } x = \text{'b'} \\
\text{'f'} & \text{if } x = \text{'c'} \\
\text{'g'} & \text{if } x = \text{'d'} \\
& \vdots \\
\text{'z'} & \text{if } x = \text{'w'} \\
\text{'a'} & \text{if } x = \text{'x'} \\
\text{'b'} & \text{if } x = \text{'y'} \\
\text{'c'} & \text{if } x = \text{'z'}
\end{cases}
\qquad
\text{DEC}(x) = \begin{cases}
\text{'a'} & \text{if } x = \text{'d'} \\
\text{'b'} & \text{if } x = \text{'e'} \\
\text{'c'} & \text{if } x = \text{'f'} \\
\text{'d'} & \text{if } x = \text{'g'} \\
& \vdots \\
\text{'w'} & \text{if } x = \text{'z'} \\
\text{'x'} & \text{if } x = \text{'a'} \\
\text{'y'} & \text{if } x = \text{'b'} \\
\text{'z'} & \text{if } x = \text{'c'}
\end{cases}
$$

Encryption works by examining each character of the plaintext message in turn. For example, where we see 'a' and want to encrypt it, we use ENC('a') to look-up the result 'd'. Or, in the other direction, if we want to decrypt 'd' then we use DEC('d') to look-up the result 'a'. The term shift cipher comes from the fact that what we are actually doing is shifting the alphabet around: in this case the shifting moves characters by three places.

To demonstrate the process on a larger example, we need something to act as plaintext. As in Chap. 1, we use text downloaded from Project Gutenberg

http://www.gutenberg.org/

There are numerous worthy examples we could use, but opt for *The Merchant of Venice* by Shakespeare. Using '△' to make it clear where the spaces are, encrypting the plaintext

't' 'h' 'e' ' △' 'm' 'e' 'r' 'c' 'h' 'a '
'n' 't' ' △' ' o ' 'f' ' △' 'v' 'e' ' n ' 'i '
'c ' 'e '

yields the ciphertext

'w ' 'k' 'h' ' △' 'p' 'h' 'u' 'f' 'k' 'd '
'q' 'w ' ' △' ' r' 'i' ' △' 'y' 'h' ' q' 'l'
'f ' 'h '

One can imagine the cipher being like a big codebook; to encrypt or decrypt messages, Caesar probably employed a trusted slave to apply the translation using tables in the codebook for reference. Obviously this is very tedious, so an important question to resolve (given we lack a slave, but on the other hand have computers) is whether encryption and decryption might be automated. One way would be to write a dedicated program for the task; since we want to focus on the concepts rather than teach programming, we will instead try to automate the process using BASH commands. First we need some plaintext to encrypt. The text for *The Merchant of Venice* will do fine: we save it as the file A.txt before translating all characters to lower-case so that our job is made a little easier (since we no longer need to consider the upper-case characters as distinct):

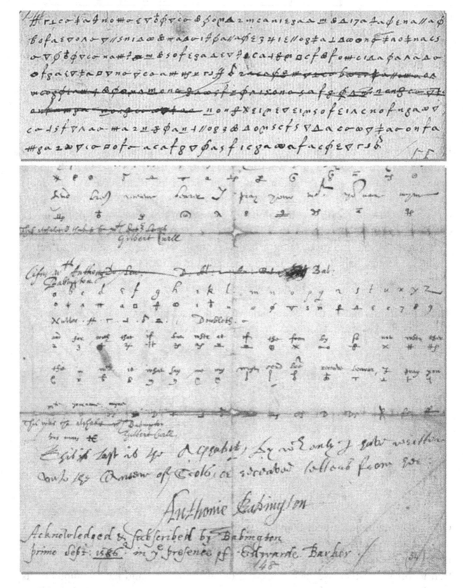

Fig. 6.1 The message that uncovered the Babington Plot: masquerading as part of a message from Mary Stewart, the postscript asks Babington to reveal the names of the conspirators using the broken cipher (public domain image, source: http://en.wikipedia.org/wiki/File: Babington_postscript.jpg)

```
bash$ wget -q -U chrome -O A.txt 'http://www.gutenberg.org/dirs/etext97/1ws1810.txt'
bash$ cat A.txt | tr [:upper:] [:lower:] > B.txt
bash$
```

Although we aim to process the whole file, this is tricky to demonstrate because of the length. Therefore, we focus on a seven line extract starting at line #274:

```
bash$ cat B.txt | tail -n +274 | head -n 7
  antonio. in sooth, i know not why i am so sad.
   it wearies me; you say it wearies you;
   but how i caught it, found it, or came by it,
   what stuff 'tis made of, whereof it is born,
   i am to learn;
   and such a want-wit sadness makes of me
   that i have much ado to know myself.
bash$
```

To encrypt and decrypt we employ the `tr` command, which we already saw in Chap. 1. Recall that `tr` reads lines of input, translates characters in those lines based on rules supplied by the user, and writes the result as output. As before, the rule is given by two sequences: all instances of a given character in the first sequence are translated into the corresponding character in the second sequence. This is easy to see with a simple example. Imagine we want to translate from ⟨'a', 'b', 'c'⟩ into ⟨'g', 'h', 'i'⟩:

```
bash$ cat | tr [a-c] [g-i]
abcdef
ghidef
bash$
```

The input "abcdef" is typed by the user; the first three characters ('a', 'b' and 'c') match those in the first sequence and are thus translated by `tr` into the corresponding characters in the second sequence ('g', 'h' and 'i'). Notice that the next three characters ('d', 'e' and 'f') do not match any in the first sequence so are passed through unaltered. Using this technique, we can encrypt and decrypt files using a 3-place shift cipher as follows:

```
bash$ cat B.txt | tr [a-cd-z] [d-za-c] > C.txt
bash$ cat C.txt | tr [d-za-c] [a-cd-z] > D.txt
bash$
```

In the first command we start with B.txt (the original file turned into lower-case), feed this to `tr`, and direct the output into the file C.txt which represents the ciphertext. The rule for translation is given by the sequences [a-cd-z], which are short-hand for

$$⟨'a', 'b', 'c', 'd', \dots, 'w', 'x', 'y', 'z'⟩,$$

i.e., the standard alphabet, and [d-za-c], meaning

$$⟨'d', 'e', 'f', 'g', \dots, 'z', 'a', 'b', 'c'⟩.$$

In other words, the first command reads input and translates 'a' into 'd', 'b' into 'e', 'c' into 'f', 'd' into 'g' and so on. In the second command we reverse the process by starting with C.txt (the ciphertext), feed this to `tr` (where the sets for translation

are reversed), and direct the output into the file D.txt. Inspecting the relevant lines
in the encrypted and decrypted files shows the result:

```
bash$ cat C.txt | tail -n +274 | head -n 7
  dqwrqlr. lq vrrwk, l nqrz qrw zkb l dp vr vdg.
   lw zhdulhv ph; brx vdb lw zhdulhv brx;
   exw krz l fdxjkw lw, irxqg lw, ru fdph eb lw,
   zkdw vwxii 'wlv pdgh ri, zkhuhri lw lv eruq,
   l dp wr ohduq;
   dqg vxfk d zdqw-zlw vdgqhvv pdnhv ri ph
   wkdw l kdyh pxfk dgr wr nqrz pbvhoi.
bash$ cat D.txt | tail -n +274 | head -n 7
  antonio. in sooth, i know not why i am so sad.
   it wearies me; you say it wearies you;
   but how i caught it, found it, or came by it,
   what stuff 'tis made of, whereof it is born,
   i am to learn;
   and such a want-wit sadness makes of me
   that i have much ado to know myself.
bash$
```

Just by looking at the text, we can see the 3-place shift cipher at work. For example,
the 'a' of "antonio" in B.txt has become a 'd' in C.txt. The file D.txt which
is the decryption *should* match the original file B.txt which was encrypted. Although the decrypted extract looks the same as the original, we can *prove* that the
whole file is the same using the diff command to perform a file comparison:

```
bash$ diff B.txt D.txt
bash$ echo ${?}
0
bash$
```

The lack of output (and exit code, as printed by the echo command) indicate there
are no differences, i.e., the encryption and subsequent decryption were successful.

Implement (task #32) This is a simple task: take any *other* plaintext of your choice
(e.g., a text file you wrote, or another one from Project
Gutenberg) and reproduce the steps above to encrypt then
decrypt it.

k-Place Shifts

At the moment, the ENC and DEC functions must be kept secret: since they are fixed
to performing 3-place shifts, if the attacker can work out their behaviour he can decrypt all messages encrypted with them. This is often called "security through ob-
scurity" and is frowned upon in modern cryptography. More usually, we try to build
schemes whose security relies only on the secrecy of some **key** rather than the actual method of encryption. This philosophy was articulated by Auguste Kerckhoffs
in the late 1800*s*, and is often called the **Kerckhoffs Principle** [5].

Kerckhoffs actually cited *six* design principles for ciphers. Find out what the others are. Based on how we communicate today compared with 1883, do you think all the principles are still relevant? If any are no longer relevant, what has changed to make this so? Are there any new principles you could add to the list?

Fortunately, we can easily generalise ENC and DEC by adding a key parameter called k that allows more general k-place shifts; the resulting functions are written ENC_k and DEC_k. To describe the generalised functions easily, we first need a way to convert characters to numbers. We could use ASCII, as in Chap. 1, but to make things easier we will use the functions

$$
\text{ORD}(x) = \begin{cases} 0 & \text{if } x = \text{`a'} \\ 1 & \text{if } x = \text{`b'} \\ 2 & \text{if } x = \text{`c'} \\ 3 & \text{if } x = \text{`d'} \\ \quad\vdots \\ 22 & \text{if } x = \text{`w'} \\ 23 & \text{if } x = \text{`x'} \\ 24 & \text{if } x = \text{`y'} \\ 25 & \text{if } x = \text{`z'} \end{cases}
\qquad
\text{CHR}(x) = \begin{cases} \text{`a'} & \text{if } x = 0 \\ \text{`b'} & \text{if } x = 1 \\ \text{`c'} & \text{if } x = 2 \\ \text{`d'} & \text{if } x = 3 \\ \quad\vdots \\ \text{`w'} & \text{if } x = 22 \\ \text{`x'} & \text{if } x = 23 \\ \text{`y'} & \text{if } x = 24 \\ \text{`z'} & \text{if } x = 25 \end{cases}
$$

where $\text{ORD}(x)$ takes a character x and returns the associated number, and $\text{CHR}(x)$ does the reverse by taking a number x and returning the associated character.

To describe what is going on, it is easier to view the scheme as another application of the **modular arithmetic** [7] we first touched on in Chap. 1. This topic appears frequently in cryptography, so it makes sense to describe it more fully now. Fortunately, we have a nice analogy to help: we are doing what is sometimes called **clock arithmetic**. Imagine someone says to you "the time is now ten o'clock; I will meet you in four hours", what time do they mean? You might say "two o'clock" instinctively, or maybe getting this answer by looking at a clock face such as Fig. 6.2 and moving clockwise 4 hours starting at 10 in order to get to 2. More formally we write this as

$$(10 + 4) = 14 \equiv 2 \pmod{12}$$

so that mod can be read to mean "remainder after division": 14 and 2 are **equivalent** modulo 12 because 14 divided by 12 gives the remainder 2. Of course, we might alter our diagram so it describes a 24-hour clock face instead; this would illustrate that the equivalence we are discussing "wraps around". We can see this easily by looking at a number line detailing x and $x \pmod{12}$:

$$
\begin{array}{llllllllllllllllll}
x & = \cdots -2 & -1 & 0 & 1 & 2 & 3 & 4 & 5 & 6 & 7 & 8 & 9 & 10 & 11 & 12 & 13 & 14 \cdots \\
x \pmod{12} & = \cdots \; 10 & 11 & 0 & 1 & 2 & 3 & 4 & 5 & 6 & 7 & 8 & 9 & 10 & 11 & 0 & 1 & 2 \cdots
\end{array}
$$

Fig. 6.2 An analogue clock
face showing the time three
o'clock

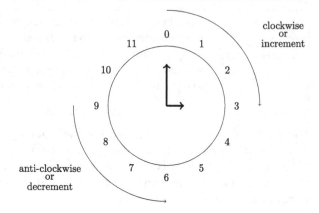

Notice that as you would expect $13 \equiv 1 \pmod{12}$, i.e., the time $13 : 00$ means one o'clock, and also that two useful facts pop out of looking at the number line:

1. Taking any x and adding 12 is the same as adding 0 because $12 \equiv 0 \pmod{12}$. For example $1 + 12 \equiv 1 \pmod{12}$.
2. If x is negative, $x \pmod{12}$ is given by $12 + x$. For example $-2 \pmod{12}$ is given by $12 + (-2) = 10$. To answer the question "the time is now four o'clock, what time was it six hours ago?" we know $4 - 6 = -2$ and hence $-2 \equiv 10 \pmod{12}$.

While talking about clock faces, 12 is the natural **modulus** to use. In general however, we can select (more or less) any integer modulus we like. What links this fact to the way we have performed encryption and decryption so far, is that both $\text{ENC}_k(x)$ and $\text{DEC}_k(x)$ can be described using modular arithmetic by setting the modulus to 26. More specifically, we can write

$$\text{ENC}_k(x) = \text{CHR}\big(\text{ORD}(x) + k \pmod{26}\big)$$

$$\text{DEC}_k(x) = \text{CHR}\big(\text{ORD}(x) - k \pmod{26}\big)$$

This is starting to get a bit complicated, so it makes sense to look at what is going on in more detail. Say we select $k = 3$ to mimic our original functions, and want to encrypt the plaintext 'a':

1. First turn 'a' into a number using $\text{ORD}('a') = 0$.
2. Next add k to get $0 + 3 = 3$, and then reduce it modulo 26 to get $3 \bmod 26 = 3$.
3. Finally, translate the number back into a character to get the result $\text{CHR}(3) = 'd'$.

In short, we have encrypted 'a' into the ciphertext 'd'. What about decryption? Essentially the same technique applies, meaning we can decrypt 'd' as follows:

1. First turn 'd' into a number using $\text{ORD}('d') = 3$.
2. Next subtract k to get $3 - 3 = 0$, and then reduce it modulo 26 to get $0 \bmod 26 = 0$.
3. Finally, translate the number back into a character to get the result $\text{CHR}(0) = 'a'$.

Notice that by opting to include the mod 26 operation we have ensured that when adding or subtracting k to a number, the result will "wrap around" to the start or end of the alphabet when turning the number back into a character. We can see this more clearly with another example, this time we encrypt the plaintext 'x':

1. First turn 'x' into a number using $\text{ORD}('x') = 23$.
2. Next add k to get $23 + 3 = 26$, and then reduce it modulo 26 to get $26 \bmod 26 = 0$.
3. Finally, translate the number back into a character to get the result $\text{CHR}(0) = 'a'$.

The corresponding decryption of the ciphertext 'a' is as follows:

1. First turn 'a' into a number using $\text{ORD}('a') = 0$.
2. Next subtract k to get $0 - 3 = -3$, and then reduce it modulo 26 to get $-3 \bmod 26 = 23$.
3. Finally, translate the number back into a character to get the result $\text{CHR}(23) = 'x'$.

One can view all this as a mechanism to generate new codebooks. Whereas before Caesar just had one codebook, he can now generate a new one for *each* value of k. Either way, we now have a situation where only k need be kept secret. An attacker might know the method of encryption but without the value of k, he cannot decrypt messages. Better still, we are free to select a *different* k for each message so that even if an attacker recovers the key for one message, he still would not necessarily know the key for another message.

6.1.2 Cryptanalysis

We already fixed one problem with the initial 3-place shift cipher by making it into a general k-place version; this gave us a cipher that at least made some attempt to comply with the Kerckhoffs Principle. You might have guessed, however, that this is not really enough, and that the cipher is *still* easy to cryptanalyse:

- Although we could have included space as a character in the plaintext alphabet, we did not do so. As such, the word structure of the plaintext is retained in the ciphertext when we encrypt it. We can identify words in both simply by spotting where the space characters are.
- A given character is translated the same way *every* time it occurs. For example if we encrypt one 'a' in the plaintext into a 'd' in the ciphertext, we know that *all* occurrences of 'a' will encrypt to 'd'.
- Even though we are free to select k, there are not that many choices. Selecting $k = 27$ and shifting the alphabet by 27 places, for example, is the same as $k = 1$ because of the "wrap around" effect. So basically there are only 26 possible keys. In fact with $k = 0$ the ciphertext is the same as the plaintext, so actually there are probably more like 25 useful keys.

How can we use these features to cryptanalyse the cipher, for example to decrypt an encrypted message we have intercepted? When presented with the ciphertext we might first employ a **brute-force** attack [1]. This means that we just try *all* the keys. Although laborious, there are only 26 of them so if the key is worth finding it could be worthwhile. Caesar would probably just have 26 slaves try one key each in order to speed things up. The problem is, how do we know when we have got the right key? In our case, we have been assuming that the underlying plaintext is English so as soon as a trial decryption yields text which forms English words we know we have got the right one.

Imagine either we do not have the time to perform the brute-force attack or are just lazy and want a short cut. The next thing we could do is apply a technique called **frequency analysis** [4]. The basic idea is that for a language like English, single characters and combinations of characters occur with varying frequencies. In fact, given a large enough sample, the frequencies are characteristic of *any* text written in that same language: this means, for example, we can make a good guess if the text is English (versus German say), or predict the frequency with which characters occur in one text given frequencies in another (if they are written in the same language).

By retrieving a fresh copy of *The Merchant of Venice*

```
bash$ wget -q -U chrome -O A.txt 'http://www.gutenberg.org/dirs/etext97/1ws1810.txt'
bash$ cat A.txt | tr [:upper:] [:lower:] > B.txt
bash$
```

we can use some further BASH commands to demonstrate this:

```
bash$ cat B.txt | fold -c -w 1 | grep [[:alpha:]] | sort | uniq -c | paste -s
   7789 a         1721 b         2427 c        3748 d        11710 e
   2174 f         1724 g         6024 h        7023 i          256 j
    799 k         4272 l         2781 m        6580 n         8816 o
   1474 p           60 q         6032 r        6395 s         8733 t
   3166 u         1002 v         2284 w         180 x         2671 y
    117 z
bash$
```

The last command in particular needs some explanation. The first part of the command pipeline feeds the file B.txt (the original text turned into lower-case) into fold which splits each line into one character per-line. Since this is the first time we have used fold, a simpler example might be helpful:

```
bash$ cat | fold -c -w 1
abcd
a
b
c
d

bash$
```

Notice that the single line input of four characters typed by the user has been split into four lines each of one character. As used originally, the output of fold is then filtered to leave only alphanumeric characters (or letters and numbers), then sorted using sort and fed to uniq to count how many duplicates appear (i.e., how many times a given character exists). Finally we format the output nicely using paste, and after all that effort, hope something useful came out! The interesting thing is that some occur much more frequently than others. For example 'e' is the most used by some distance, followed by 'o', 't', 'a' and so on. You can view the result above as being somewhat indicative of English in general. Okay, it is *Shakespearean* English but more or less the same frequencies occur in modern text as well, bar the odd "ye olde" or two.

Implement (task #34) The claim above is that our character frequencies are indicative of the language. Test this claim by performing the same type of analysis on a text file written in something other than English; Project Gutenberg offers a number of French books for instance.

So imagine someone hands us some ciphertext and challenges us to tell them the key it was encrypted with. To simulate this, we will retrieve a copy of *A Midsummer Night's Dream* again by Shakespeare

```
bash$ wget -q -U chrome -O A.txt 'http://www.gutenberg.org/dirs/etext97/1ws1710.txt'
bash$ cat A.txt | tr [:upper:] [:lower:] > B.txt
bash$
```

and imagine that someone takes the plaintext B.txt, selects a k and then encrypts B.txt to give the ciphertext C.txt. Our task is to determine the unknown k given *only* C.txt. We call this scenario a **ciphertext only** attack [3] since we are given (rather than choose) the ciphertext, and also do not get the corresponding plaintext. We do not present the file C.txt, but you could obtain your own version by encrypting some text and then following the same analysis we do; the results you obtain may be slightly different, but the general method should still work.

We first examine what happens if we apply the same frequency analysis to the ciphertext (rather than the plaintext as above). All the cipher does is shift around the alphabet, basically just rearranging the table of frequencies. Employing the method as above, we get a different set of numbers; this should not be surprising since this was a different plaintext originally:

```
bash$ cat C.txt | fold -c -w 1 | grep [[:alpha:]] | sort | uniq -c | paste -s
  5195 a       6673 b       1411 c       121 d      5114 e
  5237 f       7079 g       2763 h       783 i      1886 j
   169 k       2176 l         16 m      5984 n      1310 o
  1751 p       3173 q      10178 r      1528 s      1372 t
  5035 u       5509 v         87 w       678 x      3674 y
  2544 z
bash$
```

However, the crucial thing to notice is that the relative frequency of the characters in the new results should match those in the old results. For example, in this case 'r' is the most used by some distance, followed by 'g', 'b', 'n' and so on. If we consider 'r', 'g', 'b' and 'n' to be the only reasonable way one could have encrypted 'e' then we narrow the range of possible keys to $k = 13$, $k = 2$, $k = 23$ or $k = 9$.

Consider some more evidence in the shape of the eleven line extract of ciphertext starting at line #959:

```
bash$ cat C.txt | tail -n +959 | head -n 11
  boreba. v cenl gurr tvir vg zr.
    v xabj n onax jurer gur jvyq gulzr oybjf,
    jurer bkyvcf naq gur abqqvat ivbyrg tebjf,
    dhvgr bire-pnabcvrq jvgu yhfpvbhf jbbqovar,
    jvgu fjrrg zhfx-ebsrf, naq jvgu rtynagvar;
    gurer fyrrcf gvgnavn fbzrgvzr bs gur avtug,
    yhyy'q va gurfr sybjref jvgu qnaprf naq qryvtug;
    naq gurer gur fanxr guebjf ure ranzryy'q fxva,
    jrrq jvqr rabhtu gb jenc n snvel va;
    naq jvgu gur whvpr bs guvf v'yy fgernx ure rlrf,
    naq znxr ure shyy bs ungrshy snagnfvrf.
bash$
```

On the second line of the output, we find a 1-character word 'v'. Not many of these exist in English, so basically we know either ' a' or 'i' must encrypt to 'v' which suggests $k = 21$ or $k = 13$. By this point, $k = 13$ is looking like a good choice: we could now try to decrypt the ciphertext using this key, and see what we get. Selecting $k = 13$ means translating 'a' to ' n' and so on, which means we just need to select the right sequences for `tr` and we are done:

```
bash$ cat C.txt | tr [n-za-m] [a-mn-z] > D.txt
bash$ cat D.txt | tail -n +959 | head -n 11
   oberon. i pray thee give it me.
   i know a bank where the wild thyme blows,
   where oxlips and the nodding violet grows,
   quite over-canopied with luscious woodbine,
   with sweet musk-roses, and with eglantine;
   there sleeps titania sometime of the night,
   lull'd in these flowers with dances and delight;
   and there the snake throws her enamell'd skin,
   weed wide enough to wrap a fairy in;
   and with the juice of this i'll streak her eyes,
   and make her full of hateful fantasies.
bash$
```

Even if we did not have `diff` to confirm the result as follows

```
bash$ diff B.txt D.txt
bash$ echo ${?}
0
bash$
```

it would be fairly bad luck to have selected the wrong key and get perfect Shakespearean as output, so we can conclude $k = 13$ was the right key. If we had intercepted `C.txt` from Caesar then we could decrypt his messages and get the jump on him the next time he invaded our country.

6.2   Substitution Ciphers

After generalising the 3-place shift cipher into a k-place version and still failing to produce something which can secure our messages, the next step is something called a **substitution cipher** [11]. In The Adventure of the Dancing Men, Sir Arthur Conan Doyle had his character Sherlock Holmes, *the* arch detective, encounter a cipher of this type. Holmes and Watson are confronted with a number of pictures of dancing men:

> *These hieroglyphics have evidently a meaning. If it is a purely arbitrary one, it may be impossible for us to solve it. If, on the other hand, it is systematic, I have no doubt that we shall get to the bottom of it.*

Of course, the pictures are symbols which encode a message; Holmes and Watson eventually decode the messages and solve yet another case [12]. So if substitution ciphers are important enough for the great Sherlock Holmes to worry about, then they are good enough for us as well.

6.2.1   Encryption and Decryption

Imagine we have a sequence or list of characters

$$A = \langle\,'a',\, 'b',\, 'c',\, 'd'\,\rangle.$$

Given such a sequence, the concept of a **permutation** [9] is central: if we permute the elements in a source sequence, we basically reorder them to produce a target sequence. This means that each element occurs once, but there is some translation from the source to the target sequence. We can describe an example permutation P as follows:

$$P(X) = \langle X_1, X_2, X_3, X_0 \rangle.$$

Put more simply, if we apply P to some source sequence X then the target sequence we get back has X_1 as the 0-th element, X_2 as the 1-st element, X_3 as the 2-nd element and X_0 as the 3-rd element. Applying P to the sequence A above therefore gives us

$$P(A) = \langle\,'b',\, 'c',\, 'd',\, 'a'\,\rangle.$$

Since P is simply reordering the elements, we could write down the **inverse permutation** P^{-1} which performs translation in the opposite direction. In this case

$$P^{-1}(X) = \langle X_3, X_0, X_1, X_2 \rangle$$

which means that

$$P^{-1}(A) = \langle\,'d',\, 'a',\, 'b',\, 'c'\,\rangle$$

and, more importantly, that

$$P^{-1}\big(P(A)\big) = \langle\,'a',\, 'b',\, 'c',\, 'd'\,\rangle = A.$$

The basic idea is that the key for a substitution cipher is a permutation; we still write k as the key just for continuity, so you can think of it as a name (or index) that identifies the permutation we use among all those available. The permutation tells us how to translate characters from a source sequence (i.e., the plaintext alphabet) into characters in a target sequence (i.e., the ciphertext alphabet). Of course, one can view the shift cipher as a particular form of permutation. However, the fact that the permutation is of such a particular form makes the cipher weak. We already saw that there are only 26 possible keys, which is far from ideal: a substitution cipher generalises the idea, relaxing the need for a particular form of permutation and allowing *any* permutation at all.

How many possible keys would there be using this generalised approach? We can get the answer by looking at a more general question: say we have an n-element source sequence, how many different permutations of those elements are there? The answer is n factorial or

$$n! = n \cdot (n-1) \cdot (n-2) \cdots 3 \cdot 2 \cdot 1.$$

Fig. 6.3   An example of the "dancing men" used as a cipher in *The Adventure of the Dancing Men* (public domain image, source: http://en.wikipedia.org/wiki/File:Dancing_men.png)

Why is this is the case? We start with n elements in the source sequence, so there are n choices for the first element in the target sequence. When we remove one of those choices, there are $n - 1$ choices left for the second element in the target sequence, $n - 2$ choices left for the third element and so on. So given we have $n = 26$ possible characters in our plaintext and ciphertext alphabets there are a total of

$$26! = 403291461126605635584000000$$

possible keys for the substitution cipher. This is now too big to allow searching for the key by brute-force: we need to think a bit harder if we want to break this scheme.

Each key specifies a different permutation; you can think of this as each k specifying a different, secret pair of encryption and decryption functions. Consider an example and imagine that some k specifies the functions:

$$\text{ENC}_k(x) = \begin{cases} \text{'z'} & \text{if } x = \text{'a'} \\ \text{'y'} & \text{if } x = \text{'b'} \\ \text{'x'} & \text{if } x = \text{'c'} \\ \text{'w'} & \text{if } x = \text{'d'} \\ & \vdots \\ \text{'d'} & \text{if } x = \text{'w'} \\ \text{'c'} & \text{if } x = \text{'x'} \\ \text{'b'} & \text{if } x = \text{'y'} \\ \text{'a'} & \text{if } x = \text{'z'} \end{cases} \qquad \text{DEC}_k(x) = \begin{cases} \text{'a'} & \text{if } x = \text{'z'} \\ \text{'b'} & \text{if } x = \text{'y'} \\ \text{'c'} & \text{if } x = \text{'x'} \\ \text{'d'} & \text{if } x = \text{'w'} \\ & \vdots \\ \text{'w'} & \text{if } x = \text{'d'} \\ \text{'x'} & \text{if } x = \text{'c'} \\ \text{'y'} & \text{if } x = \text{'b'} \\ \text{'z'} & \text{if } x = \text{'a'} \end{cases}$$

Although these functions are not complete (so they can fit on a page), the general idea acts as a mechanism to generate a codebook; as was the case of the k-place shift cipher, security is based on knowledge of k rather than the actual method of encryption.

Automating *this* encryption method is almost as simple as for the shift cipher. We again fetch the text of *The Merchant of Venice* text and save it as A.txt before translating all characters to lower-case:

```
bash$ wget -q -U chrome -O A.txt 'http://www.gutenberg.org/dirs/etext97/1ws1810.txt'
bash$ cat A.txt | tr [:upper:] [:lower:] > B.txt
bash$
```

Next we set up two strings, which essentially define source and target sequences, and hence the permutation we want to use. This means we can again use tr to perform the encryption and decryption:

```
bash$ S='abcdefghijklmnopqrstuvwxyz'
bash$ T='zyxwvutsrqponmlkjihgfedcba'
bash$ cat B.txt | tr ${S} ${T} > C.txt
bash$ cat C.txt | tr ${T} ${S} > D.txt
bash$
```

What does this mean? Essentially what we are saying is that the i-th character in the source sequence S should be translated into the i-th character in target sequence T so, for example, in this case an 'a' encrypts to a 'z'.

As before, we can focus on a seven line extract starting at line #274 to show the process is working as expected:

```
bash$ cat C.txt | tail -n +274 | head -n 7
 zmglmrl. rm hllgs, r pmld mlg dsb r zn hl hzw.
  rg dvzirvh nv; blf hzb rg dvzirvh blf;
  yfg sld r xzftsg rg, ulfmw rg, li xznv yb rg,
  dszg hgfuu 'grh nzwv lu, dsvivlu rg rh ylim,
  r zn gl ovzim;
  zmw hfxs z dzmg-drg hzwmvhh nzpvh lu nv
  gszg r szev nfxs zwl gl pmld nbhvou.
bash$ cat D.txt | tail -n +274 | head -n 7
 antonio. in sooth, i know not why i am so sad.
  it wearies me; you say it wearies you;
  but how i caught it, found it, or came by it,
  what stuff 'tis made of, whereof it is born,
  i am to learn;
  and such a want-wit sadness makes of me
  that i have much ado to know myself.
bash$
```

or use `diff` to show that the decrypted file is the same as the original plaintext:

```
bash$ diff B.txt D.txt
bash$ echo ${?}
0
bash$
```

6.2.2   Cryptanalysis

Since we have improved upon the shift cipher using the stronger permutation cipher, we need to consider better forms of cryptanalysis to attack it: we cannot say it prevents the previous attack, so therefore is secure! In particular, we need to consider an improved form of frequency analysis that relies on further properties of language.

The concepts of **bigrams** and **trigrams** are special cases of something called an n-**gram** [8]. An n-gram is a sub-sequence of length n taken from some other sequence; a bigram is the case where $n = 2$ and a trigram is the case where $n = 3$. Imagine we want to find all the bigrams of

$$A = \langle \text{'a'}, \text{'b'}, \text{'c'}, \text{'d'} \rangle.$$

We can formulate a solution by saying we want all the sub-sequences which look like

$$\langle A_i, A_{i+1} \rangle.$$

That is, we want all the sub-sequences formed by taking the i-th element and the $(i + 1)$-th element of A. Of course we cannot select element three as the i-th element since the $(i + 1)$-th element would not be valid, but apart from this the sub-sequences we can form are

$$\langle \text{'a'}, \text{'b'}\rangle, \langle \text{'b'}, \text{'c'}\rangle, \langle \text{'c'}, \text{'d'}\rangle.$$

You can think of a text file as just a long string, so it is easy to imagine that we could work out all the bigrams within such a file. How can we do this in practical terms? Using only existing BASH commands demands a cunning approach; imagine we have a file called A.txt which has one character per-line:

```
bash$ cat > A.txt
a
b
c
d
bash$
```

Now imagine we take the file and paste it next to itself; we can achieve this easily using the paste command:

```
bash$ paste -d ' ' A.txt A.txt
a a
b b
c c
d d
bash$
```

Believe it or not, we are almost there. All we need now do is "skew" the second column by one character. That is, if we skewed the column so that we started at 'b' rather than 'a' we would (more or less) have the bigrams one per-line. To perform the skewing, we use tail to take A.txt and copy the content starting at the second line. Pasting the result, which we call B.txt, alongside the original A.txt gives:

```
bash$ tail -n +2 A.txt > B.txt
bash$ paste -d ' ' A.txt B.txt
a b
b c
c d
d
bash$
```

Of course, we might want to eliminate the last line (this is the result of including an "invalid" index) but other than that we can build a list of all bigrams in A.txt. The case for trigrams is quite similar but we need to skew the original file by two characters and include that in our paste command as well. Suppose we apply this to *The Merchant of Venice*. First we retrieve the text and turn it into lower-case as usual; then we split the characters from B.txt into a file called E.txt where there is one character per-line and finally skew this file by one and two lines to get F.txt and G.txt:

```
bash$ wget -q -U chrome -O A.txt 'http://www.gutenberg.org/dirs/etext97/1ws1810.txt'
bash$ cat A.txt | tr [:upper:] [:lower:] > B.txt
bash$ cat B.txt | fold -c -w 1 > E.txt
bash$ tail -n +2 E.txt > F.txt
bash$ tail -n +3 E.txt > G.txt
bash$
```

Now we are ready to construct the bigrams and trigrams. Using `paste` as above we take the files `E.txt`, `F.txt` and `G.txt` and paste them into place next to each other. Then we use `grep` to throw away any invalid lines. We do this by specifying that we only want lines with two or three alphabetic characters on them (for the respective bigram and trigram case). Finally we remove the inter-character spacing using `tr` and get the bigrams and trigrams in `H.txt` and `I.txt`:

```
bash$ paste -d ' ' E.txt F.txt        | tr -d ' ' | grep .. > H.txt
bash$ paste -d ' ' E.txt F.txt G.txt  | tr -d ' ' | grep ... > I.txt
bash$
```

Next we can apply a similar approach to analysis of the bigram and trigram frequencies as we previously applied to single character frequencies. We take the input file, sort it using `sort` and feed the output to `uniq` to count how many duplicates exists (i.e., how many times a given bigram or trigram exists). Unlike single character frequencies where there were not many (since there are not many characters), there are a huge number of bigrams and trigrams: we feed the result through `sort` and `tail` to produce only the 20 most frequent:

```
bash$ cat H.txt | sort | uniq -c | sort -n -r | head -n 20 | paste -s
  2922 th      2098 he      1814 an      1592 er      1430 ou
  1283 in      1273 re      1238 or      1181 nd      1136 ha
  1013 en       995 is       990 on       974 at       820 es
   814 to       802 it       789 me       786 ar       782 ve
bash$ cat I.txt | sort | uniq -c | sort -n -r | head -n 20 | paste -s
  1438 the      800 and      722 you      468 her      456 hat
   426 for      398 ing      376 tha      347 our      338 his
   306 thi      305 ere      297 not      281 nio      276 ith
   272 hou      262 tia      259 all      256 ear      252 wit
bash$
```

If you think about it, the results are what we would expect: "th" is obviously going to occur more often than "tz" for example, and it should not be a surprise that three character words such as "the" and "and" are the most popular trigrams.

Now imagine we play the same game as before. Someone hands us some ciphertext and challenges us to tell them the key it was encrypted with. To simulate this, we first retrieve a fresh copy of *A Midsummer Night's Dream*

```
bash$ wget -q -U chrome -O A.txt 'http://www.gutenberg.org/dirs/etext97/1ws1710.txt'
bash$ cat A.txt | tr [:upper:] [:lower:] > B.txt
bash$
```

and imagine someone takes the plaintext `B.txt`, selects k then encrypts `B.txt` to give the ciphertext `C.txt`: our task is again to determine k given only `C.txt`. To avoid having to inspect the whole file, we will again focus on the eleven lines of the ciphertext starting at line #959:

```
bash$ cat C.txt | tail -n +959 | head -n 11
  ylivyz. e xvmo tfii geri et ai.
    e czyq m lmzc qfivi tfi qebj tfoai lbyqu,
    qfivi ypbexu mzj tfi zyjjezg reybit gvyqu,
    wseti yriv-kmzyxeij qetf bsukeysu qyyjlezi,
    qetf uqiit asuc-vyuiu, mzj qetf igbmztezi;
    tfivi ubiixu tetmzem uyaiteai yh tfi zegft,
    bsbb'j ez tfiui hbyqivu qetf jmzkiu mzj jibegft;
    mzj tfivi tfi uzmci tfvyqu fiv izmaibb'j ucez,
    qiij qeji izysgf ty qvmx m hmevo ez;
    mzj qetf tfi dseki yh tfeu e'bb utvimc fiv ioiu,
    mzj amci fiv hsbb yh fmtihsb hmztmueiu.
bash$
```

By now, we have a range of techniques available to us. The first step is to run a single character frequency analysis

```
bash$ cat C.txt | fold -c -w 1 | grep [[:alpha:]] | sort | uniq -c | paste -s
   2544 a        3674 b         678 c          87 d       5509 e
   5035 f        1372 g        1528 h       10178 i       3173 j
   1751 k        1310 l        5984 m          16 n       2176 o
    169 p        1886 q         783 r        2763 s       7079 t
   5237 u        5114 v         121 w        1411 x       6673 y
   5195 z
bash$
```

and then to extract the most common bigrams and trigrams:

```
bash$ cat C.txt | fold -c -w 1 > E.txt
bash$ tail -n +2 E.txt > F.txt
bash$ tail -n +3 E.txt > G.txt
bash$ paste -d ' ' E.txt F.txt          | tr -d ' ' | grep .. > H.txt
bash$ paste -d ' ' E.txt F.txt G.txt | tr -d ' ' | grep ... > I.txt
bash$ cat H.txt | sort | uniq -c | sort -n -r | head -n 20 | paste -s
   2494 tf       1990 fi       1487 iv       1330 mz       1122 ys
   1102 ez       1026 zj        913 vi        801 fm        797 iz
    787 yv        780 yz        777 eu        728 fe        726 ai
    707 iu        705 mt        677 bb        670 mv        649 et
bash$ cat I.txt | sort | uniq -c | sort -n -r | head -n 20 | paste -s
   1186 tfi       797 mzj       505 fiv       468 oys       341 fmt
    337 tfe       333 feu       328 ezg       288 hyv       275 mbb
    273 ysv       248 tfm       242 etf       236 zyt       226 ivi
    226 imv       224 qet       219 fys       211 yri       202 ebb
bash$
```

Based on all this information we can start to make some guesses about how the ciphertext was produced:

- We still do not consider spaces during encryption, so the cipher still retains the word structure and we know that '△' decrypts to '△'.
- Based on the single character frequency analysis we can be reasonably sure about at least the three most frequent characters and say that 'i' decrypts to 'e', 't' decrypts to 't' and 'y' decrypts to 'o'.
- The bigram and trigram analysis confirms the guesses above because, for example, the most frequent trigram in the ciphertext is "tfi" and so if we match this against "the" (the most frequent trigram in some general text) we confirm the likelihood of 't' decrypting to 't'. Based on further similar matching we can guess that 'f' decrypts to 'h', 'm' decrypts to 'a', 'z' decrypts to 'n' and 'j' decrypts to 'd'.
- Given we already guessed 'm' decrypts to ' a', we can guess that 'e' decrypts to 'i' since on the second line we have a one letter word and we know it cannot decrypt to 'a'.

Based on these initial guesses, and without too much effort, we can already be fairly confident about roughly a third of the key; we can start taking the ciphertext and performing a partial decryption. Considering just the first two lines of our example text:

'y' 'l' 'i' 'v' 'y' 'z' '.' '△' 'e' '△'
'x' 'v' 'm' 'o' '△' 't' 'f' 'i' 'i' '△'
'g' 'e' 'r' 'i' '△' 'e' 't' '△' 'a' 'i'
'.' 'e' '△' 'c' 'z' 'y' 'q' '△' 'm' '△'
'l' 'm' 'z' 'c' '△' 'q' 'f' 'i' 'v' 'i'
'△' 't' 'f' 'i' '△' 'q' 'e' 'b' 'j' '△'
't' 'f' 'o' 'a' 'i' '△' 'l' 'b' 'y' 'q'
'u' ','

we can already decrypt portions of it to read:

'o' 'l' 'e' 'v' 'o' 'n' '.' '△' 'i' '△'
'x' 'v' 'a' 'o' '△' 't' 'h' 'e' 'e' '△'
'g' 'i' 'r' 'e' '△' 'i' 't' '△' 'a' 'e'
'.' 'i' '△' 'c' 'n' 'o' 'q' '△' 'a' '△'
'l' 'a' 'n' 'c' '△' 'q' 'h' 'e' 'v' 'e'
'△' 't' 'h' 'e' '△' 'q' 'i' 'b' 'd' '△'
't' 'h' 'o' 'a' 'e' '△' 'l' 'b' 'o' 'q'
'u' ','

At this point we need to start working harder ... but we can still lean on some existing tools to help us. The basic idea is to start looking at the words which we know part of and narrow down the possibilities for the parts we do not know based on which real words fit the template. This is sort of like the process of filling in a crossword. For example, we can see two partially decrypted words "ae" and "thoae". We know that 'a' probably decrypts to something which will make both of these examples real words. So first we can search the standard dictionary [13] file for all two letter words which end in 'e':

```
bash$ cat /usr/share/dict/words | grep -i ^.e$ | sort | uniq | paste -s
AE     BE    Be    CE    Ce    DE    De    EE    FE    Fe
GE     Ge    HE    He    IE    Je    KE    LE    Le    ME
Me     NE    Ne    OE    Oe    PE    QE    RE    Re    SE
Se     TE    Te    VE    Ve    Xe    ae    be    ce    de
ee     fe    ge    he    ie    le    me    ne    oe    pe
qe     re    se    te    we    ye
bash$
```

This does not help much; the dictionary does not seem much good for this case! For example, the words "ve" and "qe" might be real, but do not really seem realistic possibilities for someone writing English. If we eliminate the words beginning with characters we are already confident about, this helps to reduce the possibilities; probably only "be", "me", "we" and "ye" remain. Now we can search for all five letter words that start with "th" and end with either "be", "me", "we" or "ye":

```
bash$ cat /usr/share/dict/words | grep -i ^th.be$ | sort | uniq | paste -s
Thebe    thebe
bash$ cat /usr/share/dict/words | grep -i ^th.me$ | sort | uniq | paste -s
theme    thyme
bash$ cat /usr/share/dict/words | grep -i ^th.we$ | sort | uniq | paste -s

bash$ cat /usr/share/dict/words | grep -i ^th.ye$ | sort | uniq | paste -s

bash$
```

Although "thebe" *might* be a reasonable Shakespearean word, it seems more likely
that 'a' decrypts to 'm' given the only other two words in the dictionary support this
choice. Updating our partial decryption we get:

'o' 'l' 'e' 'v' 'o' 'n' '.' '△' 'i' '△'
'x' 'v' 'a' 'o' '△' 't' 'h' 'e' 'e' '△'
'g' 'i' 'r' 'e' '△' 'i' 't' '△' 'm' 'e'
'.' 'i' '△' 'c' 'n' 'o' 'q' '△' 'a' '△'
'l' 'a' 'n' 'c' '△' 'q' 'h' 'e' 'v' 'e'
'△' 't' 'h' 'e' '△' 'q' 'i' 'b' 'd' '△'
't' 'h' 'o' 'm' 'e' '△' 'l' 'b' 'o' 'q'
'u' ','

The process can continue in a similar way, using the frequency analysis to back
up our guesses. Although we are working in a known ciphertext scenario, we can
bend the rules a bit by considering some knowledge about the plaintext (actually we
already did this by assuming it was English). Why is this not cheating? Imagine you
get an encrypted email. In this case you know that there is a high chance that the
start of the email includes the headers "to", "from", "subject" and so on, and this
type of information can help conclude our search more quickly. Fast-forwarding a
little then, we would eventually recover the whole key and hence the method of
substitution between plaintext and ciphertext characters. Using this, and in the same
way as the shift cipher example, we can test if the result of a trial decryption looks
reasonable:

```
bash$ S='abcdefghijklmnopqrstuvwxyz'
bash$ T='mlkjihgfedcbazyxwvutsrqpon'
bash$ cat C.txt | tr ${T} ${S} > D.txt
bash$ cat D.txt | tail -n +959 | head -n 11
  oberon. i pray thee give it me.
    i know a bank where the wild thyme blows,
    where oxlips and the nodding violet grows,
    quite over-canopied with luscious woodbine,
    with sweet musk-roses, and with eglantine;
    there sleeps titania sometime of the night,
    lull'd in these flowers with dances and delight;
    and there the snake throws her enamell'd skin,
    weed wide enough to wrap a fairy in;
    and with the juice of this i'll streak her eyes,
    and make her full of hateful fantasies.
bash$
```

Implement (task #35)

Find someone to work with. One of you act as the sender
of some secret plaintext message, and the other as the cryptanalysist:

1. the sender selects k, i.e., a permutation, and encrypts the
   plaintext message to produce a ciphertext, then
2. the cryptanalysist is given the ciphertext, and asked to recover k (or at least the plaintext message, partial or otherwise).

Did it work? Several things can go wrong: can you think why
the process might fail? For example, what assumptions do we
make and therefore depend on being true?

References

1.   Wikipedia: Brute-force attack. http://en.wikipedia.org/wiki/Brute_force_attack
2.   Wikipedia: Caesar cipher. http://en.wikipedia.org/wiki/Caesar_cipher
3.   Wikipedia: Ciphertext-only attack. http://en.wikipedia.org/wiki/Ciphertext-only_attack
4.   Wikipedia: Frequency analysis. http://en.wikipedia.org/wiki/Frequency_analysis
5.   Wikipedia: Kerckhoffs' principle. http://en.wikipedia.org/wiki/Kerckhoffs'_principle
6.   Wikipedia: Mary I of Scotland. http://en.wikipedia.org/wiki/Mary_I_of_Scotland
7.   Wikipedia: Modular arithmetic. http://en.wikipedia.org/wiki/Modular_arithmetic
8.   Wikipedia: N-gram. http://en.wikipedia.org/wiki/N-gram
9.   Wikipedia: Permutation. http://en.wikipedia.org/wiki/Permutation
10.   Wikipedia: ROT13. http://en.wikipedia.org/wiki/ROT13
11.   Wikipedia: Substitution cipher. http://en.wikipedia.org/wiki/Substitution_cipher
12.   Wikipedia: The Adventure of the Dancing Men. http://en.wikipedia.org/wiki/The_Adventure_of_the_Dancing_Men
13.   Wikipedia: words. http://en.wikipedia.org/wiki/Words_(Unix)

Generation and Testing of Random Numbers   7

It might seem unlikely, but there are some really great stories about **randomness** [14]. The way Michael Larson used knowledge of the *lack* of randomness on the US game show Press Your Luck in 1984, for example, is so great that it warrants being made into a film of some sort [12]. Part of the game involved the players moving around an eighteen square board. The squares were either empty, contained a prize or contained the so-called Whammy character: landing on a prize square won you that prize, landing on the Whammy square lost all prizes won so far.

To make things exciting, the contents of the squares was updated every second or so in a "random" manner. Except it was not random at all. Larson video taped Press Your Luck episodes and played them back frame-by-frame. Then, by writing down the sequence of board states, he discovered that the board in fact cycled through just five simple patterns. Better still, during a given turn there were some squares that would never contain the Whammy. So armed with this knowledge, Larson reasoned that he could carry on playing without really gambling at all: provided he could remember the patterns and which turn he was on, he could *always* avoid the Whammy. Larson went on the game show and stayed on so long it had to be split into multiple episodes; the look on the presenters face as he consistently avoided the Whammy with seemingly steel-eyed bravery must have been priceless. Well, not exactly priceless: Larson walked off with $110, 000 after lawyers from the TV station conceded that he had not cheated. You can still find video of the now legendary episodes on YouTube:

http://www.youtube.com/results?search_query=Press+Your+Luck

I hear a more mundane story much more often: my mother has a love/hate relationship with the UK National Lottery game Lotto [10]. The idea is that she picks six numbers between 1 and 49 and then every Saturday, a machine selects six numbers at random. If her numbers match the ones the machine picked, she wins something: typically the more numbers that match, the more money she gets. But invariably the numbers do not match and she is left to contemplate the injustice of it all. This takes the form of a ritual tirade against the machine: "it's a fix, having 21 *and* 22 *cannot* be random".

D. Page, N. Smart, *What Is Computer Science?*,
Undergraduate Topics in Computer Science, DOI 10.1007/978-3-319-04042-4_7,
© Springer International Publishing Switzerland 2014

Examples like this beg some questions about what random numbers are and how we generate them. These are quite important questions because random numbers are used in lots of different areas of Computer Science. A good example is that the security of many cryptographic schemes relies on the fact that one can make random choices and choose random numbers. For example, it is common to assume that any key we choose is done so in a random way; if there was some way to predict how we selected it, the key would be more easily guessed and security more easily breached. Setting a password to "X4$ia0!l" is arguably better than "password" for example!

7.1   What *Is* Randomness?

The term **entropy** is often used by scientists to describe disorder: if a physical system has high entropy it behaves in an unpredictable way. For example as you heat up a gas, predicting how it will behave starts to become harder than if it is in a more stable, cooled state. When we say something is random we mean more or less the same thing: the behaviour we observe follows no deterministic or predictable pattern. As a result we can not write an algorithm to describe it; instead we have to describe it in terms of **probability**, or chance.

Randomness is quite an abstract concept. To make things more concrete, we will talk exclusively about sequences of random numbers. Imagine we want to generate a sequence of such numbers, e.g.,

$$X = \langle 0, 1, 0, 1 \rangle.$$

The idea is to use coin flips (or tosses) [3]: in order to generate each X_i, we first throw the coin in the air then and inspect which side it lands on. A real coin has two sides, normally called the tails side and heads side, but we can make life easier by using the number 0 with tails and 1 with heads; we also rule out any freak occurances such as the coin landing on anything other than one of the sides (e.g., on the edge). As a result, we can say each coin flip makes a random selection from the set $S = \{0, 1\}$. Clearly we cannot write down an algorithm to describe how the coin behaves, so instead we use a **probability distribution**:

$$P(x) = \begin{cases} \frac{1}{2} & \text{if } x = 0 \text{ i.e., the coin flip was a tail} \\ \frac{1}{2} & \text{if } x = 1 \text{ i.e., the coin flip was a head} \end{cases}$$

Looking at P, for a given output x we can say what the probability of selecting x from S is. In this case, we have a special name for the probability distribution: when the probability for each x is the same we say the distribution is **uniform**.

The subject of randomness is one where it is quite difficult to prove things categorically. More usually, we define randomness in terms of properties which we can measure. Typically we generate a sequence of random numbers and then use statistical tests of randomness [16] on the sequence. For example we might say that a sequence contains some feature that mean it is *not* random; we discuss two such features below.

7.1.1 Biased Versus Unbiased

Imagine we get a friend to flip a coin eight times, resulting in the sequence

$$Y = \langle 1, 1, 1, 1, 1, 1, 1, 0 \rangle.$$

We would have to ask ourselves whether or not this friend is cheating somehow: intuitively, we might say that the coin is **biased**. On the other hand, this sequence is just as probable as any other. The probability of getting Y is

$$\frac{1}{2} \cdot \frac{1}{2} \cdot \frac{1}{2} \cdot \frac{1}{2} \cdot \frac{1}{2} \cdot \frac{1}{2} \cdot \frac{1}{2} \cdot \frac{1}{2} = \frac{1}{2^8} = \frac{1}{256}$$

which is the same as any other sequence of the same length. So given Y is just as likely to occur as any other sequence, why would we conclude that the coin is unfair?

In more general terms, if we select uniformly at random from a set of m numbers the probability of selecting a number x is

$$P(x) = \frac{1}{m}.$$

If we repeat the selection n times, we would expect each of the numbers to appear roughly $\frac{n}{m}$ times *on average*. If some number x is selected significantly more or less than $\frac{n}{m}$ times, we could conclude that the selection process is not random at all: it is biased in favour or against x somehow. This means that there exists a number x with $P(x) \neq \frac{1}{m}$, but we expected that for all x we would have $P(x) = \frac{1}{m}$. This is another way of saying the selection process is biased, i.e., P is not uniform.

The "on average" part in the previous paragraph is important in the sense that we need n to be large before we start talking about average behaviour. For example if we flip a coin twice and get 1 twice, we cannot conclude that the coin is unfair because we do not have enough evidence. If we flip a coin eight hundred times and get 1 seven hundred times however, we can be more confident that something fishy is going on.

Looking again at the sequence Y, we can start to see why our friend might be cheating. We are selecting from $m = 2$ numbers and have repeated the selection $n = 8$ times so we would expect each number to occur $\frac{8}{2} = 4$ times. But they do not: we get 1 seven times and 0 just once, so we could conclude that for this limited sample the coin is biased toward 1 and is therefore unfair. Rather than being uniform, based on having seen Y we might say the behaviour of the coin is better described by

$$P(x) = \begin{cases} \frac{1}{8} & \text{if } x = 0 \\ \frac{7}{8} & \text{if } x = 1 \end{cases}$$

Maybe we should get some more trustworthy friends!

You can get some statistics about the UK National Lottery here

http://www.lottery.co.uk/statistics/

Based on the discussion above, i.e., explaining your answer in terms of Mathematics, probability in particular, is it biased or not?

7.1.2   Predictable Versus Unpredictable

Now imagine we get a different friend to flip another coin eight times, and that this time the resulting sequence is

$$Z = \langle 1, 0, 1, 0, 1, 0, 1, 0 \rangle.$$

The probability of getting this sequence is still

$$\frac{1}{2} \cdot \frac{1}{2} \cdot \frac{1}{2} \cdot \frac{1}{2} \cdot \frac{1}{2} \cdot \frac{1}{2} \cdot \frac{1}{2} \cdot \frac{1}{2} = \frac{1}{2^8} = \frac{1}{256}$$

so again we cannot really infer anything from it occurring rather than some other sequence. Also, we can see that the coin is not biased in the same way the other one was: we get 1 four times and 0 four times so the coin is not biased toward either case. On the other hand, we might intuitively say the new coin is still unfair because there is a clear pattern: if a given flip of the coin gives 1, there seems a strong chance the next flip will give 0. If we believe the pattern will continue to hold, this means we can predict the next result with some confidence.

You can think of this in terms of **conditional probability** [2]: the result of a given coin flip should not depend on anything other than the probability distribution. It especially should not depend on the results from previous coin flips: imagine you flip the coin ten times and every time you get 1. We might say a 0 was "due". But looking at our description of the behaviour, it clearly is not: the probability of getting a 0 on the eleventh flip is still $\frac{1}{2}$ and the probability of getting a 1 is still $\frac{1}{2}$. The tendency for people to ignore this is sometimes called the gambler's fallacy [5]. In our case, we can see that the result of the i-th coin flip probably is dependent on the $(i - 1)$-th coin flip. For example if $Z_{i-1} = 1$ then it is more probable that $Z_i = 0$ than $Z_i = 1$. Therefore we could conclude that the coin behaviour is not as well described by the probability distribution as expected.

There is another, perhaps neater way to think about this. Imagine we want to take Z and compress it by coming up with a shorter way to describe the sequence, just as we did in Chap. 1. For example, imagine we say that the symbol $\star$ represents the sequence $\langle 1, 0 \rangle$. We might then describe Z as the sequence

$$\bar{Z} = \langle \star, \star, \star, \star \rangle.$$

Why does this work? Well, we know what $\star$ "means" so we can take $\bar{Z}$ and reconstruct Z by just replacing each occurrence of $\star$ with $(1, 0)$. But the way we describe $\bar{Z}$ is shorter than the way we describe Z (even if we include the definition of $\star$), so in some sense we have used the fact there is a "pattern" to compress the information. We have glossed over a lot of the detail, but there is a fancy name for this general concept: we call it Kolmogorov-Chaitin complexity [7]. Very roughly, this concept says that the more we can compress a sequence the less random it must be; equivalently, the more we can compress a sequence the more usable structure there must be in the sequence.

7.1.3 Random Versus Arbitrary

There used to be a joke about messages from computers that would prompt the user to "press any key" [1]; the joke was that users would find the space key and the escape key, but could not find the "any" key. It seems debatable whether this was ever actually funny, but looking at things more closely highlights an important point: the message did not read "press a random key", the choice of key does not matter so really what we mean is "press an arbitrary key".

The difference between arbitrary and random is sometimes important however. For example, many files used within a UNIX-based operating system start with a magic number [9] which allows us to easily identify their type; if the file starts with the number 8993 this tells us that we can execute it for example. In a sense the choice of 8993 is arbitrary; there is no real reason to choose 8993 rather than say 1234 or 9999, we just needed "any" number. In this sort of situation, it is tempting to just select the numbers at random.

Test this claim using BASH. Remember, the od command can display the content of files in various ways: the option -tux1 will print the content as a sequence of hexadecimal bytes for instance. If you can locate some different file types (e.g., JPEG images, PDF documents, BASH scripts, Java class files and so on) you should be able to see the magic number in the first few bytes (the file command uses this information to guess the file type).

Implement (task #37)

In cryptography, this approach can have some disadvantages. The most famous example is illustrated by the **Data Encryption Standard (DES)** [4] which was designed and standardised in the US in the late 1970s. DES is a block cipher; it encrypts messages. One of the components in the algorithm is a large table called the S-box whose contents is chosen carefully but somewhat arbitrarily. The problem is, there was no explanation of *how* the content was generated. People began to become suspicious that the content had been chosen in a special way so that, for example, the US government could decrypt their messages. In turned out that the US government had not selected the S-box content either randomly *or* arbitrarily. They had actually been selected to prevent an attack which, at the time, only the US governments cryptographers knew about. Even so, the lack of openness over the design choices for the S-box sparked a trend toward use of so-called "nothing up my sleeve" numbers [11]. This idea is used when we want "any" number, but one which we can prove has not been selected with special properties. For example, the number π might not be a good random number, but if all you need is an arbitrary number then it is probably a good choice. For example, people would be hard pushed to prove your choice of π was underhand: it cannot have been generated in some special way.

7.2 Real Randomness

7.2.1 Generating Randomness

When we talk about *real* random numbers, we typically mean numbers that come from some physical process. The idea is that we cannot control, or to some extent understand, how these processes might work. In other words, we cannot write down an algorithm that describes them. Radioactive decay is a good candidate. The idea is that an unstable atom will decay by emitting energy in the form of radiation; we know the average rate at which this might happen, but when exactly a given atom will decay is unpredictable. So we could generate random numbers by simply taking a measuring device such as a Geiger counter [6] and have it tell us whenever radioactive decay is detected.

Another candidate is atmospheric noise. In the same way as radioactive decay, it is difficult to predict the level and characteristics of the noise around us. Sampling such noise using even a basic radio or microphone can give quite effective results: Mads Haahr, a lecturer at Trinity College, Dublin has rigged up such a system to the Internet at

$$\text{http://www.random.org/}$$

The web-site offers a neat interface which we can easily use from BASH by employing the wget command. The idea is to issue a command that mimics what happens when we type a URL into the address bar of a web-browser:

```
bash$ wget -q -U chrome -O- 'http://www.random.org/integers/?num=100&min=0&max=255&col=5&base=10&format=
       plain&rnd=new'
52      131     189     14      3
118     123     153     46      88
206     77      42      72      171
194     229     113     19      153
55      244     69      46      220
117     9       101     82      82
5       64      164     172     250
119     26      1       87      58
169     231     44      194     182
28      210     243     124     193
148     129     177     71      249
178     202     101     25      47
254     102     2       44      144
15      24      46      84      165
32      225     153     101     17
148     255     220     235     71
45      195     34      217     84
80      134     25      74      117
17      21      109     25      148
144     167     10      41      203
bash$
```

Of course having a Geiger counter attached to *every* computer is not ideal, and neither is having to access a remote computer over the Internet every time we need to generate random numbers. Fortunately there are lots of devices already connected to your local computer which could do a similar job. Most operating systems have a mechanism for collecting together random events from such devices into what is called an **entropy pool** [17]. You can think of the entropy pool as a sequence of numbers; the idea is that each time a random event happens, we mix it into the entropy pool by adding some numerical representation of the event onto the end of the sequence. You could imagine that every time someone moves the mouse, the computer might add the mouse speed and direction to the sequence. Then, when someone or something needs to generate a random number, we take one from the start of the sequence.

UNIX systems commonly have two types of entropy pool which they let users access via the /dev/random and /dev/urandom files. Except the files are not *really* files at all: when we read from them, behind the scenes we are taking random numbers from an entropy pool. The difference between the two is that /dev/random will wait for enough entropy to exist before allowing us to read from it, while /dev/urandom will let us read whenever we want. You can see this as a choice between the *quality* of the numbers we read and the length of *time* required to read them. Again, we can easily read some numbers from /dev/urandom using BASH:

```
bash$ cat /dev/urandom | od -Ad -tu1 -w5 -N50 | cut -c 9-
 32  38 155 120  79
 74  78 146 204 147
  9 206 233  35 218
 41  49 214  96  35
 25 200  21 190   9
 47 213 208 199  21
123  69 220 194 226
  6 154  57  46  78
150 244 150 225 166
 97  31 145 243  15

bash$
```

That is quite a horrible looking command, so it makes sense to look at what is going on in more detail. Basically, we take /dev/urandom and pass it through a command called od which is controlled using a number of options: we tell od to give us fifty bytes of the input using -N50, to format the output in five columns using -w5, and to format the content as unsigned decimal integers in the range 0...255 inclusive using -t with the format u1. Finally we pass the output of od through cut to remove some information we do not need, i.e., to get just the random numbers.

7.2.2 Testing Randomness

So we can generate random numbers, but can we apply similar statistical tests as those discussed earlier to *show* they are random? As an example, we will look at the tests for bias and predictability; we will compare the real random numbers against

English text, which is not random at all. Again we will use **Project Gutenberg** as a source of text:

http://www.gutenberg.org/

For the sake of argument, we fetch the text for *War and Peace* by Tolstoy (which is quite large) and save it as the file A.txt. Using the du command we can see that it weighs in at roughly 3 MB:

```
bash$ wget -q -U chrome -O A.txt 'http://www.gutenberg.org/files/2600/2600.txt'
bash$ du -b A.txt
3226645 A.txt
bash$
```

Next we take the same amount of random data from /dev/urandom (using du and cut to provide the number of bytes as an option for head), then save it as the binary file B.bin as follows:

```
bash$ cat /dev/urandom | head -c 'du -b A.txt | cut -f 1' > B.bin
bash$
```

Remember that testing for bias in A.txt and B.bin basically means testing that each possible number we could select has the same probability of selection. The test will be performed in two steps:
1. Take the input file and chop it up into decimal numbers in the range 0...255. The output will need some cleaning up, but the end result will essentially be a long sequence of decimal numbers (one per-line) that represents the file content.
2. Take the sequence and count how many times each number occurs in it.
There are two main things to notice in the output for A.txt:

```
bash$ cat A.txt | od -Ad -tu1 -w1 -v | cut -c 9- | grep [0-9]* > D.txt
bash$ cat D.txt | tr -d [:blank:] | grep -v ^$ | sort -n | uniq -c | paste -s
 65008 10     514911 32        3923 33      17970 34          1 35
     2 36           1 37        7529 39        670 40        670 41
   300 42       39891 44        6308 45       30805 46         29 47
   179 48         392 49         147 50          61 51         23 52
    55 53          57 54          40 55         193 56         35 57
  1015 58        1145 59           2 61        3137 63          2 64
  6575 65        3606 66        2107 67        2017 68       2259 69
  1946 70        1303 71        4378 72        7933 73        308 74
  1201 75         713 76        3251 77        3614 78       1635 79
  6519 80          35 81        3057 82        2987 83       6817 84
   254 85        1116 86        2888 87         673 88       1265 89
   108 90           1 91           1 93      199239 97      31052 98
 59520 99      116274 100      312990 101      52950 102      50024 103
163027 104     166351 105        2266 106      19230 107      95814 108
 58395 109     180561 110      191245 111      39014 112       2295 113
145373 114     159906 115      219591 116      65180 117      25970 118
 56319 119       3711 120       45000 121       2280 122
bash$
```

First, some numbers do not appear at all; for example the output starts at 10 so clearly 0...9 appear zero times. Second, among the numbers that do appear, some appear much more often than others. For example the number 32 appears many times whereas the number 90 appears fewer times. The reason for this is simple. Since A.txt is an ASCII text file, the numbers will be biased toward those which relate to printable ASCII codes. Looking back to Chap. 4, we find that 32 is the ASCII code for SPC, the characters 'a'...'z' have ASCII codes 97...122, and

ASCII codes 10 and 13 produce a new line; unsurprisingly these all appear *very* often! What about B.bin?

```
bash$ cat B.bin | od -Ad -tu1 -w1 -v | cut -c 9- | grep [0-9]* > D.txt
bash$ cat D.txt | tr -d [:blank:] | grep -v ^$ | sort -n | uniq -c | paste -s
  12593 0      12698 1      12513 2      12485 3      12524 4
  12627 5      12663 6      12609 7      12691 8      12535 9
  12699 10     12597 11     12683 12     12520 13     12697 14
  12525 15     12520 16     12577 17     12621 18     12477 19
  12438 20     12585 21     12594 22     12845 23     12591 24
  12688 25     12623 26     12600 27     12658 28     12692 29
  12747 30     12490 31     12476 32     12521 33     12770 34
  12739 35     12451 36     12569 37     12628 38     12666 39
  12628 40     12523 41     12579 42     12507 43     12504 44
  12634 45     12757 46     12529 47     12517 48     12602 49
  12454 50     12598 51     12409 52     12445 53     12634 54
  12723 55     12566 56     12780 57     12817 58     12737 59
  12565 60     12532 61     12641 62     12495 63     12565 64
  12661 65     12808 66     12670 67     12610 68     12685 69
  12663 70     12511 71     12692 72     12665 73     12705 74
  12639 75     12454 76     12658 77     12821 78     12702 79
  12656 80     12746 81     12542 82     12775 83     12592 84
  12413 85     12486 86     12725 87     12681 88     12574 89
  12663 90     12544 91     12716 92     12651 93     12584 94
  12729 95     12671 96     12529 97     12430 98     12499 99
  12500 100    12439 101    12662 102    12891 103    12600 104
  12581 105    12720 106    12538 107    12650 108    12599 109
  12550 110    12567 111    12512 112    12534 113    12864 114
  12449 115    12590 116    12548 117    12650 118    12779 119
  12546 120    12787 121    12548 122    12611 123    12663 124
  12577 125    12323 126    12583 127    12623 128    12757 129
  12564 130    12572 131    12780 132    12527 133    12839 134
  12487 135    12458 136    12783 137    12452 138    12570 139
  12521 140    12571 141    12699 142    12691 143    12461 144
  12835 145    12618 146    12582 147    12681 148    12657 149
  12593 150    12489 151    12859 152    12544 153    12823 154
  12513 155    12676 156    12399 157    12613 158    12379 159
  12650 160    12626 161    12693 162    12595 163    12633 164
  12773 165    12696 166    12761 167    12834 168    12472 169
  12576 170    12892 171    12496 172    12571 173    12611 174
  12353 175    12509 176    12546 177    12729 178    12777 179
  12624 180    12612 181    12480 182    12517 183    12584 184
  12395 185    12573 186    12679 187    12408 188    12597 189
  12748 190    12733 191    12360 192    12397 193    12616 194
  12503 195    12480 196    12699 197    12641 198    12487 199
  12470 200    12481 201    12609 202    12580 203    12621 204
  12598 205    12555 206    12692 207    12593 208    12426 209
  12568 210    12470 211    12630 212    12483 213    12684 214
  12665 215    12623 216    12499 217    12629 218    12312 219
  12551 220    12502 221    12749 222    12682 223    12581 224
  12787 225    12625 226    12805 227    12596 228    12505 229
  12806 230    12473 231    12608 232    12564 233    12663 234
  12747 235    12512 236    12428 237    12788 238    12456 239
  12704 240    12672 241    12575 242    12621 243    12515 244
  12542 245    12362 246    12566 247    12692 248    12496 249
  12654 250    12639 251    12853 252    12518 253    12475 254
  12626 255
bash$
```

The difference is quite obvious: all numbers appear in the output and do so roughly 12600 times on average. There are a few cases which vary a little, but basically we can conclude that there is no bias in B.bin to the same extent there was in A.txt. We might use some further statistics to back this up, for example if we were to measure the standard deviation of B.bin it would not be very large.

Measuring predictability is a little more tricky. One thing we could do quite easily is to approximate the Kolmogorov-Chaitin complexity by seeing how easy it is to compress the file content. The command bzip2 performs a full blown version of the compression ideas we discussed in Chap. 1. bzip2 processes an input file to identify patters and replaces them with shorter symbols to produce a compressed output file. It needs to define what those symbols mean so it adds a dictionary to the start of the compressed file so that we can decompress it later if we want to. Using bzip2 to compress A.txt and B.bin is simple; to be fair, we instruct bzip2 to make the best effort it can at compressing the files rather than worrying about producing the result quickly:

```
bash$ bzip2 -c -9 A.txt > A.txt.bz2
bash$ bzip2 -c -9 B.bin > B.bin.bz2
bash$
```

We then inspect how big the resulting files are, again using the du command we used earlier:

```
bash$ du -b A.txt A.txt.bz2
3226645 A.txt
883666  A.txt.bz2
bash$ du -b B.bin B.bin.bz2
3226645 B.bin
3241465 B.bin.bz2
bash$
```

Inspecting the results confirms more or less what we expected: the *War and Peace* text A.txt was compressed into A.txt.bz2, which is roughly a quarter of the size. This is what we would expect since A.txt represents English text; for example the word "and" probably appears very often so we might imagine replacing each occurrence with a one character symbol. However, the randomness produced by /dev/urandom in B.bin is processed by bzip2 to produce the file B.bin.bz2. In this case the output of /dev/urandom is so hard to compress that the overhead of adding the dictionary to the compressed file has meant the end result is larger than what we started with!

Maybe bzip2 is just not very good at compressing files (or at least this file? To test this, we can try the same thing with some other compression tools like gzip and get similar results:

```
bash$ gzip -c -9 A.txt > A.txt.gz
bash$ gzip -c -9 B.bin > B.bin.gz
bash$ du -b A.txt A.txt.gz
3226645 A.txt
1193969 A.txt.gz
bash$ du -b B.bin B.bin.gz
3226645 B.bin
3227164 B.bin.gz
bash$
```

Or perhaps using the zip compression method:

```
bash$ zip -q -9 A.zip A.txt
bash$ zip -q -9 B.zip B.bin
bash$ du -b A.txt A.zip
3226645 A.txt
1194105 A.zip
bash$ du -b B.bin B.zip
3226645 B.bin
3227300 B.zip
bash$
```

Of course, this still does not prove anything; perhaps bzip2, gzip and zip are *all* missing some obvious way to compress the files. But basically we conclude from our tests that A.txt is quite easy to compress whereas B.bin is at least harder to compress. This means the Kolmogorov-Chaitin complexity of A.txt is quite low: we can make a shorter description of A.txt, so it is not very random. On the other hand, for B.bin the Kolmogorov-Chaitin complexity is higher: it is not as easy to describe B.bin in a shorter way, so in a sense it is more random.

Implement (task #38)

Using the commands described above for compressing files, set yourself a challenge: what is the
1. *largest* file you can create that can be compressed into the *smallest* size, and
2. *smallest* file you can create that can be compressed into the *largest* size.

Put more precisely, imagine the original and compressed files have sizes x and y bytes respectively: you are trying to maximises or minimise the compression ratio x/y. In each case, explain what your strategy for constructing the original file is, i.e., what features does it have that make it a good choice?

7.3 Fake Randomness

7.3.1 Generating Randomness

The problem with real random numbers is that sometimes they are *too* random for our purposes. Yes, really: imagine we want to simulate a scientific experiment using a computer; this is a good idea if the real experiment would be impractical. For example, maybe we would like to experiment with things that expand very fast and generate large amounts of heat; usually we call these things explosions and doing real experiments can be quite hazardous! So instead, we simulate the explosion on a computer. On one hand it is quite possible we would want a source of random numbers to model parts of the experiment, for example randomness in atomic-level behaviour. On the other hand it would be a good idea if we could repeat the simulation and get the *same* results. Using real random numbers is not ideal because of the second reason: we cannot reproduce the real randomness so we would need to generate all the numbers, store them somewhere and then look them up if we needed them again.

A solution is to use **pseudo-random** numbers [13]. Whereas real randomness cannot be described using an algorithm, pseudo-randomness can. The idea is to think of the pseudo-random numbers we generate as a sequence called R. We start by specifying the first element in the sequence R_0, this is called the **seed**. Then, to generate the next element R_1 we apply the algorithm to compute it for us; we can perform this over and over again so that more generally if we have R_i, the i-th element in the sequence, we can generate the next element R_{i+1}. The thing we need to be very careful about is that the sequence we generate still passes the tests for randomness we looked at previously: although pseudo-random numbers are in a sense fake, they should still satisfy our definition of what randomness looks like. If we are successful, reproducing pseudo-random numbers becomes a matter of using the algorithm over and over again rather than storing a large amount of real random numbers: we have traded more computation for less storage.

A **Linear Congruence Generator (LCG)** is one way to generate pseudo-random numbers [8]. The algorithm we use to compute the next element of the sequence given the current element is

$$R_{i+1} = a \cdot R_i + c \pmod{p}.$$

This means that we take R_i, multiply it by some number a, and finally add another number c: the result R_{i+1} is produced by using modular arithmetic where the modulus we are using is p. Imagine we select $a = 5$, $b = 1$, $p = 8$ and set the seed value $R_0 = 2$. We can apply the LCG equation to generate successive elements in the sequence

$$
\begin{aligned}
R_0 &   &= 2 \\
R_1 &= 5 \cdot R_0 + 1 \bmod 8 &= 3 \\
R_2 &= 5 \cdot R_1 + 1 \bmod 8 &= 0 \\
R_3 &= 5 \cdot R_2 + 1 \bmod 8 &= 1 \\
R_4 &= 5 \cdot R_3 + 1 \bmod 8 &= 6 \\
R_5 &= 5 \cdot R_4 + 1 \bmod 8 &= 7 \\
R_6 &= 5 \cdot R_5 + 1 \bmod 8 &= 4 \\
R_7 &= 5 \cdot R_6 + 1 \bmod 8 &= 5 \\
R_8 &= 5 \cdot R_7 + 1 \bmod 8 &= 2 \\
R_9 &= 5 \cdot R_8 + 1 \bmod 8 &= 3 \\
&\qquad\vdots   &\vdots
\end{aligned}
$$

Think back to our example application of pseudo-randomness where we wanted to use a computer to simulate something, and imagine we want to start the simulation half way through. Normally this would be tricky: we would first have to start our random number generator at the beginning using the seed element, and then repeatedly compute the next element until we got to the point we actually wanted to start. Depending on where this is, we might waste quite a bit of time just finding the R_i we want.

Research (task #39)

The LCG is just one example of a **Pseudo-Random Number Generator (PRNG)**. Find out about at least one other type, including how it works; compare it with the LCG in terms of any advantages and disadvantages each might offer given a particular context or application.

The LCG has a nice property which allows us to avoid this wasted time by skipping ahead in the sequence. We already have a way to skip ahead by one element, namely

$$R_{i+1} = a \cdot R_i + c \pmod{p}.$$

What if we take R_{i+1} and apply the equation again? We would skip ahead two elements, and the result would look a bit like

$$R_{i+2} = a \cdot S + c \quad (\text{mod } p)$$

where $S = a \cdot R_i + c$; writing things out fully gives a way to go straight from R_i to R_{i+2}

$$R_{i+2} = a \cdot (a \cdot R_i + c) + c \quad (\text{mod } p).$$

Pulling the same trick again we can compute what the result of skipping ahead three elements would be

$$R_{i+3} = a \cdot T + c \quad (\text{mod } p)$$

where $T = a \cdot (a \cdot R_i + c) + c$; things are starting to get a bit of a mess, but we can again write things out to get straight from R_i to R_{i+3}

$$R_{i+3} = a \cdot \big(a \cdot (a \cdot R_i + c) + c\big) + c \quad (\text{mod } p).$$

The aim of all this is not to give you a headache, but rather to show that there is a pattern emerging: if we start at R_i then to skip ahead k elements means that first we multiply R_i by a a total of k times, but also add c a total of k times as we go. The problem is, the multiplications by a and additions of c are sort of mixed up. We can unravel the mess by rewriting things a bit

$$\begin{aligned}
R_{i+3} &= a \cdot \big(a \cdot (a \cdot R_i + c) + c\big) + c &&(\text{mod } p) \\
&= a \cdot \big(a^2 \cdot R_i + a \cdot c + c\big) + c &&(\text{mod } p) \\
&= a^3 \cdot R_i + a^2 \cdot c + a \cdot c + c &&(\text{mod } p)
\end{aligned}$$

The important thing to notice from the above is that given R_i we just need to compute two values which we can write down as

$$\begin{aligned}
A(k) &= a^k \\
C(k) &= a^{k-1} \cdot c + a^{k-2} \cdot c + \cdots + a^2 \cdot c + a \cdot c + c
\end{aligned}$$

and then we can use them to compute

$$R_{i+k} = A(k) \cdot R_i + C(k) \quad (\text{mod } p).$$

If we plug in the specific case of $k = 3$ the terms are as we expect, i.e.

$$\begin{aligned}
A(3) &= a^3 \\
C(3) &= a^2 \cdot c + a \cdot c + c
\end{aligned}$$

which gives

$$R_{i+3} = a^3 \cdot R_i + a^2 \cdot c + a \cdot c + c.$$

The great thing is, since a and c are constant values, so if we know k before we start then we can also compute $A(k)$ and $C(k)$ before we start. But what if we do not know k before we start? What is the best way to compute $A(k)$ and $C(k)$? Certainly we want to do this in an inexpensive way, otherwise we might as well perform k steps, skipping ahead 1 element each time.

The $A(k)$ part is quite easy, but the $C(k)$ part looks much less pleasant. We have got an expression of the form

$$a^{k-1} \cdot c + a^{k-2} \cdot c + \cdots a^2 \cdot c + a \cdot c + c$$

to compute. This looks bad because for a large value of k, the number of additions and multiplications we need to do is also quite large. However, we are saved because this large expression is actually the same as the much nicer looking

$$\frac{(a^k - 1) \cdot c}{a - 1}.$$

To see why, multiply the first expression by $(a - 1)$, to obtain

$$\left(a^{k-1} \cdot c + a^{k-2} \cdot c + \cdots + a \cdot c + c\right) \cdot (a - 1)$$
$$= \left(a^{k-1} \cdot c + a^{k-2} \cdot c + \cdots + a^2 \cdot c + a \cdot c + c\right) \cdot a$$
$$\quad - \left(a^{k-1} \cdot c + a^{k-2} \cdot c + \cdots + a^2 \cdot c + a \cdot c + c\right)$$
$$= \left(a^k \cdot c + a^{k-1} \cdot c + a^{k-2} \cdot c + \cdots + a^2 \cdot c + a \cdot c\right)$$
$$\quad - \left(a^{k-1} \cdot c + a^{k-2} \cdot c + \cdots + a^2 \cdot c + a \cdot c + c\right)$$
$$= a^k \cdot c - c$$
$$= \left(a^k - 1\right) \cdot c$$

Now dividing both sides by $(a - 1)$ we obtain

$$a^{k-1} \cdot c + a^{k-2} \cdot c + \cdots + a^2 \cdot c + a \cdot c + c = \frac{(a^k - 1) \cdot c}{a - 1}$$

This is great news because we already have to compute a^k in order to get $A(k)$, so given that $a - 1$ is also just a constant value we only need to do one subtraction, one multiplication and one division to get $C(k)$ rather than the mass of multiplications and additions that we started with. In other words we have

$$C(k) = \frac{(A(k) - 1) \cdot c}{a - 1}.$$

Computing the sequence an LCG produces by hand is somewhat tedious, so how might we automate the process? One way would be to write a dedicated program for the task; since we want to focus on the concepts rather than teach programming, we will instead try to automate the process using only existing BASH commands. Our approach is to write a small BASH **script** [15] which will generate n elements of the sequence given R_0, a, c and p. You can think of the script as creating a new command which we can use as follows:

```
bash$ ./P.sh n R a c p
```

In other words it will produce the output of the LCG for values of i in the range $1, 2, \ldots, n$, starting at position R_0. We create the script, which we call P.sh, as follows:

```
bash$ cat > P.sh
#!/bin/bash

R=${2}

for (( i = 0; i < ${1}; i += 1 )) ; do
  echo "${R}"
  R=$[ ( ( ${3} * ${R} ) + ${4} ) % ${5} ]
done
bash$ chmod 775 P.sh
bash$
```

Note that `cat` is used to capture input from the user and save it into a file called P.sh.[1] The permissions of P.sh are set using chmod so we can use it as a script (rather than just a normal file). For example, to replicate the sequence we looked at above, we might run P.sh as follows:

```
bash$ ./P.sh 100 2 5 1 8 | paste -s -d ' '
2 3 0 1 6 7 4 5 2 3 0 1 6 7 4 5 2 3 0 1 6 7 4 5 2 3 0 1 6 7 4 5 2 3 0 1 6 7 4 5
2 3 0 1 6 7 4 5 2 3 0 1 6 7 4 5 2 3 0 1 6 7 4 5 2 3 0 1 6 7 4 5 2 3 0 1 6 7 4 5
2 3 0 1 6 7 4 5 2 3 0 1 6 7 4 5 2 3 0 1
bash$
```

where we read $\${1}$ as 100 meaning $n = 100$, $\${2}$ as 2 meaning $R_0 = 2$, $\${3}$ as 5 meaning $a = 5$, $\${4}$ as 1 meaning $c = 1$, and finally $\${5}$ as 8 meaning $p = 8$.

Although overall it might seem unfamiliar, each step of the script is easy to explain: you can think of it as an algorithm, but written in a slightly different way. First we assign R to $\${2}$ which is the second option given to P.sh on the command line (i.e., the seed). Then we use a loop to iterate over a block of statements $\${1}$ times, where $\${1}$ is the first option given to P.sh on the command line (i.e., the value n). The block does two things. First it writes the current value of R (i.e., the value R_i) to standard output using the echo command, then updates R to the next value (i.e., R_{i+1}) using the method we have already seen. Note that $\${3}$, $\${4}$ and $\${5}$ are the third, forth and five options given to P.sh on the command line (i.e., the values of a, c and p).

---

[1]Using cat here is a bit awkward: we do so simply to show this example within the same BASH-based setting as the others. An easier way to create P.sh might of course be to use a text editor.

7.3.2   Testing Randomness

Hang on a second: that sequence we just generated looks like it just repeats over and over again! We call the number of elements before this repetition occurs the **period** of the sequence and in fact, the case where the period is equal to p is the best we can hope for. Since we are computing elements modulo p there are only p possibilities, i.e., numbers in the range $0 \ldots p - 1$. So in our case, after the eighth element the sequence *must* repeat because the next element *must* be one we have already seen. It turns out that depending on the choices of a, c and p things can get even worse:

```
bash$ ./P.sh 100 2 0 0  8 | paste -s -d ' '
2 0 0 0 0 0 0 0 0 0 0 0 0 0 0 0 0 0 0 0 0 0 0 0 0 0 0 0 0 0 0 0 0 0 0 0 0 0 0 0
0 0 0 0 0 0 0 0 0 0 0 0 0 0 0 0 0 0 0 0 0 0 0 0 0 0 0 0 0 0 0 0 0 0 0 0 0 0 0 0
0 0 0 0 0 0 0 0 0 0 0 0 0 0 0 0 0 0 0 0
bash$ ./P.sh 100 2 1 0  8 | paste -s -d ' '
2 2 2 2 2 2 2 2 2 2 2 2 2 2 2 2 2 2 2 2 2 2 2 2 2 2 2 2 2 2 2 2 2 2 2 2 2 2 2 2
2 2 2 2 2 2 2 2 2 2 2 2 2 2 2 2 2 2 2 2 2 2 2 2 2 2 2 2 2 2 2 2 2 2 2 2 2 2 2 2
2 2 2 2 2 2 2 2 2 2 2 2 2 2 2 2 2 2 2 2
bash$ ./P.sh 100 2 0 1  8 | paste -s -d ' '
2 1 1 1 1 1 1 1 1 1 1 1 1 1 1 1 1 1 1 1 1 1 1 1 1 1 1 1 1 1 1 1 1 1 1 1 1 1 1 1
1 1 1 1 1 1 1 1 1 1 1 1 1 1 1 1 1 1 1 1 1 1 1 1 1 1 1 1 1 1 1 1 1 1 1 1 1 1 1 1
1 1 1 1 1 1 1 1 1 1 1 1 1 1 1 1 1 1 1 1
bash$ ./P.sh 100 2 1 1  8 | paste -s -d ' '
2 3 4 5 6 7 0 1 2 3 4 5 6 7 0 1 2 3 4 5 6 7 0 1 2 3 4 5 6 7 0 1 2 3 4 5 6 7 0 1
2 3 4 5 6 7 0 1 2 3 4 5 6 7 0 1 2 3 4 5 6 7 0 1 2 3 4 5 6 7 0 1 2 3 4 5 6 7 0 1
2 3 4 5 6 7 0 1 2 3 4 5 6 7 0 1 2 3 4 5
bash$ ./P.sh 100 2 2 2  8 | paste -s -d ' '
2 6 6 6 6 6 6 6 6 6 6 6 6 6 6 6 6 6 6 6 6 6 6 6 6 6 6 6 6 6 6 6 6 6 6 6 6 6 6 6
6 6 6 6 6 6 6 6 6 6 6 6 6 6 6 6 6 6 6 6 6 6 6 6 6 6 6 6 6 6 6 6 6 6 6 6 6 6 6 6
6 6 6 6 6 6 6 6 6 6 6 6 6 6 6 6 6 6 6 6
bash$ ./P.sh 100 0 2 1 10 | paste -s -d ' '
0 1 3 7 5 1 3 7 5 1 3 7 5 1 3 7 5 1 3 7 5 1 3 7 5 1 3 7 5 1 3 7 5 1 3 7 5 1 3 7
5 1 3 7 5 1 3 7 5 1 3 7 5 1 3 7 5 1 3 7 5 1 3 7 5 1 3 7 5 1 3 7 5 1 3 7 5 1 3 7
5 1 3 7 5 1 3 7 5 1 3 7 5 1 3 7 5 1 3 7
bash$
```

The first four cases are a bit dumb: it we select a or c as zero for example, we do not really update R_i to get a new R_{i+1} as we would like. The fifth and sixth cases are a bit more subtle however. In the fifth case the period is one: we always get 6 from the generator after the seed even though, at face value, our choices of a, c and p are not very special. In the sixth case a slightly better situation occurs: the period is four which is less disastrous, but also less than the value of ten which we would hope to get given the choice of p. Hopefully it is clear that *none* of these cases are attractive: if the sequence repeats itself after p elements (or less) and we generate more than that many elements, then there will be a pattern that we can use to compress the sequence and it does not pass our tests for randomness any more. So in some sense, the smaller the period the less randomness there is for us to use.

We can use some rules of thumb to avoid these problems. An often used approach is to select the seed element R_0 as the current time and date; this ensures that we get a different starting point (more or less) every time we generate the sequence. We also need to select p so that it is large enough that there would not be any (or at least very few) cycles. Finally, we should select a and c in such a way that the sequence we generate is not trivially bad (like those above). Putting all this together we can run P.sh as follows for example:

```
bash$ ./P.sh 100 'date +'%Y%m%d'' 16807 0 2147483647  | paste -s -d ' '
20130905 1185187756 1539789167 2058583419 502486316 1381813008 1243066798 150275
5970 264415423 886348718 1916327834 1909651979 1377706638 946782912 1874061361 2
06643778 580919647 1055847867 977725508 87746112 1575122542 1053646825 492034613
 1813699741 1468661469 616270865 350798574 1029022203 1090356530 1144239859 5232
51328 339535231 704577338 606490208 1323537194 1054003932 51481021 1953093853 13
60842976 987057082 157204099 724406083 1008242138 1879638536 1600427182 11469691
99 1298112121 1084047774 339676470 930897564 1176989753 1194906154 1668147181 11
50659482 1043672739 361295677 1360173270 468726575 917528829 1974443543 15553137
57 987362615 997329936 1014369517 1783282333 1344393199 1541045506 1699036522 61
6771095 168229596 1346340520 2057414848 189666342 856477846 240271881 980247607
1674474712 123290649 1971702035 575945388 1205339087 920793058 1001765524 401369
388 569168889 1129353685 1586911609 1624000370 57065220 1317445978 1758151676 20
27719459 1462953170 1313653687 298142602 803363363 898353252 1813067954 15876355
95 907131190
bash$
```

and get an output which reassuringly looks like nonsense!

Here we selected $p = 2^{31} - 1 = 2147483647$ so we would expect there to be no repetitions in the sequence unless we generated a huge amount of output. But how can we be sure that what we have generated passes our tests for randomness? The easy answer to this is to actually run those tests. To do this we need to update our script a little. We create the new script, which we call Q.sh, as follows:

```
bash$ cat > Q.sh
#!/bin/bash

R=${2}

for (( i = 0; i < ${1}; i += 1 )) ; do
  r='printf '\134%03o' $[ ${R} % 256 ]'
  printf "${r}"
  R=$[ ( ( ${3} * ${R} ) + ${4} ) % ${5} ]
done
bash$ chmod 775 Q.sh
bash$
```

The new Q.sh script is used in exactly the same way as P.sh. There are two main differences however. Firstly, we do not write each R_i exactly, but instead compute $r_i = R_i \bmod 256$. So basically, the LCG is generating the sequence R which looks like

$$R_0 \qquad\qquad\qquad\qquad 461110000$$
$$R_1 = 16807 \cdot R_0 + 0 \bmod 2147483647 = 1754771624$$
$$R_2 = 16807 \cdot R_1 + 0 \bmod 2147483647 = 1053760317$$
$$R_3 = 16807 \cdot R_2 + 0 \bmod 2147483647 = 252011010$$
$$R_4 = 16807 \cdot R_3 + 0 \bmod 2147483647 = 711293186$$
$$R_5 = 16807 \cdot R_4 + 0 \bmod 2147483647 = 1810597900$$
$$R_6 = 16807 \cdot R_5 + 0 \bmod 2147483647 = 875627310$$
$$R_7 = 16807 \cdot R_6 + 0 \bmod 2147483647 = 2110249926$$
$$R_8 = 16807 \cdot R_7 + 0 \bmod 2147483647 = 1278076077$$
$$R_9 = 16807 \cdot R_8 + 0 \bmod 2147483647 = 1493188845$$
$$\vdots \qquad\qquad\qquad\qquad\qquad \vdots$$

but we are actually *using*

$$r_0 = R_0 \bmod 256 = 240$$
$$r_1 = R_1 \bmod 256 = 168$$
$$r_2 = R_2 \bmod 256 = 61$$
$$r_3 = R_3 \bmod 256 = 2$$
$$r_4 = R_4 \bmod 256 = 2$$
$$r_5 = R_5 \bmod 256 = 12$$
$$r_6 = R_6 \bmod 256 = 46$$
$$r_7 = R_7 \bmod 256 = 198$$
$$r_8 = R_8 \bmod 256 = 173$$
$$r_9 = R_9 \bmod 256 = 237$$

$$\vdots \qquad\qquad \vdots$$

Secondly, we do not write each r_i directly to standard output as text; instead we add some nasty looking `printf` commands that result in the script writing binary output. The idea behind both alterations is that Q.sh generates output in the same format as /dev/urandom (i.e., binary values in the range $0\ldots255$) so we can use the same testing strategy.

Running Q.sh with the parameters above that we eventually decided on for P.sh, we can generate a binary file called C.bin which is the same size as our original tests:

```
bash$ ./Q.sh 3288738 `date +'%Y%m%d'` 16807 0 2147483647 > C.bin
bash$
```

This takes quite a long time; BASH is not really intended for this sort of thing so our script is not exactly tuned for performance. Even so, it gives us a result eventually and we can perform the same analysis as before:

```
bash$ cat C.bin | od -Ad -tu1 -w1 -v | cut -c 9- | grep [0-9]* > D.txt
bash$ cat D.txt | tr -d [:blank:] | grep -v ^$ | sort -n | uniq -c | paste -s
  12817 0        12889 1        12917 2        12732 3        12948 4
  12817 5        12766 6        12713 7        12905 8        12877 9
  12935 10       12789 11       12861 12       12862 13       12675 14
  12727 15       12784 16       13027 17       12801 18       12887 19
  12780 20       12721 21       12845 22       12825 23       12980 24
  12825 25       12845 26       12963 27       13059 28       12769 29
  12698 30       12944 31       12921 32       12754 33       12822 34
  13063 35       12949 36       12859 37       12654 38       12950 39
  12866 40       12734 41       12770 42       12578 43       12701 44
  12709 45       13060 46       12726 47       12608 48       13075 49
  12990 50       12935 51       12836 52       12903 53       13034 54
  12744 55       12785 56       12768 57       13155 58       12802 59
  12830 60       12941 61       12860 62       12699 63       12874 64
  12724 65       12788 66       12957 67       12762 68       12899 69
  12813 70       12816 71       12762 72       12904 73       12836 74
  13029 75       12930 76       12794 77       12982 78       12846 79
  12992 80       12871 81       12759 82       12723 83       12951 84
  12736 85       13032 86       12762 87       12696 88       12863 89
  12754 90       12786 91       12882 92       12861 93       12959 94
  12808 95       12831 96       12805 97       12917 98       12757 99
  12744 100      12831 101      12856 102      12807 103      13047 104
  13157 105      12869 106      12858 107      12778 108      12769 109
  12932 110      12834 111      12890 112      12764 113      12713 114
  12941 115      13034 116      12922 117      12720 118      12745 119
  12759 120      12863 121      12893 122      12768 123      12848 124
  12782 125      12897 126      12924 127      12780 128      12904 129
  12925 130      12788 131      12945 132      12753 133      12854 134
  12790 135      12897 136      12746 137      12846 138      12955 139
  12942 140      12777 141      13056 142      12888 143      12870 144
```

```
12977 145     12827 146     12697 147     12737 148     12830 149
12746 150     12789 151     12972 152     12696 153     12824 154
12931 155     12947 156     12731 157     12891 158     12981 159
12798 160     12970 161     12871 162     12900 163     13020 164
12874 165     12756 166     12788 167     12946 168     12778 169
12767 170     12971 171     12926 172     12740 173     12890 174
12706 175     12712 176     12713 177     12963 178     12672 179
12781 180     12766 181     12771 182     12652 183     12790 184
12800 185     12930 186     12812 187     13014 188     12765 189
12919 190     12809 191     12869 192     12753 193     12829 194
12719 195     12605 196     12853 197     13025 198     12740 199
12593 200     12705 201     12851 202     12799 203     12704 204
12833 205     12861 206     12966 207     12959 208     13121 209
13042 210     12963 211     12719 212     12858 213     12741 214
12715 215     12757 216     12942 217     12857 218     12937 219
12898 220     12657 221     12864 222     13062 223     12912 224
13005 225     12791 226     12820 227     12764 228     12744 229
12993 230     12886 231     12770 232     12877 233     12950 234
12738 235     12881 236     12914 237     12768 238     13032 239
12903 240     12812 241     12784 242     12915 243     13039 244
12942 245     13007 246     12833 247     12856 248     12845 249
12962 250     12676 251     12726 252     12738 253     12862 254
12864 255
bash$
```

This looks good: in a similar way to B.bin, the output of /dev/urandom, we can see that every number is appears in the output and do so roughly 12800 times on average. Again there are a few cases which vary a little, but again we can conclude that there is no significant bias in C.bin. What about the test for predictability? Running bzip2 again gives a positive result:

```
bash$ bzip2 -c -9 C.bin > C.bin.bz2
bash$ du -b C.bin C.bin.bz2
3288738 C.bin
3304334 C.bin.bz2
bash$
```

The randomness produced by the LCG in C.bin is processed by bzip2 to produce the file C.bin.bz2; again slightly larger than the original. An interesting thing to note is that this *proves* bzip2 is not a perfect compression algorithm: if it *was* perfect it would have detected that the file contained the output of our LCG, and then compressed the entire file into a description of the LCG (i.e., Q.sh), plus the requisite parameters.

We know that the output of the LCG is only pseudo-random so what can we conclude? The first thing to highlight repeats what we already said: we cannot really prove anything about randomness, we can just test for features. In a way, this perhaps hints that our tests are not good enough to capture the difference between real randomness and pseudo-randomness. The second thing is that we have to be pragmatic about what we actually want: the pseudo-random results look random, and we have shown that for our application their generation is perhaps more attractive than using real randomness. So in a way, who cares? They might not really be random but as long as we can test them and they are good enough for our purposes, then their use should not be viewed as invalid.

References

1. Wikipedia: Any key. http://en.wikipedia.org/wiki/Any_key

2. Wikipedia: Bayes theorem. http://en.wikipedia.org/wiki/Bayes'_theorem
3. Wikipedia: Coin flipping. http://en.wikipedia.org/wiki/Coin_flipping
4. Wikipedia: Data Encryption Standard (DES). http://en.wikipedia.org/wiki/Data_Encryption_Standard
5. Wikipedia: Gambler's fallacy. http://en.wikipedia.org/wiki/Gambler's_fallacy
6. Wikipedia: Geiger counter. http://en.wikipedia.org/wiki/Geiger_counter
7. Wikipedia: Kolmogorov randomness. http://en.wikipedia.org/wiki/Kolmogorov_randomness
8. Wikipedia: Linear Congruence Generator (LCG). http://en.wikipedia.org/wiki/Linear_congruence_generator
9. Wikipedia: Magic number. http://en.wikipedia.org/wiki/Magic_number_(programming)
10. Wikipedia: National lottery. http://en.wikipedia.org/wiki/National_Lottery
11. Wikipedia: "Nothing up my sleeve" number. http://en.wikipedia.org/wiki/Nothing_up_my_sleeve_number
12. Wikipedia: Press Your Luck. http://en.wikipedia.org/wiki/Press_Your_Luck
13. Wikipedia: Pseudo-randomness. http://en.wikipedia.org/wiki/Pseudo_random
14. Wikipedia: Randomness. http://en.wikipedia.org/wiki/Randomness
15. Wikipedia: Script. http://en.wikipedia.org/wiki/Script_(computing)
16. Wikipedia: Statistical randomness. http://en.wikipedia.org/wiki/Statistical_randomness
17. Wikipedia: /dev/random. http://en.wikipedia.org/wiki//dev/random

Safety in Numbers: Modern Cryptography from Ancient Arithmetic

8

Think back to the k-place shift encryption scheme that was introduced in Chap. 6, and consider two **parties**, a **sender** called Alice and a **receiver** called Bob, using it to communicate with each other. We might describe how Alice and Bob behave using a diagram:

Alice	Eve	Bob
$C \leftarrow \mathrm{ENC}_k(M)$		
	$\xrightarrow{\;C\;}$	
		$M \leftarrow \mathrm{ENC}_k(C)$

This description is a simple cryptographic **protocol**: it describes the computational steps each party performs and the communication steps that occur between them. Note that we *could* have named the parties Angharad and Bryn but, somewhat bizarrely, an entire menagerie of standard names are used within protocol descriptions of this sort [1]. Unless we use Alice and Bob, cryptographers get confused as to what their roles are! In this case, the protocol that Alice and Bob engage in has three simple steps read from top-to-bottom:

1. Alice encrypts a plaintext, e.g., $M = $ 'a', using the key $k = 3$ to produce the ciphertext message

$$C = \text{`d'} = \mathrm{ENC}_{k=3}(\text{`a'}).$$

2. Alice communicates C to Bob.
3. Bob decrypts the ciphertext, e.g., $C = $ 'd', using the key $k = 3$ to recover the plaintext message

$$M = \text{`a'} = \mathrm{DEC}_{k=3}(\text{`d'}).$$

There are some important features of this protocol that demand further discussion:

- The diagram shows a third party: Eve is a passive **adversary** who hopes to learn M (or k) just by *observing* what Alice and Bob communicate to each other (in this case C). If Eve is allowed to *alter* the communication rather than just observe it, she turns into Mallory the active, malign adversary. We saw why this could be

D. Page, N. Smart, *What Is Computer Science?*,
Undergraduate Topics in Computer Science, DOI 10.1007/978-3-319-04042-4_8,
© Springer International Publishing Switzerland 2014

a problem at the start of Chap. 6: Thomas Phelippes was basically doing the same thing with messages communicated between Mary Stewart and Anthony Babington.

- With the encryption scheme we have, both M and C are single characters. Formally, we have **block cipher** [2] where each **block** is one character in size. What if Alice wants to send a *sequence* of characters (i.e., a string) to Bob? This is easy to accommodate: we simply apply the encryption scheme independently to each of the characters (i.e., the blocks) in the sequence. That is, take the i-th block of the plaintext and encrypt it to form the i-th block of the ciphertext

$$C_i = \text{ENC}_{k=3}(M_i)$$

and vice versa

$$M_i = \text{DEC}_{k=3}(C_i).$$

- Both Alice *and* Bob need to know and use the *same* shared key. We call this type of encryption scheme a **symmetric-key** [24] block cipher because the use of k is symmetric, i.e., the same for both Alice and Bob. In some circumstances this poses no problem at all, but in others it represents what we call the **key distribution problem**: given that Eve can see everything communicated between Alice and Bob, how can they decided on k in the first place?

Research (task #40)

The *way* we use a block cipher is, roughly speaking, called a **mode of operation** [3]. For example, although

$$C_i = \text{ENC}_k(M_i)$$

and

$$M_i = \text{DEC}_k(C_i).$$

Describe the **Electronic Codebook (ECB)** mode, various alternatives also exist. Find out about at least one alternative, plus when and why it might be preferred. Try to write equations, similar to those above, that describe how the mode produces a block of ciphertext from the corresponding block of plaintext (and vice versa).

The focus of this chapter relates to the final point above, and two potential solutions more specifically: **key agreement protocols** [15] and **public-key encryption schemes** [21]. Both are interesting from a historical point of view, but also underpin a widely-used application of modern cryptography: the **Secure Sockets Layer (SSL)** [25] system that permits modern e-commerce to exist in a usable form. If you open a web-browser and load a secure web-site (whose URL will often start with `https://` rather than `http://`), these technologies enable you to shop online without a *real* Eve finding out and using your credit card number!

Additionally, they both rely on a field of mathematics called **number theory** [17]. Many of the algorithms within this field have been studied for thousands of years; two of the most famous are Euclid's algorithm [8] for computing the greatest common divisor of two numbers, and the binary exponentiation algorithm [10] that we saw in Chap. 2. Both are often studied as examples in Computer Science because, aside from being useful, they have a number of attractive properties. In particular they

1. are short and fairly easy to understand (or at least explain),
2. allow simple arguments and proofs about their correctness, and
3. allow relatively simple analysis of their computational complexity.

Our aim is to demonstrate these properties and to show how these ancient algorithms support the modern cryptographic protocols on which we now rely.

8.1   Modular Arithmetic: the Theory

Chapter 6 described modular arithmetic as being like the "clock arithmetic" you need when reading the time from an analogue clock face such as Fig. 8.1a. Based on someone saying "the time is now ten o'clock; I will meet you in four hours", our example question asked what time they mean? We reasoned that since

$$(10 + 4) = 14 \equiv 2 \pmod{12},$$

the answer is two o'clock. We started being more formal by saying that the $\equiv$ symbol means **equivalent to**, so writing

$$x \equiv y \pmod{N}$$

means x and y give the same remainder after division by the **modulus** N. This is the same as saying there exists some κ so that

$$x = y + \kappa \cdot N,$$

i.e., x equals y after some multiple of the modulus is added on. We can see this from our example: we can say

$$14 \equiv 2 \pmod{12}$$

precisely because for $\kappa = 1$

$$14 = 2 + 1 \cdot 12,$$

i.e., both 14 and 2 give the remainder 2 after division by 12.

Fig. 8.1 Two analogue clock
faces, one standard 12-hour
version and a slightly odd
13-hour alternative

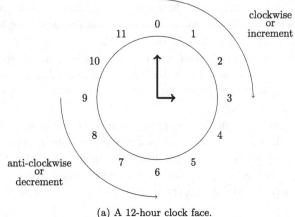

(a) A 12-hour clock face.

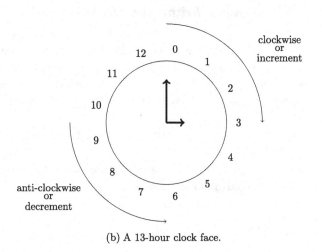

(b) A 13-hour clock face.

8.1.1   Rules for Modular Addition

Although things look more complicated, many of the rules of addition and subtraction you already know still apply to modular arithmetic:

$$\begin{aligned}
x + y &\equiv y + x &&(\text{mod } N)\\
x + (y + z) &\equiv (x + y) + z &&(\text{mod } N)\\
x + 0 &\equiv x &&(\text{mod } N)
\end{aligned}$$

In the last rule, 0 is called an **additive identity**. More generally, an **identity function** [13] gives the same output as the input. For example,

$$f(x) = x$$

means f is an identify function because whatever x we give it as input, the output is x as well. Here, you can think of the "add 0 function" as an identity function as well, i.e.,

$$f(x) = x + 0 \equiv x \quad (\text{mod } N).$$

A useful question to ask is whether for a given x we can find y, the **additive inverse** of x, which produces

$$x + y \equiv 0 \quad (\text{mod } N).$$

That is, can we find a y which when added to x produces the additive identity as a result? One way to answer this question is to just search through all possible values of y. If $x = 3$ and $N = 12$ for example, we can look at the following possibilities:

$$
\begin{array}{ll}
3 + 0 \equiv 3 \quad (\text{mod } 12) & 3 + 6 \equiv 9 \quad (\text{mod } 12) \\
3 + 1 \equiv 4 \quad (\text{mod } 12) & 3 + 7 \equiv 10 \quad (\text{mod } 12) \\
3 + 2 \equiv 5 \quad (\text{mod } 12) & 3 + 8 \equiv 11 \quad (\text{mod } 12) \\
3 + 3 \equiv 6 \quad (\text{mod } 12) & 3 + 9 \equiv 0 \quad (\text{mod } 12) \\
3 + 4 \equiv 7 \quad (\text{mod } 12) & 3 + 10 \equiv 1 \quad (\text{mod } 12) \\
3 + 5 \equiv 8 \quad (\text{mod } 12) & 3 + 11 \equiv 2 \quad (\text{mod } 12)
\end{array}
$$

The one we want is $y = 9$ which produces $3 + 9 \equiv 0$ (mod 12). But can we *always* find an additive inverse, no matter what x and N are? Ignoring modular arithmetic, the intuitive answer would be to set $y = -x$ meaning that $x + y = x - x = 0$. This also works for modular arithmetic. Remember from Chap. 6 that $-x$ (mod N) $= N - x$, so setting $y = -x$ gives us

$$x - y \equiv x + (-y) \equiv x + (N - x) \equiv N \equiv 0 \quad (\text{mod } N).$$

In our example above, this is demonstrated by

$$3 - 3 \equiv 3 + (-3) \equiv 3 + (12 - 3) \equiv 12 \equiv 0 \quad (\text{mod } N),$$

which produces exactly what we wanted.

8.1.2 Rules for Modular Multiplication

In Chap. 6 we only used modular addition, but it should be no great surprise that we can consider other operations as well. We saw in Chap. 2 that multiplication is just repeated addition, so it follows that modular multiplication could be similar.

As another example, suppose you started a job at ten o'clock and worked in three shifts each of two hours. When you finished, the time would be given by

$$10 + (3 \cdot 2) = 16 \equiv 4 \quad (\text{mod } 12),$$

i.e., you would have finished at four o'clock. Of course this is just the same as

$$10 + (2 + 2 + 2) = 16 \equiv 4 \quad (\text{mod } 12).$$

We can again rely on existing rules for multiplication:

$$
\begin{aligned}
x \cdot y &\equiv y \cdot x & (\text{mod } N) \\
x \cdot (y \cdot z) &\equiv (x \cdot y) \cdot z & (\text{mod } N) \\
x \cdot 1 &\equiv x & (\text{mod } N)
\end{aligned}
$$

This time 1 is called a **multiplicative identity**; the "multiply by 1 function" is another identity function. Since this resembles the additive identity case we saw previously, we can ask the same question: can we always find a y so that $x \cdot y \equiv 1$ (mod N)? The answer this time is no, not always. If $x = 3$ and $N = 12$, we show this by searching through all values of y again:

$$
\begin{array}{ll}
3 \cdot 0 \equiv 0 \quad (\text{mod } 12) & 3 \cdot 6 \equiv 6 \quad (\text{mod } 12) \\
3 \cdot 1 \equiv 3 \quad (\text{mod } 12) & 3 \cdot 7 \equiv 9 \quad (\text{mod } 12) \\
3 \cdot 2 \equiv 6 \quad (\text{mod } 12) & 3 \cdot 8 \equiv 0 \quad (\text{mod } 12) \\
3 \cdot 3 \equiv 9 \quad (\text{mod } 12) & 3 \cdot 9 \equiv 3 \quad (\text{mod } 12) \\
3 \cdot 4 \equiv 0 \quad (\text{mod } 12) & 3 \cdot 10 \equiv 6 \quad (\text{mod } 12) \\
3 \cdot 5 \equiv 3 \quad (\text{mod } 12) & 3 \cdot 11 \equiv 9 \quad (\text{mod } 12)
\end{array}
$$

None of the y gives us the result we want. Why?! Remember that finding such a y is the same as finding a κ which satisfies

$$3 \cdot y = 1 + 12 \cdot \kappa$$

or put another way,

$$3 \cdot y - 12 \cdot \kappa = 1.$$

The left-hand side of this equation is divisible by three, i.e., we can write it as

$$3 \cdot (y - 4 \cdot \kappa) = 1$$

instead, whereas the right-hand side is not; this means that no such κ can exist. What about some other values of x, say $x = 7$? This time things work out

$$
\begin{array}{ll}
7 \cdot 0 \equiv 0 \quad (\text{mod } 12) & 7 \cdot 6 \equiv 6 \quad (\text{mod } 12) \\
7 \cdot 1 \equiv 7 \quad (\text{mod } 12) & 7 \cdot 7 \equiv 1 \quad (\text{mod } 12) \\
7 \cdot 2 \equiv 2 \quad (\text{mod } 12) & 7 \cdot 8 \equiv 8 \quad (\text{mod } 12) \\
7 \cdot 3 \equiv 9 \quad (\text{mod } 12) & 7 \cdot 9 \equiv 3 \quad (\text{mod } 12) \\
7 \cdot 4 \equiv 4 \quad (\text{mod } 12) & 7 \cdot 10 \equiv 10 \quad (\text{mod } 12) \\
7 \cdot 5 \equiv 11 \quad (\text{mod } 12) & 7 \cdot 11 \equiv 5 \quad (\text{mod } 12)
\end{array}
$$

and we find that for $y = 7$, $x \cdot y \equiv 1$ (mod 12). The reason is that given the equation

$$7 \cdot y - 12 \cdot \kappa = 1$$

we can write, using $\kappa = 4$,

$$7 \cdot 7 - 12 \cdot 4 = 1.$$

We are allowed to call this y the **multiplicative inverse** of the corresponding x: if you take x and multiply it with its multiplicative inverse, you end up with the multiplicative identity.

8.1.3 The Sets $\mathbb{Z}$, $\mathbb{Z}_N$ and $\mathbb{Z}_N^\star$

The set of **integers** [14], or "whole numbers", is written using a special symbol:

$$\mathbb{Z} = \{\ldots, -3, -2, -1, 0, +1, +2, +3, \ldots\}.$$

Clearly this is an infinite set: the continuation dots at the right- and left-hand ends highlight the fact that we can write down infinitely many positive and negative integers. With modular arithmetic, we deal with a sub-set of the integers. By using a modulus N, we only deal with 0 through to $N-1$ because anything equal to or larger than N or less than 0 "wraps around" (as we saw with the number line in Chap. 6). More formally, we deal with the set

$$\mathbb{Z}_N = \{0, 1, 2, 3, \ldots, N-1\},$$

which for $N = 12$ would obviously be

$$\mathbb{Z}_{12} = \{0, 1, 2, 3, \ldots, 11\}.$$

When you see $\mathbb{Z}_N$, take it to mean the set of integers modulo N; the *only* numbers we can work with are 0 through to $N-1$.

Given an N we already know that for some $y \in \mathbb{Z}_N$, but not all, we can find a multiplicative inverse; this is a bit of a pain unless we know beforehand which values of y and N will work. For example, for $N = 12$ we can write out a table and fill in the multiplicative inverses for each y:

$$
\begin{array}{llll}
0 \cdot ? \equiv 1 & (\text{mod } 12) \qquad & 6 \cdot ? \equiv 1 & (\text{mod } 12) \\
1 \cdot 1 \equiv 1 & (\text{mod } 12) & 7 \cdot 7 \equiv 1 & (\text{mod } 12) \\
2 \cdot ? \equiv 1 & (\text{mod } 12) & 8 \cdot ? \equiv 1 & (\text{mod } 12) \\
3 \cdot ? \equiv 1 & (\text{mod } 12) & 9 \cdot ? \equiv 1 & (\text{mod } 12) \\
4 \cdot ? \equiv 1 & (\text{mod } 12) & 10 \cdot ? \equiv 1 & (\text{mod } 12) \\
5 \cdot 5 \equiv 1 & (\text{mod } 12) & 11 \cdot 11 \equiv 1 & (\text{mod } 12)
\end{array}
$$

The question marks in the table highlight entries that we cannot fill in, with the values $y \in \{1, 5, 7, 11\}$ being those with a multiplicative inverse.

Recall that if some p is a **prime number** [20], it can only be divided exactly by 1 and p; we say 1 and p are the only **divisors** of p. Strictly speaking 1 is a prime number based on this definition, but 1 is not usually very interesting so we tend to exclude it. Two facts explain why the result above is no accident:

1. 2 and 3 are the two **prime divisors** of 12, i.e., the divisors of 12 which are prime. For example, 6 is a divisor of 12 but not prime, 5 is not a divisor but is prime, whereas 3 is both a divisor of 12 and prime.

2. $\{1, 5, 7, 11\}$ is precisely the set of elements in $\mathbb{Z}_{12}$ which are not divisible by 2 or 3. For example, 4 is not in the set because it is divisible by 2, whereas 5 is divisible by neither 2 nor 3 so it is in the set.

The special symbol $\mathbb{Z}_N^*$ is used to represent the sub-set of $\mathbb{Z}_N$ for which we can find a multiplicative inverse; for our example this means

$$\mathbb{Z}_{12}^* = \{1, 5, 7, 11\}.$$

Interestingly, the $y \in \mathbb{Z}_{12}^*$ are integers we can safely divide by. Normally if we wrote $2/5$ you might say the result is 0.4, but keep in mind that we can *only* work with 0 through to $N - 1$: there are no fractional numbers. So actually, when we write $2/5$ (mod 12) this means

$$2/5 = 2 \cdot 1/5 = 2 \cdot 5^{-1} \equiv 2 \cdot 5 \equiv 10 \quad (\text{mod } 12)$$

which is "allowed" precisely because, as we saw, $1/5 \equiv 5^{-1} \equiv 5$ (mod 12), i.e., 5 has a multiplicative inverse modulo 12 which, coincidentally, is also 5.

Now look at a different modulus, namely $N = 13$. Something special happens, because if we follow the same reasoning as above we get

$$\mathbb{Z}_{13} = \{0, 1, 2, 3, 4, 5, 6, 7, 8, 9, 10, 11, 12\},$$
$$\mathbb{Z}_{13}^* = \quad \{1, 2, 3, 4, 5, 6, 7, 8, 9, 10, 11, 12\}.$$

$\mathbb{Z}_{13}$ and $\mathbb{Z}_{13}^*$ look fairly similar: *all* non-zero $y \in \mathbb{Z}_{13}$ have a multiplicative inverse and appear in $\mathbb{Z}_{13}^*$ as a result. We can see this by again writing out a table and filling in the multiplicative inverse for each y:

$$
\begin{array}{llll}
0 \cdot ? \equiv 1 & (\text{mod } 13) \qquad & 6 \cdot 11 \equiv 1 & (\text{mod } 13) \\
1 \cdot 1 \equiv 1 & (\text{mod } 13) & 7 \cdot 2 \equiv 1 & (\text{mod } 13) \\
2 \cdot 7 \equiv 1 & (\text{mod } 13) & 8 \cdot 5 \equiv 1 & (\text{mod } 13) \\
3 \cdot 9 \equiv 1 & (\text{mod } 13) & 9 \cdot 3 \equiv 1 & (\text{mod } 13) \\
4 \cdot 10 \equiv 1 & (\text{mod } 13) & 10 \cdot 4 \equiv 1 & (\text{mod } 13) \\
5 \cdot 8 \equiv 1 & (\text{mod } 13) & 11 \cdot 6 \equiv 1 & (\text{mod } 13)
\end{array}
$$

There are no question marks (except for 0) this time, precisely because 13 is a prime number, and means we can divide by every non-zero y. You can think of this mirroring integer arithmetic, where dividing by zero is not allowed either. It also illustrates the fact that for $p = 12$, it was just a coincidence that $y^{-1} \equiv y$ (mod 12) for all y with an inverse: clearly this is not true for $p = 13$, where we find $5^{-1} \equiv 8$ (mod 13) for instance.

8.1.4   Some Interesting Facts About $\mathbb{Z}_N^\star$

The set $\mathbb{Z}_N^\star$ is interesting because the number of elements it contains can be calcu-
lated, using just N, via the so-called **Euler** Φ (or "phi") function [9]. Specifically,

$$\Phi(N) = \prod_{i=0}^{l-1} p_i^{e_i - 1} \cdot (p_i - 1)$$

when the **prime factorisation** [19] of N is given by

$$N = \prod_{i=0}^{l-1} p_i^{e_i}$$

and where each p_i is a prime number. Basically we express N as the product of
l prime numbers (or powers thereof). This is quite a nasty looking definition, but
some examples should make things clearer:

- If we select $N = 12$, then the prime factorisation of N is

$$N = 12 = 2 \cdot 2 \cdot 3 = 2^2 \cdot 3^1.$$

  We have expressed N as the product of $l = 2$ primes, namely 2 and 3. Matching
  this description with what we had above, this means $p_0 = 2$, $e_0 = 2$, $p_1 = 3$ and
  $e_1 = 1$ so

$$N = \prod_{i=0}^{l-1} p_i^{e_i} = \prod_{i=0}^{2-1} p_i^{e_i} = p_0^{e_0} \cdot p_1^{e_1} = 2^2 \cdot 3^1 = 12.$$

  If we select $N = 13$ then things are even simpler, i.e.,

$$N = 13 = 13^1,$$

  due to the fact that 13 *is* a prime number: the prime factorisation only includes
  13 itself! That is, for $N = 13$ we just have $p_0 = 13$ and $e_0 = 1$ so

$$N = \prod_{i=0}^{l-1} p_i^{e_i} = \prod_{i=0}^{1-1} p_i^{e_i} = p_0^{e_0} = 13^1 = 13.$$

- We can now compute

$$
\begin{aligned}
\Phi(12) &= 2^{2-1} \cdot (2-1) \cdot 3^{1-1} \cdot (3-1) \\
&= 2^1 \quad \cdot 1 \quad\quad \cdot 3^0 \quad \cdot 2 \\
&= 2 \quad\quad\quad\quad\quad\quad \cdot 2 \\
&= 4
\end{aligned}
$$

and

$$\Phi(13) = 13^{1-1} \cdot (13 - 1)$$
$$= 13^0 \quad \cdot 12$$
$$= 12$$

Both these results make sense because looking back we know that

$$\mathbb{Z}^{*}_{12} = \{1, 5, 7, 11\}$$
$$\mathbb{Z}^{*}_{13} = \{1, 2, 3, 4, 5, 6, 7, 8, 9, 10, 11, 12\}$$

which match up: $\mathbb{Z}^{*}_{12}$ contains $\Phi(12) = 4$ elements, and $\mathbb{Z}^{*}_{13}$ contains $\Phi(13) = 12$ elements.

Another way to look at things is that $\Phi(N)$ represents the number of integers less than N which are also **coprime** [4] to N. Two integers a and b are coprime if their **Greatest Common Divisor (GCD)** is 1; some examples again make the idea clearer:

- If $a = 3$ and $b = 12$, the divisors of a are 1 and 3 while the divisors of b are 1, 2, 3 and 6. The greatest divisor they have in common is 3 so we can write

$$\gcd(a, b) = \gcd(3, 12) = 3$$

and say a and b are not coprime.

- If $a = 3$ and $b = 13$, the divisors of a are 1 and 3 while the divisors of b are 1 and 13. The greatest divisor they have in common is 1 so we can write

$$\gcd(a, b) = \gcd(3, 13) = 1$$

and say a and b are coprime.

So, if $N = 12$ how many integers y exist that are less than N and also coprime to N? If we list all the options (except 0)

	$\gcd(12, 6) = 6$
$\gcd(12, 1) = 1$	$\gcd(12, 7) = 1$
$\gcd(12, 2) = 2$	$\gcd(12, 8) = 4$
$\gcd(12, 3) = 3$	$\gcd(12, 9) = 3$
$\gcd(12, 4) = 4$	$\gcd(12, 10) = 2$
$\gcd(12, 5) = 1$	$\gcd(12, 11) = 1$

the answer is four, i.e., 1, 5, 7 and 11, so $\Phi(12) = 4$. Notice that the values of y which produce $\gcd(N, y) = 1$ are precisely those which make up the set $\mathbb{Z}^{*}_{N}$. We need not go through the same task for $N = 13$: *all* positive integers less than 13 are coprime to 13 because it is prime, so $\Phi(13) = 12$.

Another interesting fact is that if you take any $x \in \mathbb{Z}^{*}_{N}$ and raise it to the power $\Phi(N)$ modulo N, the result is 1. In short, for every $x \in \mathbb{Z}^{*}_{N}$ we have

$$x^{\Phi(N)} \equiv 1 \pmod{N}.$$

For example, consider $x = 5$ which is an element of both $\mathbb{Z}_{12}^{\star}$ and $\mathbb{Z}_{13}^{\star}$. In these cases we have

$$
\begin{aligned}
x^{\Phi(12)} &= 5^4 = 625 \equiv 1 \quad (\text{mod } 12), \\
x^{\Phi(13)} &= 5^{12} = 244140625 \equiv 1 \quad (\text{mod } 13).
\end{aligned}
$$

 Implement (task #41) Demonstrate this fact is also true for other elements of $\mathbb{Z}_{12}^{\star}$ and $\mathbb{Z}_{13}^{\star}$ by working out similar results for them.

8.2   Modular Arithmetic: the Practice

In Chap. 2, one of the goals was to convince ourselves that we could write down an algorithm for multiplication: the premise was that if we could do this, we were closer to writing a program to do the same thing on a computer.

You can easily imagine having a similar motivation with respect to modular arithmetic and cryptographic protocols based on it. The goal is to show that you can write algorithms to compute *all* the modular arithmetic operations we need using *only* integer arithmetic as a starting point. Put another way, all the theory that surrounds modular arithmetic is important, but if all you want to do is make some cryptographic protocol work on a computer then there is no magic involved: we can describe such computation entirely in terms of what you already know.

8.2.1   Addition and Subtraction

Imagine we start off with $0 \leq x, y < N$, i.e., both x and y are in the set $\mathbb{Z}_N = \{0, 1, \ldots, N - 1\}$. If we add x and y together to get $t = x + y$, we end up with a result that satisfies

$$0 \leq t \leq 2 \cdot (N - 1).$$

The smallest result we can end up with is $t = 0$ which happens when x and y are as small as they can be, i.e., $x = y = 0$; the largest result we can end up with is $t = 2 \cdot (N - 1)$ which happens when x and y are as large as then can be, i.e., $x = y = N - 1$. We would like to apply a modular reduction to t, i.e., compute $t' \equiv t$ (mod N). This is simple in that to get

$$0 \leq t' \leq N - 1,$$

we just subtract N from t if $t \geq N$. This is captured in Algorithm 8.2a, and demonstrated in action by some examples:

```
1  algorithm ADD-MOD(x, y, N) begin
2  |   t ← x + y
3  |   if t ≥ N then
4  |   |   t' ← t − N
5  |   end
6  |   else
7  |   |   t' ← t
8  |   end
9  |   return t'
10 end
```

(a) $x + y \pmod{N}$

```
1  algorithm SUBTRACT-MOD(x, y, N) begin
2  |   t ← x − y
3  |   if t < 0 then
4  |   |   t' ← t + N
5  |   end
6  |   else
7  |   |   t' ← t
8  |   end
9  |   return t'
10 end
```

(b) $x - y \pmod{N}$

Fig. 8.2 Some algorithms for modular arithmetic

- Imagine $x = 8$, $y = 7$ and $N = 12$: we compute $t = 8 + 7 = 15$, and then $t' = 15 - 12 = 3$ since $t \geq 12$. Checking the modular reduction, we can see that

$$3 \equiv 15 \pmod{12}.$$

- Imagine $x = 1$, $y = 7$ and $N = 12$: we compute $t = 1 + 7 = 8$, and then $t' = 8$ since $t < 12$, i.e., no modular reduction is needed in this case because we know

$$8 \equiv 8 \pmod{12}.$$

So to cut a long story short, computing a modular addition relies only on integer addition and subtraction.

Things work more or less the same way for modular subtraction: if we subtract y from x to get $t = x - y$, we end up with a result that satisfies

$$-(N - 1) \leq t \leq (N - 1).$$

The smallest result we can end up with is $t = -(N - 1)$ which happens when x is as small as it can be and y is as large as it can be, i.e., $x = 0$ and $y = N - 1$; the largest result we can end up with is $t = N - 1$ which happens when x is as large as it can be and y is as small as it can be, i.e., $x = N - 1$ and $y = 0$. Again, we would like to apply a modular reduction to get

$$0 \leq t' \leq N - 1$$

which is again simple: we just add N to t if $t < 0$. This is captured in Algorithm 8.2b, and demonstrated in action by some examples:

- Imagine $x = 8$, $y = 7$ and $N = 12$: we compute $t = 8 - 7 = 1$, and then $t' = 1$ since $t \geq 0$. No modular reduction is required in this case because we know

$$1 \equiv 1 \pmod{12}.$$

- Imagine $x = 1$, $y = 7$ and $N = 12$: we compute $t = 1 - 7 = -6$, and then $t' = -6 + 12 = 6$ since $t < 0$. Checking the modular reduction, we can see that

$$6 \equiv -6 \pmod{12}.$$

Once more it is clear that to compute a modular subtraction, integer addition and subtraction are all we need.

8.2.2 Multiplication

Imagine we start off with $0 \leq x, y < N$, i.e., both x and y are in the set $\mathbb{Z}_N = \{0, 1, \ldots, N - 1\}$. Following the cases for addition and subtraction above, if we now multiply x and y together to get $t = x \cdot y$, we end up with a result that satisfies

$$0 \leq t \leq (N - 1)^2.$$

The smallest result we can end up with is $t = 0$ which happens when x and y are as small as they can be, i.e., $x = y = 0$; the largest result we can end up with is $t = (N - 1)^2$ which happens when x and y are as large as then can be, i.e., $x = y = N - 1$.

We would like to apply a modular reduction to t, but this time things are more tricky. For addition and subtraction, the t we compute is only ever wrong by at most N, i.e., we only need to subtract or add N *once* to get the right result; here we might need to subtract N *many* times. Consider an example: imagine we set $N = 12$ and select $x = 10$ and $y = 11$. If we compute $t = x + y = 10 + 11 = 21$, then we only need to subtract N once from t to get the result $t' = 9 \equiv 21 \pmod{12}$. If however we compute $t = x \cdot y = 10 \cdot 11 = 110$, then we need to subtract N *nine* times to get $t' = 2 \equiv 110 \pmod{12}$. So basically, instead of

```
1  if t ≥ N then
2  |   t' ← t − N
3  end
4  else
5  |   t' ← t
6  end
```

```
1  algorithm MULTIPLY-MOD(x, y, N) begin
2  │   t ← x · y
3  │   t' ← t − (N · ⌊t/N⌋)
4  │   return t'
5  end
```

(a) $x \cdot y \pmod{N}$

```
1   algorithm EXPONENTIATE-MOD(x, y, N) begin
2   │   t ← 1
3   │   for i from |y| − 1 downto 0 do
4   │   │   │   t ← MULTIPLY-MOD(t, t, N)
5   │   │   │   if y_i = 1 then
6   │   │   │   │   t ← MULTIPLY-MOD(t, x, N)
7   │   │   │   end
8   │   │   end
9   │   return t
10  end
```

(b) $x^y \pmod{N}$

Fig. 8.3 Some algorithms for modular arithmetic

we need something that *repeatedly* subtracts N until we get the right result, i.e., something more like

```
1  t' ← t
2  while t' ≥ N do
3  │   t' ← t' − N
4  end
```

Potentially this will be *very* inefficient however; the reason is more or less the same as when we talked about repeated addition in Chap. 2. Instead, we can calculate how many multiples of N we *would* need to subtract using this approach, and then simply do them all in one go. The idea is basically to compute

$$t' = t - \left(N \cdot \left\lfloor \frac{t}{N} \right\rfloor \right).$$

The term $\lfloor \frac{t}{N} \rfloor$ is the number of times N goes into t; this is basically the number of times we would go around the loop above. As a result $N \cdot \lfloor \frac{t}{N} \rfloor$ tells us what to subtract from t, which we can now do in one step. This is captured in Algorithm 8.3a, and demonstrated in action by some examples:

- Imagine $x = 8$, $y = 7$ and $N = 12$: we compute $t = 8 \cdot 7 = 56$, and then

$$t' = 56 - (12 \cdot 4) = 8$$

since $\lfloor \frac{56}{12} \rfloor = 4$. Checking the modular reduction, we can see that

$$8 \equiv 56 \pmod{12}.$$

- Imagine $x = 1$, $y = 7$ and $N = 12$: we compute $t = 1 \cdot 7 = 7$, and then

$$t' = 7 - (12 \cdot 0) = 7$$

since $\lfloor \frac{7}{12} \rfloor = 0$, i.e., no modular reduction is needed in this case because we know that

$$7 \equiv 7 \pmod{12}.$$

Things are more involved here than in the case of modular addition and subtraction, but to compute a modular multiplication we *still* only rely on integer multiplication, division and subtraction.

8.2.3   Exponentiation

The case of modular exponentiation is (believe it or not) one of the easiest to resolve. What we end up with is Algorithm 8.3b, which should look at least a bit familiar: basically we have just taken the old algorithm based on Horner's Rule from Chap. 2 and replaced the normal, integer multiplications with modular multiplications instead. The idea is that if each multiplication applies a modular reduction, then of course the exponentiation algorithm as a whole will be sane.

Consider an example where $x = 3$ and $y = 6_{(10)} = 110_{(2)}$. We know that $3^6 = 729$ and that $729 \equiv 9 \pmod{12}$, so the question is whether the new algorithm will give us the same result. The steps it performs demonstrate that it does:

Step #1   Assign $t \leftarrow 1$.
Step #2   Assign $t \leftarrow t^2 \pmod{N}$, i.e., $t \leftarrow 1^2 \pmod{12} = 1$.
Step #3   Since $y_2 = 1$, assign $t \leftarrow t \cdot x \pmod{N}$, i.e., $t \leftarrow 1 \cdot 3 \pmod{12} = 3$.
Step #4   Assign $t \leftarrow t^2 \pmod{N}$, i.e., $t \leftarrow 3^2 \pmod{12} = 9$.
Step #5   Since $y_1 = 1$, assign $t \leftarrow t \cdot x \pmod{N}$, i.e., $t \leftarrow 9 \cdot 3 \pmod{12} = 3$.
Step #6   Assign $t \leftarrow t^2 \pmod{N}$, i.e., $t \leftarrow 3^2 \pmod{12} = 9$.
Step #7   Since $y_0 = 0$, skip the assignment $t \leftarrow t \cdot x \pmod{N}$.
Step #8   Return $t = 9$.

All we are relying on to do this is modular multiplication, and we already know that modular multiplication can be described using integer operations only.

8.2.4   Division (via Inversion)

We have already seen that in modular arithmetic, dividing by some y only makes sense if y has a multiplicative inverse. This is only true if $y \in \mathbb{Z}_N^{\star}$ which, in turn, is only true if N and y are coprime, i.e., $\gcd(N, y) = 1$. When this all works out, we can write

$$x/y = x \cdot 1/y = x \cdot y^{-1} \pmod{N}$$

which implies that modular division of x by y boils down to finding the multiplicative inverse of y modulo N, and multiplying this by x modulo N.

Problem #1: Computing gcd(N, y)

The first challenge is to test whether y has a multiplicative inverse or not: for large values of N we cannot simply write out the whole set $\mathbb{Z}_N^{\star}$, we need to compute and test whether $\gcd(N, y) = 1$ or not.

One way would be to write out the prime factorisation of N and y and simply pick out the greatest divisor they have in common; if this turns out to be 1, we know N and y are coprime. We performed this exact task when we originally discussed coprimality, but imagine we now select the larger examples

$$N = 1426668559730 = 2^1 \cdot 5^1 \cdot 157^1 \cdot 271^1 \cdot 743^1 \cdot 4513^1,$$
$$y = \quad 810653094756 = 2^2 \cdot 3^2 \cdot \quad 61^1 \cdot 157^1 \cdot 521^1 \cdot 4513^1.$$

Using their prime factorisations (the right-hand part of each line), we can deduce that

$$\gcd(N, y) = \gcd(1426668559730, 810653094756)$$
$$= 2 \cdot 157 \cdot 4513$$
$$= 1417082$$

because both N and y have 2, 157 and 4513 as common divisors. However factoring is relatively hard work, particularly if N and y are large; if this *was* the best way to compute $\gcd(N, y)$, we would need a very fast computer or plenty of time on our hands! Luckily the **Euclidean algorithm** [8], an ancient algorithm due to Greek mathematician Euclid, can compute the same result rather more quickly.

Imagine we want to compute

$$\gcd(a, b)$$

assuming $a \geq b$ (swapping a and b if not). Understanding how the Euclidean algorithm works hinges on writing

$$a = b \cdot q + r$$

where q is called the quotient and r is called the remainder. This is the same as saying that if we divide a by b, we get a quotient (how many times b divides into a) and a remainder (what is left after such a division). An important fact is that $0 \leq r < b \leq a$ because if r *were* larger, b would divide into a one more time than q says it should. Taking this as our starting point, we can formulate two rules:

1. If you divide a by b and the remainder is 0, then a is a multiple of b (because b divides a exactly): this implies that b is a common divisor of a and b.

2. If you divide a by b and the remainder is not 0, then we can say that

$$\gcd(a, b) = \gcd(b, r).$$

Why is this? Imagine we write out the prime factorisation of a as follows:

$$a = p_0^{e_0} \cdot p_1^{e_1} \cdots p_{l-1}^{e_{l-1}}.$$

One of those terms will be $d = \gcd(a, b)$. Therefore you could imagine a written instead as

$$a = d \cdot a'$$

where a' represents all the "other" terms. We can do the same thing with b, because we know d must divide it as well, to get

$$b = d \cdot b'.$$

As a result

$$a - b = (d \cdot a') - (d \cdot b') = d \cdot (a' - b')$$

and hence d clearly divides $a - b$. Now going back to what we know from above, i.e.,

$$r = a - b \cdot q,$$

it follows that

$$a - b \cdot q = (d \cdot a') - (d \cdot b' \cdot q) = d \cdot (a' - b' \cdot q).$$

So basically

$$r = d \cdot (a' - b' \cdot q)$$

which means that d also divides r. To cut a long story short, $\gcd(b, r)$ will therefore give us the same result as $\gcd(a, b)$; because r is smaller than a and b, computing $\gcd(b, r)$ retains the restrictions we had to start with that said $a \geq b$. Based on these two rules, the Euclidean algorithm computes the following sequence:

$$r_0 = a$$
$$r_1 = b$$
$$r_2 = r_0 - r_1 \cdot q_2$$
$$r_3 = r_1 - r_2 \cdot q_3$$
$$\vdots$$

Basically the sequence is describing repeated application of the second rule above: the i-th remainder r, which we call r_i, is computed via

$$r_i = r_{i-2} - r_{i-1} \cdot q_i$$

```
1  algorithm EUCLIDEAN(a, b) begin
2      r_0 ← a
3      r_1 ← b
4      i ← 2
5      forever
6          if (r_{i-2} mod r_{i-1}) = 0 then
7              | return r_{i-1}
8          end
9          q_i ← ⌊r_{i-2}/r_{i-1}⌋
10         r_i ← r_{i-2} − r_{i-1} · q_i
11         i ← i + 1
12     end
13 end
```

(a) $\gcd(a, b)$

```
1  algorithm EXTENDED-EUCLIDEAN(a, b) begin
2      r_0 ← a, s_0 ← 1, t_0 ← 0
3      r_1 ← b, s_1 ← 0, t_1 ← 1
4      i ← 2
5      forever
6          if (r_{i-2} mod r_{i-1}) = 0 then
7              | return r_{i-1}, s_{i-1}, t_{i-1}
8          end
9          q_i ← ⌊r_{i-2}/r_{i-1}⌋
10         r_i ← r_{i-2} − r_{i-1} · q_i
11         s_i ← s_{i-2} − s_{i-1} · q_i
12         t_i ← t_{i-2} − t_{i-1} · q_i
13         i ← i + 1
14     end
15 end
```

(b) $\mathrm{xgcd}(a, b)$

Fig. 8.4 Some algorithms for modular arithmetic

where the i-th quotient is $q_i = r_{i-2}/r_{i-1}$. The sequence will finish in some m-th step when r_{m-1} divides r_{m-2} exactly (meaning we compute $r_m = 0$), at which point the answer we want is r_{m-1}; this corresponds to the first rule above. There are plenty of ways to write this down as an algorithm; one simple approach is shown in Algorithm 8.4a.

If we invoke

$$\text{EUCLIDEAN}(21, 12),$$

i.e., try to compute $\gcd(a, b)$ with $a = 21$ and $b = 12$ as in the example above, the algorithm computes the sequence

$$
\begin{aligned}
r_0 &= 21 \\
r_1 &= 12 \\
r_2 &= 21 - 12 \cdot 1 = 9 \\
r_3 &= 12 - 9 \cdot 1 = 3 \\
r_4 &= 9 - 3 \cdot 3 = 0
\end{aligned}
$$

meaning that $m = 4$ and hence $r_{m-1} = r_3 = 3$. The algorithm itself does this via the following steps:

Step #1   Assign $r_0 \leftarrow 21$.
Step #2   Assign $r_1 \leftarrow 12$.
Step #3   Assign $i \leftarrow 2$.
Step #4   Since $r_0 \bmod r_1 = 21 \bmod 12 \neq 0$, skip the return.
Step #5   Assign $r_2 \leftarrow r_0 \bmod r_1 \cdot \lfloor \frac{r_0}{r_1} \rfloor = 21 - 12 \cdot \lfloor \frac{21}{12} \rfloor = 21 - 12 \cdot 1 = 9$.
Step #6   Assign $i \leftarrow i + 1 = 3$.
Step #7   Since $r_1 \bmod r_2 = 12 \bmod 9 \neq 0$, skip the return.
Step #8   Assign $r_3 \leftarrow r_1 \bmod r_2 \cdot \lfloor \frac{r_1}{r_2} \rfloor = 12 - 9 \cdot \lfloor \frac{12}{9} \rfloor = 12 - 9 \cdot 1 = 3$.
Step #9   Assign $i \leftarrow i + 1 = 4$.
Step #10   Since $r_2 \bmod r_3 = 9 \bmod 3 = 0$, return $r_3 = 3$.

What about the example we started off with originally? The a and b are larger so we have a longer sequence, but by invoking

$$\text{EUCLIDEAN}(1426668559730, 810653094756)$$

we get

$$
\begin{aligned}
r_0 &= 1426668559730 \\
r_1 &= 810653094756 \\
r_2 &= 1426668559730 - 810653094756 \cdot 1 = 616015464974 \\
r_3 &= 810653094756 - 616015464974 \cdot 1 = 194637629782 \\
r_4 &= 616015464974 - 194637629782 \cdot 3 = 32102575628 \\
r_5 &= 194637629782 - 32102575628 \cdot 6 = 2022176014 \\
r_6 &= 32102575628 - 2022176014 \cdot 15 = 1769935418 \\
r_7 &= 2022176014 - 1769935418 \cdot 1 = 252240596 \\
r_8 &= 1769935418 - 252240596 \cdot 7 = 4251246 \\
r_9 &= 252240596 - 4251246 \cdot 59 = 1417082 \\
r_{10} &= 4251246 - 1417082 \cdot 3 = 0
\end{aligned}
$$

via similar steps, meaning that $m = 10$ and hence $r_{m-1} = r_9 = 1417082$ which matches the original result.

Problem #2: Computing y^{-1} (mod N)

Now we can tell whether or not y has a multiplicative inverse modulo N, the next challenge is to compute the inverse itself, i.e., y^{-1} (mod N). One option is to use the fact that we know

$$y^{\Phi(N)} \equiv 1 \quad (\text{mod } N).$$

Based on this, it also makes sense that

$$
\begin{aligned}
&\vdots \qquad \vdots \\
y^{\Phi(N)-2} &\equiv y^{-2} \equiv 1/y^2 \quad (\text{mod } N) \\
y^{\Phi(N)-1} &\equiv y^{-1} \equiv 1/y \quad (\text{mod } N) \\
y^{\Phi(N)+0} &\equiv y^0 \quad \equiv 1 \quad (\text{mod } N) \\
y^{\Phi(N)+1} &\equiv y^1 \quad \equiv y \quad (\text{mod } N) \\
y^{\Phi(N)+2} &\equiv y^2 \quad \equiv y^2 \quad (\text{mod } N) \\
&\vdots \qquad \vdots
\end{aligned}
$$

Or, put another way, we can easily compute y^{-1} (mod N) if we know $\Phi(N)$ because we already know how to do modular exponentiation. On the other hand, we already said that computing $\Phi(N)$ is relatively hard because we need to factor N.

An alternative option is to use a variant of the Euclidean algorithm, called the Extended Euclidean Algorithm (EEA) [11]; sometimes this is called "XGCD" as in "eXtended". Recall that the Euclidean algorithm used

$$r_i = r_{i-2} - r_{i-1} \cdot q_i.$$

The idea of the extended Euclidean algorithm is to unwind the steps and write each r_i in terms of a and b. This produces

$$
\begin{aligned}
r_0 &= a \\
r_1 &= b \\
r_2 &= r_0 - r_1 \cdot q_2 \\
    &= a - b \cdot q_2 \\
r_3 &= r_1 - r_2 \cdot q_3 \\
    &= b - (a - b \cdot q_2) \cdot q_3 \\
    &= -a \cdot q_3 + b \cdot (1 + q_2 \cdot q_1) \\
&\vdots
\end{aligned}
$$

This quickly starts to look nasty, so we simplify it by saying that in the i-th step we have

$$r_i = a \cdot s_i + b \cdot t_i$$

where s_i and t_i collect together all the nasty looking parts in one place. The sequence again finishes in the m-th step. But if we keep track of s_i and t_i, as well as getting r_{m-1} we also get s_{m-1} and t_{m-1}. Algorithm 8.4b shows the updated algorithm that keeps track of the extra parts.

If we invoke the new algorithm via EXTENDED-EUCLIDEAN(21, 12), we get

$$
\begin{aligned}
r_0 &= 21 \\
s_0 &= 1 \\
t_0 &= 0 \\
r_1 &= 12 \\
s_1 &= 0 \\
t_1 &= 1 \\
r_2 &= 21 - 12 \cdot 1 = 9 \\
s_2 &= 1 - 0 \cdot 1 = 1 \\
t_2 &= 0 - 1 \cdot 1 = -1 \\
r_3 &= 12 - 9 \cdot 1 = 3 \\
s_3 &= 0 - 1 \cdot 1 = -1 \\
t_3 &= 1 - -1 \cdot 1 = 2 \\
r_4 &= 9 - 3 \cdot 3 = 0 \\
s_4 &= 1 - -1 \cdot 3 = 4 \\
t_4 &= -1 - 2 \cdot 3 = -7
\end{aligned}
$$

meaning that $m = 4$. We can verify that this is sane because

$$
\begin{aligned}
r_{m-1} = 3 = a \quad &\cdot s_{m-1} + b \quad \cdot t_{m-1} \\
= 21 \quad &\cdot -1 \quad + 12 \cdot 2 \\
= -21 \quad &\quad\quad + 24 \\
= 3
\end{aligned}
$$

as expected. The point is that the extra parts the algorithm computes turn out to be very useful because given

$$r_{m-1} = \gcd(a, b) = 1$$

if a and b are coprime, we therefore know

$$1 = a \cdot s_{m-1} + b \cdot t_{m-1}.$$

As a result, we can compute the multiplicative inverse of x modulo N by setting $a = x$ and $b = N$. This means we get

$$1 = x \cdot s_{m-1} + N \cdot t_{m-1}$$

and, if we look at this modulo N,

$$1 \equiv x \cdot s_{m-1} \pmod{N}$$

since $N \cdot t_{m-1} \equiv 0 \pmod{N}$ (in fact any multiple of N is equivalent to 0 when reduced modulo N) or rather

$$x^{-1} \equiv s_{m-1} \pmod{N}$$

meaning that s_{m-1} is the multiplicative inverse we want.

8.3   From Modular Arithmetic to Cryptographic Protocols

As we saw in the introduction, a cryptographic protocol is a description of how the parties involved accomplish some task (e.g., sending messages between each other securely). The two tasks we focus on relate to the key distribution problem: can Alice and Bob communicate in a secure way *without* having to agree on a shared key before they start? We can describe two potential solutions using just the modular arithmetic studied so far:

1. key agreement protocols [15], and
2. public-key encryption schemes [21].

One of the motivations for solving this problem is that we, as Alice say, often want to communicate with a non-human Bob. Imagine for example if Bob were a web-site we want to buy something from; it is not feasible for us to agree a shared key with *every* possible web-site, so solutions like those above are critically important.

8.3.1   Diffie-Hellman Key Exchange

Suppose Alice wants to send a message to Bob, but they do not have a shared key; they *could* use the protocol we saw in the introduction, but first they need a secure way to agree on a shared key. The Diffie-Hellman key exchange [5] protocol, invented in 1976 by cryptographers Whitfield Diffie and Martin Hellman, offers one solution to this problem. A historically interesting fact is that the same protocol was invented independently, and around the same time, by Malcolm Williamson, a cryptographer at GCHQ [12] in the UK; this only became apparent when the intelligence agency declassified the work, making it public in 1997.

Before they start, Alice and Bob agree on two public values: a large prime number p, and some $g \in \mathbb{Z}_p$. The values are made available to *everyone*, e.g., by publishing them on a web-site. You can think of them as fixed settings which allow the protocol to work, a bit like the settings that tell a web-browser how to work. As a result, Alice and Bob can agree on a key as follows:

Alice	Eve	Bob
$x \xleftarrow{\$} \mathbb{Z}_p$		$y \xleftarrow{\$} \mathbb{Z}_p$
$a \leftarrow g^x \pmod{p}$		$b \leftarrow g^y \pmod{p}$
	$\xrightarrow{a}$	
	$\xleftarrow{b}$	
$k \leftarrow b^x \pmod{p}$		$k \leftarrow a^y \pmod{p}$

The protocol Alice and Bob engage in has five simple steps:

1. Alice selects x, a random element in $\mathbb{Z}_p$; at the same time Bob selects y, a random element in $\mathbb{Z}_p$.
2. Alice computes $a = g^x \pmod{p}$; at the same time Bob computes $b = g^y \pmod{p}$.
3. Alice communicates a to Bob .
4. Bob communicates b to Alice.
5. Alice computes $k = b^x \pmod{p}$; at the same time Bob computes $k = a^y \pmod{p}$.

Notice that at the end of the protocol Alice and Bob end up with the *same* shared key k; this is because for Alice

$$
\begin{aligned}
k &\equiv b^x & \pmod{p} \\
&\equiv \left(g^y\right)^x & \pmod{p} \\
&\equiv g^{y \cdot x} & \pmod{p}
\end{aligned}
$$

while for Bob we find

$$
\begin{aligned}
k &\equiv a^y & \pmod{p} \\
&\equiv \left(g^x\right)^y & \pmod{p} \\
&\equiv g^{x \cdot y} & \pmod{p}
\end{aligned}
$$

A concrete example demonstrates that crucially, this happens even though Alice does not know y, Bob does not know x and Eve knows neither y nor x. Imagine we make the settings $p = 13$ and $g = 7$ available to everyone. The protocol can then proceed as follows:

1. Alice selects $x = 9$; at the same time Bob selects $y = 3$.
2. Alice computes $a = g^x \pmod{p} = 7^9 \pmod{13} = 8$; at the same time Bob computes $b = g^y \pmod{p} = 7^3 \pmod{13} = 5$.
3. Alice communicates $a = 8$ to Bob .
4. Bob communicates $b = 5$ to Alice.
5. Alice computes $k = b^x \pmod{p} = 5^9 \pmod{13} = 5$; at the same time Bob computes $k = a^y \pmod{p} = 8^3 \pmod{13} = 5$.

Research (task #42)

What if all you have is a block cipher? Clearly Alice and Bob cannot rely on the fact they know k before they start, but what if they each share a different key with some trusted third-party Trent (call them k_{Alice} and k_{Bob} say): can you write down a protocol whereby they end up with a shared k using Trent to help out?

8.3.2 RSA Encryption

Now suppose Alice wants to send a message to Bob, without the need to agree on a shared key *at all*. The RSA public-key encryption [22], invented in 1978 by Ron Rivest, Adi Shamir and Leonard Adleman (who lend their initials to the name), represents an efficient and widely-used solution. In short, it allows us to avoiding the need for shared keys entirely, and hence side-step the key distribution problem. Again, cryptographers at GCHQ [12] produced similar results behind closed doors: Clifford Cocks had developed a similar scheme independently in 1973, but this was not declassified until 1997.

Before Alice can encrypt a message, Bob has to do some work. He picks two large prime numbers p and q and uses them to first compute $N = p \cdot q$, then

$$\Phi(N) = (p - 1) \cdot (q - 1).$$

Notice that only Bob can do this because only he knows p and q, the prime factors of N. He then selects a small number e which is coprime to $\Phi(N)$, and solves

$$e \cdot d \equiv 1 \quad \left(\mathrm{mod}\ \Phi(N)\right),$$

that is, he computes d, the multiplicative inverse of e modulo $\Phi(N)$. Remember, this means there exists a κ (known only by Bob in this case) such that

$$e \cdot d = 1 + \kappa \cdot \Phi(N).$$

The pair (N, e) is the **public-key** for Bob, while (N, d) is the **private-key**. The idea is that Bob can make his public-key available to *everyone* (e.g., by publishing it on his web-site), and that by downloading it doing so *anyone* can encrypt messages for him. Only Bob knows the corresponding private-key, so only he will be able to decrypt said messages.

As a result, Alice can send $M \in \mathbb{Z}_N^\star$ to Bob as follows:

Alice	Eve	Bob
$C \leftarrow M^e \pmod{N}$		
	$\xrightarrow{\ \ C\ \ }$	
		$M \leftarrow C^d \pmod{N}$

As in the introduction, the protocol that Alice and Bob engage in has three simple steps:

1. Alice encrypts a plaintext M using the public-key (N, e) to produce the ciphertext message

$$C = M^e \pmod{N}.$$

2. Alice communicates C to Bob.

3. Bob decrypts the ciphertext C using the private-key (N, d) to recover the plaintext message

$$M = C^d \quad (\text{mod } N).$$

But why does this work? Well, it follows from a fact we saw earlier: for any $x \in \mathbb{Z}_N^*$ we have that

$$x^{\Phi(N)} \equiv 1 \quad (\text{mod } N).$$

This means

$$
\begin{aligned}
C^d &\equiv \left(M^e\right)^d & (\text{mod } N) \\
&\equiv M^{e \cdot d} & (\text{mod } N) \\
&\equiv M^{1 + \kappa \cdot \Phi(N)} & (\text{mod } N) \\
&\equiv M \cdot M^{\kappa \cdot \Phi(N)} & (\text{mod } N) \\
&\equiv M \cdot \left(M^{\Phi(N)}\right)^{\kappa} & (\text{mod } N) \\
&\equiv M \cdot 1^{\kappa} & (\text{mod } N) \\
&\equiv M \cdot 1 & (\text{mod } N) \\
&\equiv M & (\text{mod } N)
\end{aligned}
$$

and so we get the message M as a result! The crucial difference between this and what we saw in the introduction is that Alice and Bob no longer use a shared key: *everyone* knows the public-key owned by Bob that was used for encryption, but *only* Bob knows the corresponding private-key used for decryption. We can demonstrate this using another concrete example. Imagine Bob selects

$$
\begin{aligned}
p &= 5 \\
q &= 11
\end{aligned}
$$

meaning $N = 55$ and $\Phi(N) = (p - 1) \cdot (q - 1) = 40$. He also selects $e = 7$, noting that $\gcd(e, \Phi(N)) = 1$, and computes $d = 23$, again noting that $e \cdot d = 161 \equiv 1$ (mod $\Phi(N)$). The protocol can then proceed as follows:

1. Alice encrypts a plaintext $M = 46$ using the public-key $(N, e) = (55, 7)$ to produce the ciphertext message

$$C = M^e \quad (\text{mod } N) = 46^7 \quad (\text{mod } 55) = 51.$$

2. Alice communicates C to Bob.
3. Bob decrypts the ciphertext $C = 51$ using the private-key $(N, d) = (55, 23)$ to recover the plaintext message

$$M = C^d \quad (\text{mod } N) = 51^{23} \quad (\text{mod } 55) = 46.$$

The ElGamal [7] public-key encryption scheme is an alternative to RSA; it also makes use of modular arithmetic. Three public values, namely g, p and q, are known to everyone:
- Alice chooses a random private-key x from the set $\{1, 2, \ldots q - 1\}$ and computes

$$h = g^x \quad (\text{mod } p)$$

Research (task #43)

which is her public-key made available to everyone.
- Bob wants to send a message m to Alice: he first chooses a random k from the set $\{1, 2, \ldots q - 1\}$ and computes

$$c_1 = g^k \quad (\text{mod } p)$$
$$c_2 = h^k \cdot m \quad (\text{mod } p)$$

The pair (c_1, c_2) is the ciphertext sent to Alice.
How can Alice decrypt (c_1, c_2) to recover the plaintext m? Work out the steps required, and show that the overall scheme works using an example (e.g., using the public values $g = 105$, $p = 107$ and $q = 53$).

8.3.3 Functional Versus Secure

In describing the protocols above, we showed they do what they should: they satisfy the functional requirements. But we forgot about (or more like ignored) Eve: how can we be sure the protocols are secure? We need to be able to reason about what Eve can do as well: it is not good enough to say in the case of RSA "Eve does not see M communicated between Alice and Bob so the protocol is secure". A standard approach is to model all the things that Eve must do in order that a protocol is insecure, and relate them to a "hard" Mathematical problem: if we can prove things about the problem, those proofs mean something in terms of Eve. For example, if we can reason about *how* hard the problem is (e.g., how many steps an algorithm will take to solve it), we can reason about how easily Eve will be able to attack the protocol.

Both of the protocols we introduced rely on a common building block, namely the computation of

$$z = x^y \quad (\text{mod } N)$$

for various x, y and N. This allows us to consider (at least) two problems:
- If N is prime, say $N = p$, then given N, x and z computing y is believed to be hard (for large values of N). This is called the **Discrete Logarithm Problem (DLP)** [6]; we write down an instance of this problem as $\text{DLP}(z, x, N)$.

- If N is a product of two primes, say $N = p \cdot q$, then given N, y and z computing x is believed to be hard without also knowing p and q. This is called the **RSA problem** [23]; we write down an instance of this problem as RSA(z, y, N).

In both cases, a problem instance is simply a challenge to Eve. When you see DLP(z, x, N) this should be read as "find y such that $z \equiv x^y$ (mod N)"; when you see RSA(z, y, N) this should be read as "find an x such that $z \equiv x^y$ (mod N)".

In general, a function f which is easy to compute but which is hard to invert or "reverse" (meaning f^{-1} is hard to compute) is called a **one-way function** [18]. Our examples fall exactly into this category: it is easy to compute $z = x^y$ (mod N), but (depending on the N we choose) hard to solve either DLP(z, x, N) or RSA(z, y, N). The question is, what do we mean by "hard"? Usually we try to answer this by using the same ideas as in Chap. 2. By saying that computing f should be easy, we mean that for a problem of size n (for example the number of bits in N), we might have an algorithm which does not take too many steps to compute f. So maybe f is $O(n)$ or $O(n^2)$ or even $O(n^3)$. In contrast, computing f^{-1} should be much harder; for example we might select f so that the *best known* algorithm to compute f^{-1} takes $O(2^n)$ steps.

So how does this relate to what Eve might do? Consider a model where Eve observes the communication between Alice and Bob (in addition to getting any publicly available values). How might she attack the protocol?

1. In the Diffie-Hellman example, Eve (like everyone else) gets access to the settings p and g and sees a and b communicated from Alice to Bob and vice versa.

   Assuming Eve wants to recover the shared key k, one approach would be to solve the problem instance DLP(a, g, p); this yields x and means Eve can compute

$$b^x = k$$

   just like Bob did. Alternatively, Eve could solve the problem instance DLP(b, g, p) to get y and compute

$$a^y = k$$

   just like Alice did. But both problem instances are as hard as each other, so either way we might argue that if solving them is hard then Diffie-Hellman key exchange is secure.

2. In the RSA example, Eve (like everyone else) gets access to the public-key for Bob, i.e., (N, e) and sees C communicated by Alice to Bob.

   Assuming Eve wants to recover the message M, one can imagine two approaches:

   (a) Factor N to recover p and q, then compute $\Phi(N)$. By doing this, d can be computed and Eve can decrypt C just like Bob did.

   (b) Solve the problem instance RSA(C, e, N) which gives the result M.

   and solving instances of the RSA problem is hard.

This seems great: if Eve wants to do anything we might regard as "bad", she has to work out how to solve what we are assuming are hard mathematical problems. If the problems really are hard, then we can say the protocols are secure.

But what if Eve does something other than what we expect? What if she acts outside our current model, which assumes she can only observe the communication between Alice and Bob? For example, imagine Eve has cut the network cable that links Alice and Bob and placed her own computer in between them; this is known as a **man-in-the-middle** attack [16]. Now Eve becomes the active adversary Mallory, and can do all sorts of other things. The question is, are the two protocols still secure?

1. For the Diffie-Hellman example, imagine the protocol changes because of how Mallory behaves; Alice and Bob behave in exactly the same way. The result is as follows:

Alice	Mallory	Bob
	$x' \xleftarrow{\$} \mathbb{Z}_p$	
$x \xleftarrow{\$} \mathbb{Z}_p$	$y' \xleftarrow{\$} \mathbb{Z}_p$	$y \xleftarrow{\$} \mathbb{Z}_p$
	$a' = g^{x'} \pmod{p}$	
$a \leftarrow g^x \pmod{p}$	$b' = g^{y'} \pmod{p}$	$b \leftarrow g^y \pmod{p}$
	$\xrightarrow{a}$ $\xrightarrow{a'}$	
	$\xleftarrow{b'}$ $\xleftarrow{b}$	
	$k_1 = a^{y'} \pmod{p}$	
$k_1 \leftarrow b'^x \pmod{p}$	$k_2 = b^{x'} \pmod{p}$	$k_2 \leftarrow a'^y \pmod{p}$

Since

$$
\begin{aligned}
k_1 &= b'^x && \pmod{p} \\
&= \left(g^{y'}\right)^x && \pmod{p} \\
&= g^{y' \cdot x} && \pmod{p} \\
&= \left(g^x\right)^{y'} && \pmod{p} \\
&= a^{y'} && \pmod{p}
\end{aligned}
$$

and

$$
\begin{aligned}
k_2 &= a'^y && \pmod{p} \\
&= \left(g^{x'}\right)^y && \pmod{p} \\
&= g^{x' \cdot y} && \pmod{p} \\
&= \left(g^y\right)^{x'} && \pmod{p} \\
&= b^{x'} && \pmod{p}
\end{aligned}
$$

Mallory agrees one key with Alice and one with Bob: Alice *thinks* she is communicating with Bob and vice versa, but actually they are communicating *through* Mallory. When Alice sends a message to Bob encrypted using k_1, Mallory can simply decrypt the message and read it, then re-encrypt it using k_2 and send it on: neither Alice nor Bob are any the wiser because from their point of view, nothing has gone wrong.

2. For the RSA example, imagine the protocol changes to the following:

Alice	Mallory	Bob
$C \leftarrow M^e \pmod{N}$		

$$\xrightarrow{C}$$

$$C' \leftarrow 2^e \cdot C \pmod{N}$$

$$\xrightarrow{C'}$$

$$M' \leftarrow C'^d \pmod{N}$$

Since

$$
\begin{aligned}
C' &\equiv 2^e \cdot C &&\pmod{N} \\
& 2^e \cdot M^e &&\pmod{N} \\
& (2 \cdot M)^e &&\pmod{N},
\end{aligned}
$$

when Bob decrypts C', he gets an M' equal to $2 \cdot M$. That seems quite bad: if M was a message saying "Alice owes Bob $100" then Alice might actually end up owing twice as much!

Both cases are meant to illustrate that Eve (now Mallory) has avoided the hard mathematical problems: in order to do "something bad", there was no need to solve an instance of the RSA problem for example. What does this mean: is the protocol insecure? Or is the security model wrong? The combined difficulty of

1. understanding what a protocol should do,
2. understanding and modelling what any adversaries can do, and
3. designing a protocol that is efficient while also matching all functional requirements

make *good* cryptography very challenging. The fact that people are constantly developing new capabilities for Eve (e.g., new ways to factor numbers or solve the RSA problem) adds even more of a challenge; what is secure today may not be secure in ten or twenty years time, and equally the types of protocol parties want to engage in might change. But these challenges also make cryptography a fascinating subject: it must, by definition, constantly evolve to keep pace with both functionality and attack landscapes.

References

1. Wikipedia: Alice and Bob. http://en.wikipedia.org/wiki/Alice_and_Bob
2. Wikipedia: Block cipher. http://en.wikipedia.org/wiki/Block_cipher
3. Wikipedia: Block cipher modes of operation. http://en.wikipedia.org/wiki/Block_cipher_modes_of_operation
4. Wikipedia: Coprime. http://en.wikipedia.org/wiki/Coprime
5. Wikipedia: Diffie-Hellman. http://en.wikipedia.org/wiki/Diffie-Hellman
6. Wikipedia: Discrete logarithm. http://en.wikipedia.org/wiki/Discrete_logarithm
7. Wikipedia: ElGamal encryption. http://en.wikipedia.org/wiki/ElGamal_encryption
8. Wikipedia: Euclidean algorithm. http://en.wikipedia.org/wiki/Euclidean_algorithm
9. Wikipedia: Euler's totient function. http://en.wikipedia.org/wiki/Euler's_totient_function

10. Wikipedia: Exponentiation by squaring. http://en.wikipedia.org/wiki/Exponentiation_by_squaring

11. Wikipedia: Extended Euclidean algorithm. http://en.wikipedia.org/wiki/Extended_Euclidean_algorithm

12. Wikipedia: GCHQ. http://en.wikipedia.org/wiki/Government_Communications_Headquarters

13. Wikipedia: Identity function. http://en.wikipedia.org/wiki/Identity_function

14. Wikipedia: Integer. http://en.wikipedia.org/wiki/Integer

15. Wikipedia: Key agreement protocol. http://en.wikipedia.org/wiki/Key-agreement_protocol

16. Wikipedia: Man-in-the-middle attack. http://en.wikipedia.org/wiki/Man-in-the-middle_attack

17. Wikipedia: Number theory. http://en.wikipedia.org/wiki/Number_theory

18. Wikipedia: One-way function. http://en.wikipedia.org/wiki/One-way_function

19. Wikipedia: Prime factor. http://en.wikipedia.org/wiki/Prime_factor

20. Wikipedia: Prime number. http://en.wikipedia.org/wiki/Prime_number

21. Wikipedia: Public key cryptography. http://en.wikipedia.org/wiki/Public-key_cryptography

22. Wikipedia: RSA. http://en.wikipedia.org/wiki/RSA

23. Wikipedia: RSA Problem. http://en.wikipedia.org/wiki/RSA_problem

24. Wikipedia: Symmetric key cryptography. http://en.wikipedia.org/wiki/Symmetric_key_algorithm

25. Wikipedia: Transport Layer Security (TLS). http://en.wikipedia.org/wiki/Transport_Layer_Security

Hiding a Needle in a Haystack: Concealed Messages

9

Imagine you are employed as a spy or, to add a modicum of glamour to the story, *the* spy, James "007" Bond himself [5]. You have two suspects under surveillance and are tasked with identifying which one is plotting to end the world. The usual laser pen and exploding pants were loaned to 006, but you *do* have a watch that can intercept the emails people send; you use the watch to capture some evidence:

<table>
<tr><td align="center">Email from suspect #1:</td><td align="center">Email from suspect #2:</td></tr>
<tr><td>

```
Dear Mum,

I am having a strange holiday.  The
weather here is nice enough, but there
is a weird man in the next room who does
nothing but drink vodka martinis and
smile at women.

Love, David.
```

</td><td>

```
DE259236 4D503352 8D9ABE72 818B4040
856ECEC7 C9DB0FF2 7E854F98 9B0DF034
D14EC5DC 683D69C5 49C7AA7D AB6BD65A
77DDE93E 815275EC 6F66DD23 22A0333A
B1641A64 FCB533FA E8E210B7 81115EF2
7DB41239 4A942DCF E2C59A6E DC6DB547
3B0F1BC2 23D1E844 FDFD474A 9B0C9D30
FAD65181 3EEAD4FB 5D71AE10 28F8702B

Love, Mr. X.
```

</td></tr>
</table>

Which suspect should you throw in the shark infested swimming pool? Clearly suspect #2: by the look of it he is sending encrypted emails so if he does not want people to know what they say, he *must* be up to no good. What went wrong for suspect #2? Cryptography was meant to solve all his secrecy problems! In short, the problem here is not really one of secrecy because the message suspect #2 sent is still secure in the sense that it cannot be read. Rather, the problem is that the message he is sending stands out and therefore attracts attention. It would be nice if the message was also secret, but in this case *hiding* the message is perhaps more important to suspect #2. The topic of **steganography** [16], a Greek word meaning "concealed writing", gives us a solution. As we have described previously, cryptography is all about preserving the secrecy of data; steganography on the other hand relates to hiding secret data, typically within non-secret data. For example, imagine we intercept a million emails with the watch. Suspect #2 could hide a secret message inside an innocuous email similar to the one suspect #1 sent: the secret message in this case is one needle in a haystack of a million emails, and we may totally overlook it as a result.

D. Page, N. Smart, *What Is Computer Science?*,
Undergraduate Topics in Computer Science, DOI 10.1007/978-3-319-04042-4_9,
© Springer International Publishing Switzerland 2014

Although steganography is more generally interesting, one reason it makes a good topic is the connection to use within digital media: we get to look at some pictures for a change, rather than long lists of numbers! In this context, steganography can be used as a way to **watermark** [4] digital media. Imagine we have taken a brilliant photograph, and upload it to our web-site. What is to stop a competitor downloading the image, making a copy of it on their web-site, and claiming *they* took the photograph not us? The answer is not much because the beauty (and curse) of digital media is that it is so easy to copy. In Chap. 1 we already saw that CDs and DVDs are just well organised sequences of numbers; digital images and MP3 files are the same thing. So, unlike an oil painting or an analogue cassette tape, it is trivial to make a perfect copy of most digital media. One way to combat this problem is to hide a message within whatever we want to protect: imagine we hide the message "this photograph was taken by X on the date Y" inside the image. Even if someone else copies it, they would have a hard time convincing a court of law that they had taken the image and just happened to put our name in it!

Of course, real digital watermarking techniques usually have additional and complicated requirements that we will not worry about; obviously we require the watermark to be robust, in the sense that it cannot easily be removed, for instance. Our aim here is to use the scenario above as a motivation to look at two types of digital image, and two forms of steganography that follow quite naturally from how such images are represented.

9.1 Digital Images

It pains me to say it, but I am old enough to remember a time before digital photography existed. The question is, how do modern digital cameras do the same thing as older ones that were based mainly on chemical processes? That is, how do they represent a physical image using numbers so that we can store and manipulate them using a computer? The answer is not *too* involved, but it turns out that there are (at least) two quite different varieties of digital image.

9.1.1 Rasterised Images

A **rasterised image** (or "bitmap" image) measures or **samples** the colour of the physical image at regular intervals; the samples are the digital representation we keep. You can think of a rasterised image as being a matrix where each element represents one sample called a **pixel** (or **picture element**) [11].

The number of rows and columns for a particular image is usually fixed; if we have a $(m \times n)$-pixel image then the **resolution** is n by m, meaning it has n columns and m rows. You might have seen images described as "1024 by 768" for example, which would mean $n = 1024$ and $m = 786$. When talking about digital cameras, it is also common to refer to the *total* number of pixels rather than the number of rows and columns. So a camera described as "having 10 megapixels" produces images where $n \cdot m \sim 10 \cdot 10^6$, i.e., we might have a matrix with just over $n = 3000$ columns and just over $m = 3000$ rows.

In a sense, the total number of pixels tells us something about the image detail. Basically, if there are more pixels, more samples have been taken from the physical image and therefore there is more detail:

- A 1 megapixel digital camera produces a (1000×1000)-pixel image, i.e., one million pixels in total. Imagine we use the camera to take a picture of an object that is 5 m long: we sample about one pixel every 5 mm or so. What if there is an ant on the object which is only 2 mm long? Chances are we might miss him out if he happens to fall between two samples.
- A 10 megapixel digital camera produces an image with ten times as many pixels, i.e., ten million pixels in total. Now, taking a picture of the same 5 m object means we sample about one pixel every 1.6 mm. There is more detail in this image: we can capture smaller features within the physical image.

The next question is how we describe the pixels themselves; remember that they are meant to represent samples, or colours, from the physical image. To do this, we use a **colour model** [3] which tells us which numbers represent which colours.

The RGB Colour Model

The **RGB** colour model [14] represents colours by mixing together red, green and blue (i.e., "R", "G" and "B"). The idea is to write a sequence of three numbers, i.e., a triple

$$\langle r, g, b \rangle$$

where each of r, g and b is called a **channel** and represents the proportion of red, green or blue in the pixel. There are several ways we could specify r, g and b; for example we could use a percentage, e.g., 100 % red, which is both easy to read and understand. However, it is more common to see them specified as an n-bit integer between zero and some maximum $2^n - 1$. Imagine we set $n = 8$: this means each channel is some number x in the range $0 \ldots 255$ and the proportion specified is $x/(2^n - 1)$, in this case $x/255$. Here are some examples to make things clearer:

1. The triple $\langle 255, 255, 255 \rangle$ is white: it specifies $255/255$ (or 100 % red), $255/255$ (or 100 %) green and $255/255$ (or 100 %) blue.
2. The triple $\langle 255, 0, 0 \rangle$ is a pure red colour: it specifies $255/255$ (or 100 % red), $0/255$ (or 0 %) green and $0/255$ (or 0 %) blue.
3. The triple $\langle 255, 255, 0 \rangle$ is a pure yellow colour: it specifies $255/255$ (or 100 % red), $255/255$ (or 100 %) green and $0/255$ (or 0 %) blue.
4. The triple $\langle 51, 255, 102 \rangle$ is a pea green colour: it specifies $51/255$ (or 20 % red), $255/255$ (or 100 %) green and $102/255$ (or 40 %) blue.

Since we need an n-bit integer for each channel, and we need three channels to specify the colour of each pixel, we need $3n$ bits for each pixel. This is sometimes called the **colour depth** because it tells us how many colours we can represent, i.e., the number of bits-per-pixel (sometimes abbreviated as "bpp"). With $n = 8$, each pixel needs 24 bits and we can represent nearly 17 million colours. This is enough colours to approximate physical images, and is used by many image formats that are produced by digital cameras.

The obvious next step is to put the two concepts together and arrange the RGB triples in a matrix to represent the pixels of an image. Figure 9.1 demonstrates what this actually looks like, both as a matrix of numbers and the pixels they represent. We can write the numbers that represent each colour channel in *any* base, so the matrix

$$
\begin{pmatrix}
\langle 11111111_{(2)}, 11111111_{(2)}, 11111111_{(2)} \rangle & \langle 00000000_{(2)}, 00000000_{(2)}, 00000000_{(2)} \rangle \\
\langle 11111111_{(2)}, 00000000_{(2)}, 00000000_{(2)} \rangle & \langle 00000000_{(2)}, 11111111_{(2)}, 00000000_{(2)} \rangle \\
\langle 00000000_{(2)}, 00000000_{(2)}, 11111111_{(2)} \rangle & \langle 11111111_{(2)}, 11111111_{(2)}, 00000000_{(2)} \rangle \\
\langle 11111111_{(2)}, 00000000_{(2)}, 11111111_{(2)} \rangle & \langle 00000000_{(2)}, 11111111_{(2)}, 11111111_{(2)} \rangle
\end{pmatrix}
$$

is equivalent: it is just written down in a different way.

You might be used to creating images using software that allows you to "paint" interactively (using a mouse). When we need careful control over pixel values, however, it can be easier to describe images using a text format such as PPM [9]. For example,

```
P3              # this is an ASCII PPM file
2               # there are 2 columns
4               # there are 4    rows
255             # maximum R, G or B is 255

255 255 255 # P_{0,0}
  0   0   0 # P_{0,1}
255   0   0 # P_{1,0}
  0 255   0 # P_{1,1}
  0   0 255 # P_{2,0}
255 255   0 # P_{2,1}
255   0 255 # P_{3,0}
  0 255 255 # P_{3,1}
```

Implement
(task #44)

is a PPM description of Fig. 9.1. The first four lines specify information about the image, namely
- the PPM file identifier (which ensures any software reading the file can interpret the associated content correctly),
- the image dimensions, first the number of columns then the number of rows, and
- the maximum value any colour channel can have.

The subsequent lines specify image content: each line specifies a pixel, from top-left to bottom-right in the image. So the first pixel in the top-left corner is $(255, 255, 255)$ (meaning white).

Try to reproduce this example using image manipulation software of your choice to view the result.

$$
\begin{pmatrix}
\langle 255, 255, 255 \rangle & \langle 0, 0, 0 \rangle \\
\langle 255, 0, 0 \rangle & \langle 0, 255, 0 \rangle \\
\langle 0, 0, 255 \rangle & \langle 255, 255, 0 \rangle \\
\langle 255, 0, 255 \rangle & \langle 0, 255, 255 \rangle
\end{pmatrix}
$$

(a) Representation as a (4 × 2)-element matrix of RGB triples.

(b) Representation as a (4 × 2)-pixel image.

Fig. 9.1   An example rasterised image in two representations

Research (task #45)

As well as the red, green and blue channels, it is common to include an **alpha** channel. This forms the **RGBA colour space** [15], and typically means that each pixel is represented by 32 rather than 24 bits. Find out about the purpose of this addition, then try to show the effect it has using some experimental images.

The CMYK Colour Model

RGB is not the *only* colour model; you might reasonably argue that it is not even the most sensible since it does not correspond to what happens when paints are mixed together. Consider some examples:

1. To get green coloured paint you need to mix yellow and blue paint together. With RGB on the other hand, you can get a green colour "for free"; adding red gives a yellow colour. Try mixing red and green paint together: you do not get yellow paint!
2. If you mix together all colours of paint together you get black (or maybe just a mess), but in RGB you end up with a white colour.

So why the difference? Think about what a computer monitor is doing in a physical sense: basically it just emits light. If it emits no light, then we as the viewer see a black colour. If it emits red, green and blue then these "add up" to white. So, with the RGB model, colours are additive. Now think about how we see paint: white light hits the paint, the paint absorbs selected parts of the spectrum and reflects what is left so that we as the viewer can see it. If white light, $\langle 255, 255, 255 \rangle$ as an RGB triple, hits yellow paint, it absorbs all the blue component and we get reflected $\langle 255, 255, 0 \rangle$ back; if white light hits cyan paint, it absorbs all the red component and we get $\langle 0, 255, 255 \rangle$ reflected back. So if we mix yellow and cyan paint the result will absorb all the blue *and* red components from the spectrum and hence reflect $\langle 0, 255, 0 \rangle$, i.e. green, back. Hence, paint absorbs (i.e., subtracts) colours of light, whereas a computer monitor emits (i.e., adds) colours of light.

The idea of using cyan, magenta and yellow as primary colours is standard in the printing world since it deals with ink (which is like paint). So whereas we use red, green and blue as primary colours and hence the RGB colour model *within* computers, when we print rather than display images it is common to use the **CMYK** colour model [2] instead.

If you are *really* serious about printing and typesetting, the name **Pantone** [10] will crop up a lot: the **Pantone Matching System** (**PMS**) is a standard colour model used in most commercial settings. Do some research about this colour model, and the legal issues which mean it often cannot be used (e.g., within the open source GIMP software mentioned in Chap. 1).

9.1.2 Vector Images

A **vector image** describes a physical image using a combination of geometric primitives such as points and lines. It is also possible to include more complicated curved surfaces (e.g., circles and ellipses), and even to extend from 2-dimensions into 3-dimensions. An example makes this easy to explain. Imagine you have a large sheet of graph paper: a 2-dimensional point on our graph paper is just a pair of coordinates that we write as (x, y). We can draw such a point on the graph paper; scale is not important, but you can imagine the paper has unit sized or 1 cm squares on it if that helps. Using two such points, we can write

$$(x, y) \rightsquigarrow (p, q)$$

to describe a 2-dimensional line segment between points (x, y) and (p, q). Again, we can draw such a line on the graph paper: just get a ruler and join up the points. Using lots of lines, we can start to draw basic images. Imagine we start with this one

$$(1.0, 1.0) \rightsquigarrow (2.0, 1.0)$$
$$(2.0, 1.0) \rightsquigarrow (2.0, 2.0)$$
$$(2.0, 2.0) \rightsquigarrow (1.0, 2.0)$$
$$(1.0, 2.0) \rightsquigarrow (1.0, 1.0)$$
$$(3.0, 1.0) \rightsquigarrow (4.0, 1.0)$$
$$(4.0, 1.0) \rightsquigarrow (3.5, 2.0)$$
$$(3.5, 2.0) \rightsquigarrow (3.0, 1.0)$$

which describes seven lines in total. The first four lines form a square with sides of length one unit, the last three form an isosceles triangle of base and altitude one unit. It does not look very impressive when written like this, but if we were to draw it on our graph paper, it would look like Fig. 9.2a. On one hand, this is still a fairly unimpressive image; we could make it more complicated by drawing more lines,

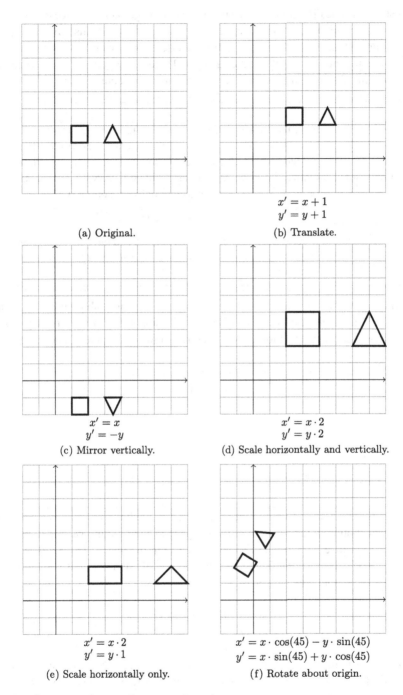

(a) Original.

$x' = x + 1$
$y' = y + 1$

(b) Translate.

$x' = x$
$y' = -y$

(c) Mirror vertically.

$x' = x \cdot 2$
$y' = y \cdot 2$

(d) Scale horizontally and vertically.

$x' = x \cdot 2$
$y' = y \cdot 1$

(e) Scale horizontally only.

$x' = x \cdot \cos(45) - y \cdot \sin(45)$
$y' = x \cdot \sin(45) + y \cdot \cos(45)$

(f) Rotate about origin.

Fig. 9.2 Some example vector image transformations

but it still might be difficult to represent a physical image such as a face or a flower. On the other hand, what we might have sacrificed in terms of realism we recoup in terms of precision: since the image is effectively described in terms of Mathematics, we can manipulate it via Mathematics as well. There are applications where this is a real benefit; if you are designing a new car or building, accuracy is vital!

It is not as common now, but a system called **Logo** [7] has been used extensively as a way to teach programming. The idea is that a program controls an on-screen **turtle** that is guided around, drawing as it moves. In a sense, the Mathematical description of images above is very close to a Logo program: see if you can use an online resource such as

http://turtleacademy.com/

to reproduce our simple example. If you have no background in programming, this is a good chance to explore what else is possible.

Implement (task #47)

To demonstrate the significance of this, we can start to think about taking a point (x, y) and translating it into a new point (x', y') using some form of **transformation**. Three such transformations, which describe how to compute x' and y', are

$$\text{TRANSLATE} : \begin{array}{l} x' = x + i \\ y' = y + j \end{array}$$

$$\text{SCALE} \quad : \begin{array}{l} x' = x \cdot i \\ y' = y \cdot j \end{array}$$

$$\text{ROTATE} \quad : \begin{array}{l} x' = x \cdot \cos\theta - y \cdot \sin\theta \\ y' = x \cdot \sin\theta + y \cdot \cos\theta \end{array}$$

Imagine we select an example point $(1.0, 2.0)$, i.e., we have $x = 1.0$ and $y = 2.0$, which is the bottom left-hand corner of our square. The first thing we might try is to translate (or "move") the point to somewhere else in the image. To do this we *add* a vector (i, j). To move the point one unit horizontally and one unit vertically for example, we compute the new point as

$$x' = 1.0 + 1.0 = 2.0$$
$$y' = 2.0 + 1.0 = 3.0$$

In isolation this probably does not seem very exciting. But if we repeat the transformation for all the points in the image, we end up with the result in Fig. 9.2b. And that is just for starters! We can reflect an image in either axis. For example by negating the y coordinate we can mirror the image in the y-axis, as in Fig. 9.2c.

If we want to scale a point (x, y) by a factor of i horizontally and j vertically we multiply x and y by i and j. Imagine we want to double the size of the image; setting $i = 2$ and $j = 2$ we compute the new point as

$$x' = 1.0 \cdot 2.0 = 2.0$$
$$y' = 2.0 \cdot 2.0 = 4.0$$

Again, doing the same thing with all the points in our image gives the result in Fig. 9.2d. This time the result is a bit more impressive: we have doubled the image size, but we have not degraded the quality *at all*. The Mathematics to describe the lines, and hence our image, is "perfect". We can play about even more, and stretch the image horizontally; setting $i = 2$ and $j = 1$ gives Fig. 9.2e.

As a final trick we can think about rotating the image, the result of which is shown in Fig. 9.2f. If we want to rotate the point by θ, say $\theta = 45$ for instance, we compute the new point (to three decimal places) as follows:

$$x' = 1.0 \cdot \cos(45) - 2.0 \cdot \sin(45) = -0.325$$
$$y' = 1.0 \cdot \sin(45) + 2.0 \cdot \cos(45) =   1.376$$

Research (task #48)

What *other* types of useful transformation can you think of? As a hint, think about a shearing transform which produces a slanting result. Find out how such transformations can be specified and applied by using matrices [17].

Rotation is the first point where we hit a problem: the "perfectness" of the Mathematics fails us when we want to write down actual values for x' and y', because of the limit on **precision** (put simply, we only have a fixed number of decimal places available). Until then, we can manipulate everything perfectly without ever having to see a number! In a sense, the same problem crops up when we want to print or view a vector image.

Most laser printers [6] or plotters [12] can draw vector images. Many accept **PostScript** [13], a language for describing vector images, as input: programs written in PostScript are essentially lists of geometry, such as the line segments we started off with. But, eventually, physical constraints will cause problems. Such a printer cannot usually draw infinitely small images, for example, since there is a limit to how accurate mechanical parts can ever be. Some other types of display device [18] can also render vector images; early video games like Asteroids [1] used this sort of technology. These are rare however, and most modern computer monitors work in a different way: they first **rasterise** the vector image, turning it into a format that can be displayed. And there lies the problem: the process of rasterisation throws away the "perfect" nature of the Mathematics and forces us to do things like round-up the coordinates of a point, which might be represented using many decimal places of precision, so they match the nearest integer pixel location.

9.2   Steganography

Back to James Bond, or rather the problem of stopping his pesky snooping. Remember that the idea is to hide some secret data in non-secret data and, by doing so, throw him off the scent. The secret message will be a string of characters (an email if you like) and the non-secret data will be a digital image. Each type of digital image we have looked at gives quite a neat way to do this.

9.2.1   Rasterised Images: "Stolen LSBs"

We have already learned that a rasterised image can be represented as a matrix of numbers, and ideally binary numbers. For example, our original (4 × 2)-pixel example image was

$$
\left(
\begin{array}{c|c}
\langle 11111111_{(2)}, 11111111_{(2)}, 11111111_{(2)} \rangle & \langle 00000000_{(2)}, 00000000_{(2)}, 00000000_{(2)} \rangle \\
\hline
\langle 11111111_{(2)}, 00000000_{(2)}, 00000000_{(2)} \rangle & \langle 00000000_{(2)}, 11111111_{(2)}, 00000000_{(2)} \rangle \\
\hline
\langle 00000000_{(2)}, 00000000_{(2)}, 11111111_{(2)} \rangle & \langle 11111111_{(2)}, 11111111_{(2)}, 00000000_{(2)} \rangle \\
\hline
\langle 11111111_{(2)}, 00000000_{(2)}, 11111111_{(2)} \rangle & \langle 00000000_{(2)}, 11111111_{(2)}, 11111111_{(2)} \rangle
\end{array}
\right).
$$

Some of the bits are given special names:

- The bits at the right-hand end of each number (those coloured red), are termed the **least-significant** bits or LSBs: they contribute weights of 2^1 and 2^0 to the overall value, the smallest weights of all.
- The bits at the left-hand end of each number (those coloured blue), are termed the **most-significant** bits or MSBs: they contribute weights of 2^7 and 2^6 to the overall value, the largest weights of all.

What happens if we alter either the LSBs or MSBs of the pixels in an image? Imagine we look at each pixel and set the two LSBs of each colour channel to zero. Or, maybe we look at each pixel and randomise the two MSBs of each colour channel. Figure 9.3 demonstrates four images that were created by taking an original and slightly altering each pixel along these lines. Figures 9.3b and 9.3c had the two LSBs in each pixel altered, either set to zero or a random 2-bit value respectively. Although the images are marginally different (perhaps a little darker), without the original you would be hard pressed to pick them out as having been altered at all. This should make sense: we are altering the LSBs and these have the least impact on the value of each colour, so changing them does not have a lot of impact.

In Figs. 9.3d and 9.3e, the two MSBs rather than the LSBs were altered and the results are quite striking: if the MSBs are altered, the images are clearly corrupted. In Fig. 9.3d, each pixel has become *much* darker: the image is more or less intact and understandable, but in Fig. 9.3e is much less understandable; there is still some structure if you look closely, but it is really quite random. Again, this should make sense, we are altering the MSBs and these have the most impact on the value of

Fig. 9.3 Four images, each created by altering the pixels from an original image

(a) Original.

(b) Two LSBs zeroed.   (c) Two LSBs randomised.

(d) Two MSBs zeroed.   (e) Two MSBs randomised.

each colour. In particular, if we zero the two MSBs we are basically saying that each colour channel can only take a value $0 \ldots 63$ rather than $0 \ldots 255$ so at *best*, it can only be about a quarter as bright.

The question is, how can we use our findings as a steganographic mechanism? The answer is reasonably simple. We are going to "steal" the LSBs from their original purpose of contributing to an image, and use them to conceal a message. The theory is that altering the LSBs will not corrupt the image too much: we have already seen that *even* if we randomise them, the end result is very close to the original. Our original (4×2)-pixel example image had eight pixels in total; we are stealing six bits from each pixel (two from each of the colour channels), so 48 bits in total. Chapter 4 already showed us than an ASCII character can be stored using 8 bits. Therefore, we can store a 6-character message in the 48 bits we have at our disposal.

First, we need to choose a message: the 6-character string "hello." (note the trailing full stop) is not particularly exciting, but will do the job here. Writing the ASCII representation of the string as a sequence we have

$$\langle 104, 101, 108, 108, 111, 46 \rangle.$$

If we write this in binary instead our message is

$$\langle 01101000_{(2)}, 01100101_{(2)}, 01101100_{(2)}, 01101100_{(2)}, 01101111_{(2)}, 00101110_{(2)} \rangle$$

and if we split it up into 2-bit chunks then, reading left-to-right and top-to-bottom, we get

$$\left\langle \begin{array}{l} 01_{(2)}, \ 10_{(2)}, \ 10_{(2)}, \ 00_{(2)}, \ 01_{(2)}, \ 10_{(2)}, \\ 01_{(2)}, \ 01_{(2)}, \ 01_{(2)}, \ 10_{(2)}, \ 11_{(2)}, \ 00_{(2)}, \\ 01_{(2)}, \ 10_{(2)}, \ 11_{(2)}, \ 00_{(2)}, \ 01_{(2)}, \ 10_{(2)}, \\ 11_{(2)}, \ 11_{(2)}, \ 00_{(2)}, \ 10_{(2)}, \ 11_{(2)}, \ 10_{(2)} \end{array} \right\rangle$$

which is now ready to be injected into the image. Again, this is reasonably simple: we just start with the example image and replace the red LSBs with the sequence of 2-bit chunks derived from our message. The result is as follows:

$$\left(\begin{array}{c|c} \langle 11111101_{(2)}, 11111110_{(2)}, 11111110_{(2)} \rangle & \langle 00000000_{(2)}, 00000001_{(2)}, 00000010_{(2)} \rangle \\ \hline \langle 11111101_{(2)}, 00000001_{(2)}, 00000001_{(2)} \rangle & \langle 00000010_{(2)}, 11111111_{(2)}, 00000000_{(2)} \rangle \\ \hline \langle 00000001_{(2)}, 00000010_{(2)}, 11111111_{(2)} \rangle & \langle 11111100_{(2)}, 11111101_{(2)}, 00000010_{(2)} \rangle \\ \hline \langle 11111111_{(2)}, 00000011_{(2)}, 11111100_{(2)} \rangle & \langle 00000010_{(2)}, 11111111_{(2)}, 11111110_{(2)} \rangle \end{array} \right)$$

If we turn this back into decimal to make it easier to read, and render the matrix as pixels as well, the end result is Fig. 9.4. The left-hand side shows the two matrices: clearly there *is* a difference as a result of the LSBs having been commandeered to store the message.

Reversing the process to extract the message is just as simple: we take the pixels, extract the LSBs and then recombine the 2-bit chunks into 8-bit bytes which represent the characters. But the point is that we would have to know the message was there in the first place before we even attempted to extract it. Looking at the comparison, it is difficult to see *any* difference in the images themselves: marginal changes in the colour channels are not easily detected *even* when we have the original image

$$\begin{pmatrix} \langle 255, 255, 255 \rangle & \langle 0, 0, 0 \rangle \\ \hline \langle 255, 0, 0 \rangle & \langle 0, 255, 0 \rangle \\ \hline \langle 0, 0, 255 \rangle & \langle 255, 255, 0 \rangle \\ \hline \langle 255, 0, 255 \rangle & \langle 0, 255, 255 \rangle \end{pmatrix}$$

(a) Original (4×2)-element matrix.

(b) Original (4×2)-pixel image.

$$\begin{pmatrix} \langle 253, 254, 254 \rangle & \langle 0, 1, 2 \rangle \\ \hline \langle 253, 1, 1 \rangle & \langle 2, 255, 0 \rangle \\ \hline \langle 1, 2, 255 \rangle & \langle 252, 253, 2 \rangle \\ \hline \langle 255, 3, 252 \rangle & \langle 2, 255, 254 \rangle \end{pmatrix}$$

(c) Altered (4×2)-element matrix.

(d) Altered (4×2)-pixel image.

Fig. 9.4 The result of injecting a 6-character ASCII message into the LSBs of an eight pixel image

(which of course we would ordinarily lack).

Research (task #49) If you *know* the message (or watermark) has been embedded in an image, it is of course easy to extract it. What about if you just suspect such a watermark is there? Can you think of a way to detect watermarks of this (or some other, similar) type?

9.2.2 Vector Images: "Microdots"

You Only Live Twice [19] is the first film to feature cat lover Ernst Blofeld, the head of SPECTRE, as a main character (in previous films you only see a character stroking a white cat, never his face). Part way through the film, Bond recovers a photograph of a cargo ship; on the photograph is something called a **microdot** [8]. A microdot is basically a very tiny image. The idea is to scale one image until it is *so* small it can be placed, in an inconspicuous way, within another image. Because it is so small, the premise is that it will be overlooked by a casual observer. So we take a secret message, scale it until it looks like a barnacle on the side of the cargo

Fig. 9.5 A "real" microdot
embedded into a full stop

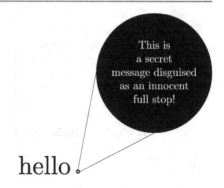

ship and then only someone looking for it (or who is far too interested in barnacles) will be able to recover the message.

Far from being limited to science fiction, there is plenty of evidence to suggest microdots being used as a real steganographic mechanism. Various sources have claimed invention, but it was almost certainly used by German intelligence agents in WW2 to send covert messages. British counter-intelligence nicknamed the microdots "duff" because they were mixed into letters like raisins were mixed into in the steamed pudding "plum duff". More modern uses include identification of physical resources such as car parts: the car manufacturer prints a unique number on each part in order to trace it in the event it is stolen. Of course a car thief might try to cover their tracks by etching off any obvious markings, but if they cannot even see the microdot then the chances of removing it are slim.

From the terminology we have used so far, it perhaps is not a surprise that we can try to create a real microdot using vector images: remember they these can be scaled without loss of quality, so are an ideal match. Figure 9.5 shows a somewhat basic example where we have scaled a message so that it is small enough to fit inside a full stop. If you are reading an electronic PDF version of this document, you can actually zoom in and enlarge the dot to see for yourself. If you are reading a version of the document printed on paper, this clearly would not work. Why not? We already talked about the problem: a given printer has limits as to how accurate the print mechanism is. So, in printing the electronic version that includes the perfect Mathematical description of our message, we have lost all the detail. Real microdots are therefore created using a traditional photographic process in which (very roughly) a special camera is used which shrinks an image of the message using magnification.

References

1. Wikipedia: Asteroids. http://en.wikipedia.org/wiki/Asteroids_(game)
2. Wikipedia: CMYK color model. http://en.wikipedia.org/wiki/CMYK_color_model
3. Wikipedia: Colour model. http://en.wikipedia.org/wiki/Color_model
4. Wikipedia: Digital watermarking. http://en.wikipedia.org/wiki/Digital_watermarking
5. Wikipedia: James Bond. http://en.wikipedia.org/wiki/James_Bond
6. Wikipedia: Laser printer. http://en.wikipedia.org/wiki/Laser_printer

7. Wikipedia: Logo. http://en.wikipedia.org/wiki/Logo_(programming_language)
8. Wikipedia: Microdot. http://en.wikipedia.org/wiki/Microdot
9. Wikipedia: Netpbm format. http://en.wikipedia.org/wiki/Netpbm_format
10. Wikipedia: Pantone. http://en.wikipedia.org/wiki/Pantone
11. Wikipedia: Pixel. http://en.wikipedia.org/wiki/Pixel
12. Wikipedia: Plotter. http://en.wikipedia.org/wiki/Plotter
13. Wikipedia: PostScript. http://en.wikipedia.org/wiki/PostScript
14. Wikipedia: RGB color model. http://en.wikipedia.org/wiki/RGB_color_model
15. Wikipedia: RGBA color space. http://en.wikipedia.org/wiki/RGBA_color_space
16. Wikipedia: Steganography. http://en.wikipedia.org/wiki/Steganography
17. Wikipedia: Transformation matrix. http://en.wikipedia.org/wiki/Transformation_matrix
18. Wikipedia: Vector monitor. http://en.wikipedia.org/wiki/Vector_monitor
19. Wikipedia: You Only Live Twice. http://en.wikipedia.org/wiki/You_Only_Live_Twice_(film)

Picking Digital Pockets

10

The 1983 film *WarGames* saw lead character David Lightman faced with a problem [9]. David had already hooked his computer up to the telephone system and broken into the school computer to change his grades. He succeeded because someone left the **password** on a desk in the school office. He then set about finding *other* computers by performing an automated search (we call this **war dialing** [8]) of all telephone numbers in the region. After a while he hit the jackpot: an interesting looking computer answered his call. But he could not gain access because this time he did not have the password.

It is easy to model this problem in a more formal way. Imagine the remote computer C has a password P embedded inside it, and that P is a sequence of characters (lower-case alphabetic characters only, to make things easier). Our job as the attacker Eve is to guess P. We can make successive attempts, each of which means sending a guess G to the computer: the computer takes P and G and uses an algorithm called MATCH-PWD to compare them. If P and G are the same then MATCH-PWD(P, G) returns **true**, otherwise it returns **false**. We know whether or not a guess was correct, because if we guessed correctly we obviously then get access to the computer. The following diagram tries to capture this model:

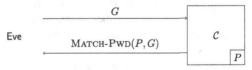

So how do we, as the attacker, proceed? One method might be to try *all* possible passwords; this is called a **brute-force** attack [1]. Imagine the password has n characters in it, and for the sake of argument say $n = 6$. With our brute-force attack we would perform guesses of the form

$$\text{MATCH-PWD}(P, \text{``aaaaaa''})$$

$$\text{MATCH-PWD}(P, \text{``baaaaa''})$$

$$\text{MATCH-PWD}(P, \text{``caaaaa''})$$

D. Page, N. Smart, *What Is Computer Science?*,
Undergraduate Topics in Computer Science, DOI 10.1007/978-3-319-04042-4_10,
© Springer International Publishing Switzerland 2014

$$\vdots$$

MATCH-PWD(P, "zaaaaa")

MATCH-PWD(P, "abaaaa")

MATCH-PWD(P, "bbaaaa")

MATCH-PWD(P, "cbaaaa")

$$\vdots$$

MATCH-PWD(P, "zbaaaa")

$$\vdots$$

MATCH-PWD(P, "zzzzzz")

until eventually one of them matched. There are two problems: first, we do not know what n is (but we can solve this later); second, the number of possible passwords is 26^n which grows quickly even if n grows slowly. With $n = 6$ for example, $26^6 = 308915776$ passwords are possible: not only will it take some time to make all those guesses, but after the first thousand or so wrong guesses someone in charge of the system *should* notice there is a problem. On the other hand, there *are* advantages in the sense that although the brute-force attack might take a long time it at least guarantees success if we wait long enough.

The next thing we could do is try common passwords. This is often called a **dictionary** attack [2]. The idea is that we have or make a dictionary of words, and use those words (including combinations of them) as our guesses. It turns out that people often select weak (i.e., easy to guess) passwords [4], so this approach can be effective. This is particularly true if we include various common passwords in our dictionary such as system defaults (e.g., "password" or "admin"), names of family and pets, football teams and so on. In fact David Lightman eventually solved his problem in exactly this way: the designer of the computer he had contacted, Prof. Stephen Falken, set the password to the name of his dead son Joshua. Clearly a similar approach could reduce the number of attempts versus a brute-force attack, but on the other hand it does not guarantee success: the actual password might not occur in our dictionary.

As we saw in Chaps. 6 and 8 however, when we design cryptographic schemes we do so in a way that should prevent these two forms of attack. For example, the key (which is of course analogous to the password) should be large enough to prevent a brute-force attack. More often than not, an attacker would need to cryptanalyse the system, usually attempting to find some weakness in the underlying Mathematics. Within this context, the concept of **side-channel** attacks [6] is relatively new. The idea is that rather than studying just the mathematics of a cryptographic scheme "on paper", we consider the fact that the scheme must be implemented as a program which executes on a computer. The idea is that as an attacker we might be able to passively monitor, or actively influence, how the computer executes the program.

Based on this activity we hope that cryptanalysis could be easier; of course, how feasible this is depends on the exact scenario. However, motivating examples are easy to come by: modern computers (e.g., a chip-and-pin card) are increasingly carried around with us, contain sensitive information (e.g., your banking details) and are used in a setting controlled by other people (e.g., the terminal of a supermarket checkout). So it is not too hard to imagine that side-channel attacks are sometimes a feasible and useful addition to the range of approaches on offer. Our aim in this chapter is to look at side-channel and fault attacks in a non-technical way: some of the examples do not *exactly* match what would happen in real life, but act as good metaphors for the concepts involved.

In the description above, there are some hints that our simplified model is *not* how real access control systems work. Within a system that controls access to a large web-site for instance, it would normally be a bad idea to store P itself somewhere.

Find out about why this choice is made, e.g., using the LinkedIn web-site breach in 2012 as motivation, and how it is supported: write out a set of requirements, and then steps that describe a better access control system than the one modelled.

Research (task #50)

10.1 Passive Physical Attacks

10.1.1 Attack

Imagine we represent strings as sequences of characters, for example we might have a sequence

$$A = \langle \text{'a'}, \text{'b'}, \text{'c'}, \text{'d'} \rangle.$$

Instead of writing $\langle \text{'a'}, \text{'b'}, \text{'c'}, \text{'d'} \rangle$ for example, we would normally write "abcd" instead. Based on this, how might we write an algorithm to check whether two strings (in our case P and G) are the same or not? Easy! We already saw algorithms in Chap. 4 that do this. If we ignore the *type* of string, since we are not really interested in that, the algorithm is (re)shown in Fig. 10.1. Recapping on Chap. 4 a little, have a look at it one step at a time. The first thing that happens is a conditional: if the number of characters in P is not the same as the number of characters in G then the two strings cannot be the same, so we return **false** as the result. If P and G are the same length then we need to check each character. To do this, we use a loop which iterates over a block for values of i in the range $0 \ldots n-1$. By this point we know $n = m$ so there is no danger of the i-th element of P or G being invalid. For each value of i, we test if $P_i = G_i$, i.e., if the i-th character of P is equal to the i-th character of G. If they are not equal, then clearly the two strings are not equal and we can return **false** as the result; if they are equal, we need to test all the

```
 1  algorithm MATCH-PWD(P, G) begin
 2      n ← STRING-LENGTH(P)
 3      m ← STRING-LENGTH(G)
 4      if n ≠ m then
 5          return false
 6      end
 7      for i from 0 upto n − 1 do
 8          if P_i ≠ G_i then
 9              return false
10          end
11      end
12      return true
13  end
```

Fig. 10.1 An algorithm to test whether the guess G matches some password P (where both G and P are strings)

other possible values of i. Finally, after we have completed all our tests we can be confident that the two strings are the same and return **true**.

Obviously it takes some time for the computer to execute an implementation of the MATCH-PWD algorithm. Thinking back to Chap. 4, you will remember that the algorithm is $O(n)$, i.e., the number of steps it takes is tied to the number of times the loop iterates. But a subtle issue is at the crux of what we are interested in: the loop does not *always* make n iterations because if there is a case where $P_i \neq G_i$, then the algorithm terminates early. Some examples make this clear:

- MATCH-PWD("joshua", "bob") returns **false** and takes 1 step because $n \neq m$.
- MATCH-PWD("joshua", "daniel") returns **false** and takes 2 steps because $n = m$ but at $i = 0$, $P_0 = $ 'j' $\neq$ 'd' $= G_0$.
- MATCH-PWD("joshua", "joanne") returns **false** and takes 4 steps because $n = m$ but at $i = 2$, $P_2 = $'s' $\neq$ 'a' $= G_2$; obviously for $i = 0$ and $i = 1$ we have $P_i = G_i$.
- MATCH-PWD("joshua", "joshua") returns **true** and takes 7 steps because $n = m$ and for all i we have $P_i = G_i$.

The idea is now to imagine that we can actually time how long it takes the computer to execute MATCH-PWD and hence recover the information above. This is not difficult: since we are communicating with the remote computer, we just measure the time that elapses between sending it a guess and getting a response back. We can redraw the original diagram to look more like this:

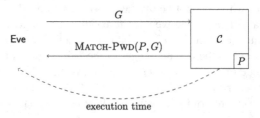

An aside: other, everyday analogies for information leakage

The example of guessing passwords *might* sound a little contrived, especially if you know a little more about how such systems are really implemented. Even so, the problem of information leakage is ubiquitous enough that many other everyday analogies exist. Consider for example

1. a burglar who opens a safe using a stethoscope to collect audible information leaked while operating the lock,
2. a burglar who guesses a door entry code by noting leaked information in the form of worn buttons on the keypad, or
3. a TV license detector van who reasons about your use of a TV set by monitoring the electro-magnetic emission from your house.

In each case, unintentional information leakage of different forms (i.e., different from execution time, which we used for guessing passwords) is the common issue.

The question is, how can we exploit this side-channel to help us solve the original problem of guessing the password? Notice that the more characters at the start of our guess that match those in the password, the longer the computer will take to give us this result. We say that information has leaked through a side-channel related to execution time; we still do not know P, but we *do* know a bit more than we thought we did. Also notice that we have solved the problem of how long P is: if the algorithm takes more than one step then we know our guess is the right length.

So let us return to the brute-force attack, but each time we make a guess we time how long it takes to get the result back and use this information to help us. We start by cycling though guesses of G_0:

$$\text{MATCH-PWD}(P, \text{``aaaaaa''}) \mapsto 2 \text{ steps}$$
$$\text{MATCH-PWD}(P, \text{``baaaaa''}) \mapsto 2 \text{ steps}$$
$$\text{MATCH-PWD}(P, \text{``caaaaa''}) \mapsto 2 \text{ steps}$$
$$\vdots$$
$$\text{MATCH-PWD}(P, \text{``jaaaaa''}) \mapsto 3 \text{ steps}$$
$$\vdots$$
$$\text{MATCH-PWD}(P, \text{``zaaaaa''}) \mapsto 2 \text{ steps}$$

One of the guesses will take slightly longer to return a result than the rest. This is because one of the guesses will make $P_0 = G_0$ and so will take 3 steps rather than 2 steps as in the cases where $P_i \neq G_i$. So we know this guess must be the real value of P_0. We carry on, but now we keep G_0 set to P_0, which we now know, and cycle through guesses at G_1:

$$\text{MATCH-PWD}(P, \text{``jaaaaa''}) \mapsto 3 \text{ steps}$$
$$\text{MATCH-PWD}(P, \text{``jbaaaa''}) \mapsto 3 \text{ steps}$$
$$\text{MATCH-PWD}(P, \text{``jcaaaa''}) \mapsto 3 \text{ steps}$$

$\vdots$

$\text{MATCH-PWD}(P, \text{``joaaaa''}) \mapsto 4 \text{ steps}$

$\vdots$

$\text{MATCH-PWD}(P, \text{``jzaaaa''}) \mapsto 3 \text{ steps}$

Again, one of the guesses will take slightly longer to return a result than the rest. This time one of the guesses will make $P_1 = G_1$ and so will take 4 steps rather than 3. Again we know this guess must be the real value of P_1; we carry on by keeping G_1 set to P_1, which we now know, and cycle through guesses at G_2:

$\text{MATCH-PWD}(P, \text{``joaaaa''}) \mapsto 4 \text{ steps}$
$\text{MATCH-PWD}(P, \text{``jobaaa''}) \mapsto 4 \text{ steps}$
$\text{MATCH-PWD}(P, \text{``jocaaa''}) \mapsto 4 \text{ steps}$

$\vdots$

$\text{MATCH-PWD}(P, \text{``josaaa''}) \mapsto 5 \text{ steps}$

$\vdots$

$\text{MATCH-PWD}(P, \text{``jozaaa''}) \mapsto 4 \text{ steps}$

If we follow this approach, we eventually guess correctly. The crucial thing to realise is that by using the side-channel information we have dramatically decreased the number of guesses we need to make. In the brute-force attack we needed 26^n guesses in the worst case, whereas now we need $26 \cdot n$; more formally, the brute-force attack can be described as $O(26^n)$ whereas the side-channel attack is $O(n)$. The latter is *clearly* better since it is at least somewhat feasible even with quite large n: with $n = 6$ that is only 156 guesses rather than 308915776.

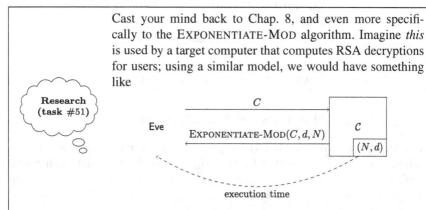

Cast your mind back to Chap. 8, and even more specifically to the EXPONENTIATE-MOD algorithm. Imagine *this* is used by a target computer that computes RSA decryptions for users; using a similar model, we would have something like

Research (task #51)

Eve

$\text{EXPONENTIATE-MOD}(C, d, N)$

C

C

(N, d)

execution time

Think about this setting: given Eve can still measure the execution time, what information leaks from C? Based on what you know about RSA, do you think this alone is a problem or not? Whatever your answer is, explain why.

```
 1  algorithm MATCH-PWD(P, G) begin
 2      if c > t then
 3      |   return false
 4      end
 5      n ← STRING-LENGTH(P)
 6      m ← STRING-LENGTH(G)
 7      if n ≠ m then
 8      |   c ← c + 1
 9      |   return false
10      end
11      for i from 0 upto n − 1 do
12      |   if P_i ≠ G_i then
13      |   |   c ← c + 1
14      |   |   return false
15      |   end
16      end
17      c ← 0
18      return true
19  end
```

(a) Detect the attack

```
 1  algorithm MATCH-PWD(P, G) begin
 2      Pause for c steps
 3      n ← STRING-LENGTH(P)
 4      m ← STRING-LENGTH(G)
 5      if n ≠ m then
 6      |   c ← c + 1
 7      |   return false
 8      end
 9      for i from 0 upto n − 1 do
10      |   if P_i ≠ G_i then
11      |   |   c ← c + 1
12      |   |   return false
13      |   end
14      end
15      c ← 0
16      return true
17  end
```

(b) Slow down the attack

```
 1  algorithm MATCH-PWD(P, G) begin
 2      f ← true
 3      n ← STRING-LENGTH(P)
 4      m ← STRING-LENGTH(G)
 5      if n ≠ m then
 6      |   f ← false
 7      end
 8      for i from 0 upto min(n, m) − 1 do
 9      |   if P_i ≠ G_i then
10      |   |   f ← false
11      |   end
12      end
13      return f
14  end
```

(c) Take a fixed number of steps

```
 1  algorithm MATCH-PWD(P, G) begin
 2      Pause for r steps, where r is random
 3      n ← STRING-LENGTH(P)
 4      m ← STRING-LENGTH(G)
 5      if n ≠ m then
 6      |   return false
 7      end
 8      for i from 0 upto n − 1 do
 9      |   if P_i ≠ G_i then
10      |   |   return false
11      |   end
12      end
13      return true
14  end
```

(d) Take a random number of steps

Fig. 10.2 Four example countermeasures to harden MATCH-PWD against side-channel attack

10.1.2 Countermeasures

If we wanted to prevent this sort of side-channel leakage, what could we do? Rather than come up with a totally different algorithm for checking passwords, one idea is to add some **countermeasures** to our existing MATCH-PWD algorithm: they are like a bandage which should patch up the algorithm and prevent the attack working. There are lots of potential ideas; the plan here is to explore four of them, plus any advantages or disadvantages they might have. To highlight the differences, we have collected the altered algorithms together in Fig. 10.2.

Detect the Attack

We have already mentioned one idea that could be quite effective: if we notice that numerous incorrect guesses have been made, we assume they are being made by an attacker and shut down the computer to prevent access. A basic version is captured by Fig. 10.2a. Of course it is a little simplistic, but the central idea is that we maintain a counter somewhere called c and initially set it to zero when the computer is turned on. Notice that each time the algorithm detects an incorrect guess it adds one to c, so if lots and lots of incorrect guesses are made in a row then c will grow quite large. When a correct guess is registered, we set c back to zero again and we forget about any incorrect guesses up to that point.

The algorithm capitalises on this behaviour by checking c before it does anything else: if c is larger than some threshold value t it instantly returns **false** and denies access to the computer, in effect denying access *forever* or at least until we manually reset c back to zero somehow. So basically what we are saying is that if t incorrect guesses in a row are made, then the computer will shut down. Choosing a suitable value for t will result in the attack becoming much less feasible.

Slow Down the Attack

If you were the administrator of the computer, you might be having a heart attack after reading the previous idea: even legitimate users make mistakes, so you would probably be called out at all hours of the day to reset c after someone forgot the password! Another less problematic idea is not to *shut* down the computer, but to *slow* it down: in short, the more incorrect guesses the attacker makes the longer the computer takes to use MATCH-PWD. This is a simple alteration from our previous algorithm, and is shown in Fig. 10.2b.

The alteration is simply in the first step: instead of testing c against a threshold, we wait for c steps. This means as more and more incorrect guesses are made, c grows larger and larger and the computer is slower and slower to respond: making many incorrect guesses, as necessitated by the attack, thus becomes laborious at best! This approach is a variant of something called **exponential back-off** [3]; you would see similar approaches to controlling network congestion for example.

Take a Fixed Number of Steps

We could force MATCH-PWD to take the same, fixed number of steps no matter what values of P and G are given to it. *If* this is possible, the idea is that information previously leaked is hidden: if the attacker cannot determine the number of steps taken, they cannot use the same strategy.

Figure 10.2c implements this idea. To keep track of when a difference is found, it maintains a flag called f: it starts with $f = $ **true**, then when it finds a difference sets $f = $ **false** to note this fact. The flag is only returned once the algorithm finishes checking characters in P and G: it *always* checks *all* characters to determine f, meaning it *always* takes a fixed number of steps. Or at least it does if P and G are the same length. Imagine we have $P = $ "joshua" for example, and make two guesses

G = "daniel" and G' = "joanne". The algorithm will take 8 steps in *both* cases, so the original attack strategy fails.

Of course, we have paid a price for this improved security: previously, if P and G were long strings then our algorithm was efficient in the sense that as soon as we definitely knew the result, we returned it straight away. With our new algorithm, we are *always* looking at the worst case; the algorithm always takes the longest possible time it could.

 With reference to Task 51, how could you apply this same idea as a countermeasure for EXPONENTIATE-MOD? Do you think this is a good approach? For instance, does using this countermeasure imply any disadvantages (versus an alternative say)?

Implement (task #52)

Take a Random Number of Steps

Another approach would be to force MATCH-PWD to take a random number of steps no matter what values of P and G are given to it. The end result is similar: the information previously leaked is now masked, meaning the attacker cannot use the same strategy.

Figure 10.2d shows that only a simple alteration is required (although, in reality, we also need a way to generate suitable random numbers). The main algorithm is the same, so the matching process is the same. However, there is an additional line before we start: by waiting a random amount of time, the actual number of steps observed by the attacker is randomised. For example, imagine we have P = "joshua" and make the two guesses G = "daniel" and G' = "joanne"; if the algorithm takes 8 steps, which guess did this come from? It could be G if the algorithm waits for $r = 6$ steps initially, then takes 2 steps in the matching phase; on the other hand, it could be G' if the algorithm waits for $r = 4$ steps initially, then takes 4 steps in the matching phase. The point is that we cannot relate the number of steps *observed* to the value of P being used; again, we have prevented the use of execution time as a useful side-channel.

Is this a *robust* countermeasure though? We could try to filter out the randomness using elementary statistics. Imagine we take our two guesses and use them each 100 times, capturing the results. If we find the *average* time taken by attempts with G and G', this might tell us something that comparing the time taken by a single attempt could not. For example, if *on average* the number of steps for guess G is *significantly* longer than the number of steps for G' then we might reason there is a good chance that more characters at the start of G are correct than G'. We cannot say for definite, but by capturing more and more results we can get more and more confident. So we have partially removed the effect of the randomness by simply using enough attempts that a general trend emerges.

10.2   Active Physical Attacks

10.2.1 Attack

Imagine a real scenario; things get a little more technical but we will try to keep the discussion simple. A mobile telephone uses a different type of password to a computer login screen: normally the telephone can be configured to ask for and test a four digit **Personal Identification Number (PIN)** when turned on [5]. There are not that many different four digit PIN numbers, only 10000 in fact, so one might immediately start to think a brute-force attack could work here. Usually the telephone would be equipped with a countermeasure to prevent such an attack. Do not try this at home, but after a few wrong attempts the telephone usually locks itself and refuses further attempts before you take it to the shop to be unlocked. This prevents a brute-force attack unless the shopkeeper is willing to reactivate a telephone for you thousands of times!

In the previous example, we had a computer with a password P embedded inside it. Here we have a telephone with a PIN number P and a counter c embedded inside it; this is more or less the same as our example countermeasure where we wanted to shut down the computer if there were lots of incorrect password guesses. In this new context, we can be a bit more accurate about the details. Typically the P and c values are stored on the SIM card [7] which means their values are retained even if the telephone is turned off. The PIN number plays the same role as the password did: the telephone is supposed to take a guess G, compare P and G and allow access if they are equal. This time we will use an algorithm called CHECK-PIN detailed in Fig. 10.3a.

Again, look at the algorithm one step at a time. The first thing that happens is that the counter c is read from where it is stored and tested: if $c = 0$ we have run out of attempts and the telephone is locked. In this case we return **false** to indicate that the attempt at accessing the telephone failed. However, if $c > 0$ then the telephone is unlocked and we are allowed at least one more attempt. In this case we call the algorithm REQUEST-PIN to read a guess G from the user and then proceed to check it. Next we check if the guess G is the same as the real PIN number P stored in the telephone. If the two are equal then we return **true** to indicate that the attempt succeeded. If they are not equal then we first subtract one from the counter c to indicate there is one less incorrect attempt allowed, and then return **false**.

As the attacker, our goal is to guess P without the telephone locking itself. Maybe we have "acquired" a telephone from somewhere, or maybe we have forgotten our own PIN number. Unlike the MATCH-PWD function, there is not really anything we can infer by timing CHECK-PIN since the actual test (i.e., $P \neq G$) takes the same time no matter what P and G are (P and G here are numbers, not strings). But imagine that rather than just passively monitoring CHECK-PIN, we could actively *influence* how it is executed. This should not sound too amazing, for example we have the telephone in our hand so we could do all sorts of things to it: we might pull out the battery, detach the keypad, or put the telephone in the oven. Of course, the goal is not to destroy the telephone but to aid cryptanalysis, so imagine we are restricted to turning the telephone off mid-execution.

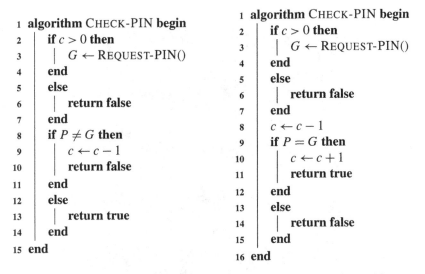

(a) The original CHECK-PIN algorithm

(b) A CHECK-PIN variant with countermeasures against fault attack

Fig. 10.3 Two algorithms to test whether the guess G matches some PIN P (where both G and P are numbers)

The trick is to turn off the power at just the right point. A good point would be just before line #9 (which updates c) gets executed. If we turn off the power before c is updated then basically it never changes: the new value of c is not stored on the SIM card. So if we had a way to sound an alarm when line #9 is going to be executed and then turn off the power whenever the alarm sounds, then c will never be updated and we have unlimited attempts at guessing P without the telephone being locked. This turns out to be very feasible. A suitable alarm can be rigged up by monitoring the telephone communicating with the SIM card, both of which we have easy access to. One can imagine an attacker that can now perform a brute-force attack on the telephone:

1. Set the current guess $G = 0$.
2. Take G and enter it into the telephone as a guess at P.
3. Monitor communication between the telephone and the SIM card:
   - If the telephone sends a command to update c, turn off the power then wait for a few seconds and skip forward to line #4.
   - If the telephone does not send a command to decrement c then G was the correct guess and we have access to the telephone.
4. Add one to G and go back to line #2.

10.2.2 Countermeasures

This is not good news for whoever made and/or sold the telephone: they would claim the PIN number password and associated locking mechanism is offering some level

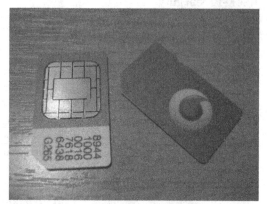

(a) Vodafone branded SIM cards.

(b) A Vodafone branded Sony-Ericsson V600i mobile telephone ...

(c) ... which when opened, exposes the power and SIM card interfaces.

Fig. 10.4 Demonstrating viability of the SIM card physical attack

of security, but with only reasonable assumptions we can circumvent that security with some ease. So how might we go about solving the problem? Have a look at the slightly modified version of CHECK-PIN in Fig. 10.3b.

At face value the two algorithms are quite similar, but now we alter c in two places: on line #8 where one is taken away from it, and then in line #10 when one is added to it again *if* it turns out that the guess was correct. What happens if we set the original attacker to work on the new algorithm? If the alarm sounds just before line #8 is executed the we can prevent one being subtracted from c. However c is *always* updated at this point regardless of whether $P = G$ or not, so if we turn off the power when the telephone communicates with the SIM then we can never get access to the telephone: we would turn off the power even if the guess was correct. On the other hand, if the alarm sounds just before line #10 is executed then it is already too late to turn off the power since c will already have been updated in line #8.

Research (task #53) Think about the types of electronic device you carry around with you: can you identify any other environmental factors (other than the power supply) that could be manipulated by Eve?

References

1. Wikipedia: Brute-force attack. http://en.wikipedia.org/wiki/Brute_force_attack
2. Wikipedia: Dictionary attack. http://en.wikipedia.org/wiki/Dictionary_attack
3. Wikipedia: Exponential backoff. http://en.wikipedia.org/wiki/Exponential_backoff
4. Wikipedia: Password strength. http://en.wikipedia.org/wiki/Password_strength
5. Wikipedia: Personal Identification Number (PIN). http://en.wikipedia.org/wiki/Personal_identification_number
6. Wikipedia: Side-channel attack. http://en.wikipedia.org/wiki/Side-channel_attack
7. Wikipedia: Subscriber Identity Module. http://en.wikipedia.org/wiki/Subscriber_Identity_Module
8. Wikipedia: War dialing. http://en.wikipedia.org/wiki/War_dialing
9. Wikipedia: WarGames. http://en.wikipedia.org/wiki/WarGames

Index

D. Page, N. Smart, *What Is Computer Science?*,
Undergraduate Topics in Computer Science, DOI 10.1007/978-3-319-04042-4,
© Springer International Publishing Switzerland 2014